Mastering MongoDB 3.x

An expert's guide to building fault-tolerant MongoDB applications

Alex Giamas

BIRMINGHAM - MUMBAI

Mastering MongoDB 3.x

First published: November 2017

Production reference: 1151117

Published by Packt Publishing Ltd.
Livery Place
35 Livery Street
Birmingham
B3 2PB, UK.
ISBN 978-1-78398-260-8

www.packtpub.com

Credits

Author
Alex Giamas

Reviewers
Juan Tomás Oliva Ramos
Nilap Shah

Commissioning Editor
Amey Varangaonkar

Acquisition Editor
Vinay Argekar

Content Development Editor
Mayur Pawanikar

Technical Editor
Prasad Ramesh

Copy Editors
Safis Editing

Project Coordinator
Nidhi Joshi

Proofreader
Safis Editing

Indexer
Aishwarya Gangawane

Graphics
Tania Dutta

Production Coordinator
Shantanu Zagade

About the Author

Alex Giamas is a Senior Software Engineer at the Department for International Trade, UK Government. He has also worked as a consultant for various startups. He is an experienced professional in systems engineering, NoSQL and big data technologies, with experience spanning from co-founding a digital health startup to Fortune 15 companies.

He has been developing using MongoDB since 2009 and early 1.x versions, using it for several projects around data storage and analytical processing. He has been developing in Apache Hadoop since 2007 while working on its incubation.

He has worked with a wide array of NoSQL and big data technologies, building scalable and highly available distributed software systems in C++, Java, Ruby and Python.

Alex holds an MSc from Carnegie Mellon University in Information Networking and has attended professional courses in Stanford University. He is a graduate from National Technical University of Athens, Greece in Electrical and Computer Engineering. He is a MongoDB Certified developer, a Cloudera Certified Developer for Apache Hadoop and Data Science essentials.

He publishes regularly for the past 4 years at InfoQ in NoSQL, big data and data science topics.

I would like to thank my parents for their support and advice all these years.

I would like to thank my fiancé Mary for her patience and support throughout the time, days and nights, weekdays and weekends I spent writing this book.

About the Reviewers

Juan Tomás Oliva Ramos is an environmental engineer from the University of Guanajuato, Mexico, with a master's degree in administrative engineering and quality. He has more than 5 years of experience in the management and development of patents, technological innovation projects, and the development of technological solutions through the statistical control of processes.

He has been a teacher of statistics, entrepreneurship, and the technological development of projects since 2011. He became an entrepreneur mentor and started a new department of technology management and entrepreneurship at Instituto Tecnológico Superior de Purisima del Rincon Guanajuato, Mexico.

Juan is an Alfaomega reviewer and has worked on the book Wearable Designs for Smart Watches, Smart TVs and Android Mobile Devices.

Juan has also developed prototypes through programming and automation technologies for the improvement of operations, which have been registered for patents.

I want to thank God for giving me wisdom and humility to review this book.

I thank Packt for giving me the opportunity to review this amazing book and to collaborate with a group of committed people

I want to thank my beautiful wife, Brenda, our two magic princesses (Maria Regina and Maria Renata) and our next member (Angel Tadeo), all of you, give me the strength, happiness, and joy to start a new day. Thanks for being my family.

Nilap Shah is a lead software consultant with experience across various fields and technologies. He is an expert in .NET, Uipath (robotics), and MongoDB. He is a certified MongoDB developer and DBA. He is a technical writer as well as a technical speaker. He also provides MongoDB corporate training. Currently, Nilap is working as a lead MongoDB consultant and provides solutions with MongoDB (DBA and developer projects). His LinkedIn profile can be found at `https:/ /www.linkedin.com/in/nilap-shah-8b6780a/` and you can reach him on WhatsApp at +91-9537047334.

www.PacktPub.com

For support files and downloads related to your book, please visit www.PacktPub.com. Did you know that Packt offers eBook versions of every book published, with PDF and ePub files available? You can upgrade to the eBook version at www.PacktPub.com and as a print book customer, you are entitled to a discount on the eBook copy. Get in touch with us at service@packtpub.com for more details. At www.PacktPub.com, you can also read a collection of free technical articles, sign up for a range of free newsletters and receive exclusive discounts and offers on Packt books and eBooks.

https://www.packtpub.com/mapt

Get the most in-demand software skills with Mapt. Mapt gives you full access to all Packt books and video courses, as well as industry-leading tools to help you plan your personal development and advance your career.

Why subscribe?

- Fully searchable across every book published by Packt
- Copy and paste, print, and bookmark content
- On demand and accessible via a web browser

Customer Feedback

Thanks for purchasing this Packt book. At Packt, quality is at the heart of our editorial process. To help us improve, please leave us an honest review on this book's Amazon page at `https://www.amazon.com/dp/1783982608`.

If you'd like to join our team of regular reviewers, you can email us at `customerreviews@packtpub.com`. We award our regular reviewers with free eBooks and videos in exchange for their valuable feedback. Help us be relentless in improving our products!

Table of Contents

Preface

MongoDB has grown to become the de facto NoSQL database with millions of users, from small start-ups to Fortune 500 companies. Addressing the limitations of SQL schema-based databases, MongoDB pioneered a shift of focus for DevOps and offered sharding and replication maintainable by DevOps teams. This book is based on MongoDB 3.x and covers topics ranging from database querying using the shell, built-in drivers, and popular ODM mappers, to more advanced topics such as sharding, high availability, and integration with big data sources.

You will get an overview of MongoDB and how to play to its strengths, with relevant use cases. After that, you will learn how to query MongoDB effectively and make use of indexes as much as possible. The next part deals with the administration of MongoDB installations on-premise or on the cloud. We deal with database internals in the next section, explaining storage systems and how they can affect performance. The last section of this book deals with replication and MongoDB scaling, along with integration with heterogeneous data sources. By the end this book, you will be equipped with all the required industry skills and knowledge to become a certified MongoDB developer and administrator.

What this book covers

Chapter 1, *MongoDB – A Database for the Modern Web*, takes us on a journey through web, SQL, and NoSQL technologies from inception to current state.

Chapter 2, *Schema Design and Data Modeling*, teaches schema design for relational databases and MongoDB, and how we can achieve the same goal starting from a different point.

Chapter 3, *MongoDB CRUD Operations*, gives a bird's-eye view of CRUD operations.

Chapter 4, *Advanced Querying*, covers advanced querying concepts using Ruby, Python, and PHP, using both the official drivers and an ODM.

Chapter 5, *Aggregation*, dives deep into the aggregation framework. We also discuss why and when we should use aggregation, as opposed to MapReduce and querying the database.

Chapter 6, *Indexing*, explores one of the most important properties of every database, which is indexing.

Chapter 7, *Monitoring, Backup, and Security*, discusses the operational aspects of MongoDB. Monitoring, backup, and security should not be an afterthought but rather a necessary process before deploying MongoDB in a production environment.

Chapter 8, *Storage Engines*, teaches about different storage engines in MongoDB. We identify the pros and cons of each one and the use cases for choosing each storage engine.

Chapter 9, *Harnessing Big Data with MongoDB*, shows more about how MongoDB fits into the wider big data landscape and ecosystem.

Chapter 10, *Replication*, discusses replica sets and how to administer them. Starting from an architectural overview of replica sets and replica set internals around elections, we dive deep into setting up and configuring a replica set.

Chapter 11, *Sharding*, explores sharding, one of the most interesting features of MongoDB. We start from an architectural overview of sharding and move on to how we can design a shard, and especially choose the right shard key.

Chapter 12, *Fault Tolerance and High Availability*, tries to fit in the information that we didn't manage to discuss in the previous chapters, and places emphasis on some others.

What you need for this book

You will need the following software to be able to smoothly sail through the chapters:

- MongoDB version 3+
- Apache Kafka 1
- Apache Spark 2+
- Apache Hadoop 2+

Who this book is for

Mastering MongoDB 3.x is a book for database developers, architects, and administrators who want to learn how to use MongoDB more effectively and productively.
If you have experience in, and are interested in working with, NoSQL databases to build apps and websites, then this book is for you.

Conventions

In this book, you will find a number of text styles that distinguish between different kinds of information. Here are some examples of these styles and an explanation of their meaning.

Code words in text, database table names, folder names, filenames, file extensions, pathnames, dummy URLs, user input, and Twitter handles are shown as follows: "In a sharded environment, each mongod applies its own locks, thus greatly improving concurrency."

When we wish to draw your attention to a particular part of a code block, the relevant lines or items are set in bold:

```
> db.types.find().sort({a:-1})
{ "_id" : ObjectId("5908d59d55454e2de6519c4a"), "a" : [ 2, 5 ] }
{ "_id" : ObjectId("5908d58455454e2de6519c49"), "a" : [ 1, 2, 3 ] }
```

Any command-line input or output is written as follows:

```
> db.types.insert({"a":4})
WriteResult({ "nInserted" : 1 })
```

New terms and **important words** are shown in bold.

Warnings or important notes appear like this.

Tips and tricks appear like this.

Reader feedback

Feedback from our readers is always welcome. Let us know what you think about this book-what you liked or disliked. Reader feedback is important for us as it helps us develop titles that you will really get the most out of. To send us general feedback, simply email feedback@packtpub.com, and mention the book's title in the subject of your message. If there is a topic that you have expertise in and you are interested in either writing or contributing to a book, see our author guide at www.packtpub.com/authors.

Customer support

Now that you are the proud owner of a Packt book, we have a number of things to help you to get the most from your purchase.

Downloading the example code

You can download the example code files for this book from your account at http://www. packtpub.com. If you purchased this book elsewhere, you can visit http://www.packtpub. com/support and register to have the files emailed directly to you. You can download the code files by following these steps:

1. Log in or register to our website using your email address and password.
2. Hover the mouse pointer on the **SUPPORT** tab at the top.
3. Click on **Code Downloads & Errata**.
4. Enter the name of the book in the **Search** box.
5. Select the book for which you're looking to download the code files.
6. Choose from the drop-down menu where you purchased this book from.
7. Click on **Code Download**.

Once the file is downloaded, please make sure that you unzip or extract the folder using the latest version of:

- WinRAR / 7-Zip for Windows
- Zipeg / iZip / UnRarX for Mac
- 7-Zip / PeaZip for Linux

The code bundle for the book is also hosted on GitHub at https://github.com/ PacktPublishing/Mastering-MongoDB-3x and https://github.com/agiamas/mastering-mongodb. We also have other code bundles from our rich catalog of books and videos available at https://github.com/PacktPublishing/. Check them out!

Errata

Although we have taken every care to ensure the accuracy of our content, mistakes do happen. If you find a mistake in one of our books-maybe a mistake in the text or the code- we would be grateful if you could report this to us. By doing so, you can save other readers from frustration and help us improve subsequent versions of this book. If you find any errata, please report them by visiting `http://www.packtpub.com/submit-errata`, selecting your book, clicking on the **Errata Submission Form** link, and entering the details of your errata. Once your errata are verified, your submission will be accepted and the errata will be uploaded to our website or added to any list of existing errata under the Errata section of that title. To view the previously submitted errata, go to `https://www.packtpub.com/books/content/support` and enter the name of the book in the search field. The required information will appear under the **Errata** section.

Piracy

Piracy of copyrighted material on the internet is an ongoing problem across all media. At Packt, we take the protection of our copyright and licenses very seriously. If you come across any illegal copies of our works in any form on the internet, please provide us with the location address or website name immediately so that we can pursue a remedy. Please contact us at `copyright@packtpub.com` with a link to the suspected pirated material. We appreciate your help in protecting our authors and our ability to bring you valuable content.

Questions

If you have a problem with any aspect of this book, you can contact us at `questions@packtpub.com`, and we will do our best to address the problem.

1
MongoDB – A Database for the Modern Web

In this chapter, we will lay the foundations for understanding MongoDB and how it is a database designed for the modern web. We will cover the following topics:

- The web, SQL, and MongoDB's history and evolution.
- MongoDB from the perspective of SQL and other NoSQL technology users.
- MongoDB's common use cases and why they matter.
- Configuration best practices:
    - Operational
    - Schema design
    - Write durability
    - Replication
    - Sharding
    - Security
    - AWS

- Learning to learn. Nowadays, learning how to learn is as important as learning in the first place. We will go through references that have the most up to date information about MongoDB for both new and experienced users.

Web history

In March 1989, more than 28 years ago, Sir Tim Berners-Lee unveiled his vision for what would later be named the **World Wide Web** (**WWW**) in a document called *Information Management: A Proposal* (`http://info.cern.ch/Proposal.html`). Since then, the WWW has grown to be a tool of information, communication, and entertainment for more than two of every five people on our planet.

Web 1.0

The first version of the WWW relied exclusively on web pages and hyperlinks between them, a concept kept until present times. It was mostly read-only, with limited support for interaction between the user and the web page. Brick and mortar companies were using it to put up their informational pages. Finding websites could only be done using hierarchical directories like Yahoo! and DMOZ. The web was meant to be an information portal.

This, while not being Sir Tim Berners-Lee's vision, allowed media outlets such as the BBC and CNN to create a digital presence and start pushing out information to the users. It revolutionized information access as everyone in the world could get first-hand access to quality information at the same time.

Web 1.0 was totally device and software independent, allowing for every device to access all information. Resources were identified by address (the website's URL) and open protocols (`GET`, `POST`, `PUT`, `DELETE`) could be used to access content resources.

Hyper Text Markup Language (**HTML**) was used to develop web sites that were serving static content. There was no notion of **Cascading Style Sheets** (**CSS**) as positioning of elements in a page could only be modified using tables and framesets were used extensively to embed information in pages.

This proved to be severely limiting and so browser vendors back then started adding custom HTML tags like `<blink>` and `<marquee>` which lead to the first browser wars, with rivals Microsoft (Internet Explorer) and Netscape racing to extend the HTTP protocol's functionality. Web 1.0 reached 45 million users by 1996.

Here is the Lycos start page as it appeared in Web 1.0 `http://www.lycos.com/`:

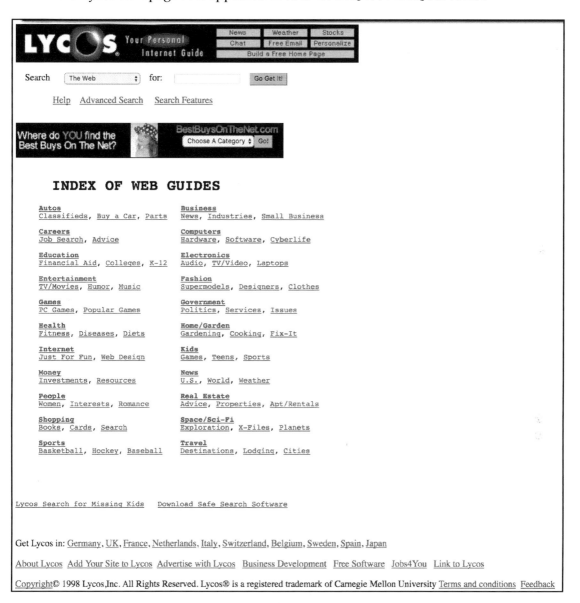

Yahoo as appeared in Web 1.0 `http://www.yahoo.com`:

Web 2.0

A term first defined and formulated by Tim O'Reilly, we use it to describe our current WWW sites and services. Its main characteristic is that the web moved from being read-only to the read-write state. Websites evolved into services and human collaboration plays an ever important part in Web 2.0.

From simple information portals, we now have many more types of services such as:

- Audio
- BlogPod
- Blogging
- Bookmarking

- Calendars
- Chat
- Collaboration
- Communication
- Community
- CRM
- E-commerce
- E-learning
- Email
- Filesharing
- Forums
- Games
- Images
- Knowledge
- Mapping
- Mashups
- Multimedia
- Portals
- RSS
- Wikis

Web 2.0 reached 1+ billion users in 2006 and 3.77 billion users at the time of writing this book (late 2017). Building communities was the differentiating factor for Web 2.0, allowing internet users to connect on common interests, communicate, and share information.

Personalization plays an important part of Web 2.0 with many websites offering tailored content to its users. Recommendation algorithms and human curation decides the content to show to each user.

Browsers can support more and more desktop applications by using Adobe Flash and **Asynchronous JavaScript and XML (AJAX)** technologies. Most desktop applications have web counterparts that either supplement or have completely replaced the desktop versions. Most notable examples are office productivity (Google Docs, Microsoft Office 365), Digital Design Sketch, and image editing and manipulation (Google Photos, Adobe Creative Cloud).

Moving from websites to web applications also unveiled the era of **Service Oriented Architecture (SOA)**. Applications can interconnect with each other, exposing data through **Application Programming Interfaces (API)** allowing to build more complex applications on top of application layers.

One of the applications that defined Web 2.0 are social apps. Facebook with 1.86 billion monthly active users at the end of 2016 is the most well known example. We use social networks and many web applications share social aspects that allow us to communicate with peers and extend our social circle.

Web 3.0

It's not yet here, but Web 3.0 is expected to bring Semantic Web capabilities. Advanced as Web 2.0 applications may seem, they all rely mostly on structured information. We use the same concept of searching for keywords and matching these keywords with web content without much understanding of context, content and intention of user's request. Also called **Web of Data**, Web 3.0 will rely on inter-machine communication and algorithms to provide rich interaction via diverse human computer interfaces.

SQL and NoSQL evolution

Structured Query Language existed even before the WWW. Dr. EF Codd originally published the paper *A Relational Model of Data for Large Shared Data Banks*, in June 1970, in the **Association of Computer Machinery (ACM)** journal, Communications of the ACM. SQL was initially developed at IBM by Chamberlin and Boyce in 1974. Relational Software (now Oracle Corporation) was the first to develop a commercially available implementation of SQL, targeted at United States governmental agencies.

The first **American National Standards Institute (ANSI)** SQL standard came out in 1986 and since then there have been eight revisions with the most recent being published in 2016 (SQL:2016).

SQL was not particularly popular at the start of the WWW. Static content could just be hard coded into the HTML page without much fuss. However, as functionality of websites grew, webmasters wanted to generate web page content driven by offline data sources to generate content that could change over time without redeploying code.

Common Gateway Interface (**CGI**) scripts in Perl or Unix shell were driving early database driven websites in Web 1.0. With Web 2.0, the web evolved from directly injecting SQL results into the browser to using two- and three-tier architecture that separated views from business and model logic, allowing for SQL queries to be modular and isolated from the rest of a web application.

Not only SQL (NoSQL) on the other hand is much more modern and supervenes web evolution, rising at the same time as Web 2.0 technologies. The term was first coined by Carlo Strozzi in 1998 for his open source database that was not following the SQL standard but was still relational.

This is not what we currently expect from a NoSQL database. Johan Oskarsson, a developer at Last.fm at the time, reintroduced the term in early 2009 to group a set of distributed, non-relational data stores that were being developed. Many of them were based on Google's Bigtable and MapReduce papers or Amazon's Dynamo highly available key-value based storage system.

NoSQL foundations grew upon relaxed **ACID** (**atomicity, consistency, isolation, durability**) guarantees in favor of performance, scalability, flexibility and reduced complexity. Most NoSQL databases have gone one way or another in providing as many of the previously mentioned qualities as possible, even offering tunable guarantees to the developer.

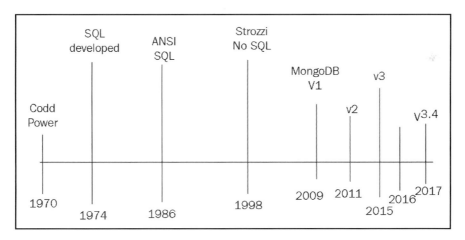

Timeline of SQL and NoSQL evolution

MongoDB evolution

10gen started developing a cloud computing stack in 2007 and soon realized that the most important innovation was centered around the document oriented database that they built to power it, MongoDB. MongoDB was initially released on August 27th, 2009.

Version 1 of MongoDB was pretty basic in terms of features, authorization, and ACID guarantees and made up for these shortcomings with performance and flexibility.

In the following sections, we can see the major features along with the version number with which they were introduced.

Major feature set for versions 1.0 and 1.2

- Document-based model
- Global lock (process level)
- Indexes on collections
- CRUD operations on documents
- No authentication (authentication was handled at the server level)
- Master/slave replication
- MapReduce (introduced in v1.2)
- Stored JavaScript functions (introduced in v1.2)

Version 2

- Background index creation (since v.1.4)
- Sharding (since v.1.6)
- More query operators (since v.1.6)
- Journaling (since v.1.8)
- Sparse and covered indexes (since v.1.8)
- Compact command to reduce disk usage
- Memory usage more efficient
- Concurrency improvements

- Index performance enhancements
- Replica sets are now more configurable and data center aware
- MapReduce improvements
- Authentication (since 2.0 for sharding and most database commands)
- Geospatial features introduced

Version 3

- Aggregation framework (since v.2.2) and enhancements (since v.2.6)
- TTL collections (since v.2.2)
- Concurrency improvements among which DB level locking (since v.2.2)
- Text search (since v.2.4) and integration (since v.2.6)
- Hashed index (since v.2.4)
- Security enhancements, role based access (since v.2.4)
- V8 JavaScript engine instead of SpiderMonkey (since v.2.4)
- Query engine improvements (since v.2.6)
- Pluggable storage engine API
- WiredTiger storage engine introduced, with document level locking while previous storage engine (now called MMAPv1) supports collection level locking

Version 3+

- Replication and sharding enhancements (since v.3.2)
- Document validation (since v.3.2)
- Aggregation framework enhanced operations (since v.3.2)

- Multiple storage engines (since v.3.2, only in Enterprise Edition)

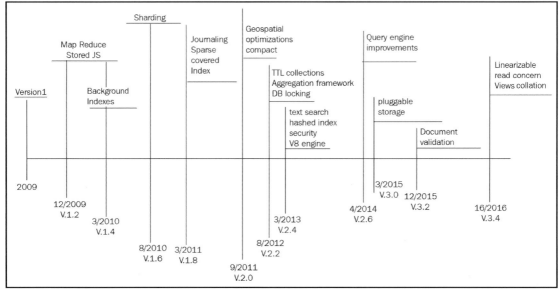

MongoDB evolution diagram

As one can observe, version 1 was pretty basic, whereas version 2 introduced most of the features present in the current version such as sharding, usable and special indexes, geospatial features, and memory and concurrency improvements.

On the way from version 2 to version 3, the aggregation framework was introduced, mainly as a supplement to the ageing (and never up to par with dedicated frameworks like Hadoop) MapReduce framework. Then, adding text search and slowly but surely improving performance, stability, and security to adapt to the increasing enterprise load of customers using MongoDB.

With WiredTiger's introduction in version 3, locking became much less of an issue for MongoDB as it was brought down from process (global lock) to document level, almost the most granular level possible.

At its current state, MongoDB is a database that can handle loads ranging from startup MVPs and POCs to enterprise applications with hundreds of servers.

MongoDB for SQL developers

MongoDB was developed in the Web 2.0 era. By then, most developers had been using SQL or **Object-relational mapping (ORM)** tools from their language of choice to access RDBMS data. As such, these developers needed an easy way to get acquainted with MongoDB from their relational background.

Thankfully, there have been several attempts at SQL to MongoDB cheat sheets that explain MongoDB terminology in SQL terms.

On a higher level there are:

- Databases, indexes just like in SQL databases
- Collections (SQL tables)
- Documents (SQL rows)
- Fields (SQL columns)
- Embedded and linked documents (SQL Joins)

Some more examples of common operations:

SQL	MongoDB
Database	Database
Table	Collection
Index	Index
Row	Document
Column	Field
Joins	Embed in document or link via DBRef
CREATE TABLE employee (name VARCHAR(100))	db.createCollection("employee")
INSERT INTO employees VALUES (Alex, 36)	db.employees.insert({name: "Alex", age: 36})
SELECT * FROM employees	db.employees.find()
SELECT * FROM employees LIMIT 1	db.employees.findOne()
SELECT DISTINCT name FROM employees	db.employees.distinct("name")

UPDATE employees SET age = 37 WHERE name = 'Alex'	db.employees.update({name: "Alex"}, {$set: {age: 37}}, {multi: true})
DELETE FROM employees WHERE name = 'Alex'	db.employees.remove({name: "Alex"})
CREATE INDEX ON employees (name ASC)	db.employees.ensureIndex({name: 1})

http://s3.amazonaws.com/info-mongodb-com/sql_to_mongo.pdf

MongoDB for NoSQL developers

As MongoDB has grown from being a niche database solution to the Swiss Army knife of NoSQL technologies, more developers are coming to it from a NoSQL background as well.

Setting the SQL to NoSQL differences aside, users from columnar type databases face the most challenges. Cassandra and HBase being the most popular column oriented database management systems, we will examine the differences and how a developer can migrate a system to MongoDB.

- **Flexibility**: MongoDB's notion of documents that can contain sub-documents nested in complex hierarchies is really expressive and flexible. This is similar to the comparison between MongoDB and SQL, with the added benefit that MongoDB can map easier to plain old objects from any programming language, allowing for easy deployment and maintenance.

- **Flexible query model**: A user can selectively index some parts of each document, query based on attribute values, regular expressions or ranges, and have as many properties per object as needed by the application layer. Primary, secondary indexes as well as special types of indexes like sparse ones can help greatly with query efficiency. Using a JavaScript shell with MapReduce makes it really easy for most developers and many data analysts to quickly take a look into data and get valuable insights.

- **Native aggregation**: The aggregation framework provides an ETL pipeline for users to extract and transform data from MongoDB and either load them in a new format or export it from MongoDB to other data sources. This can also help data analysts and scientists get the slice of data they need performing data wrangling along the way.

- **Schemaless model**: This is a result of MongoDB's design philosophy to give applications the power and responsibility to interpret different properties found in a collection's documents. In contrast to Cassandra's or HBase's schema based approach, in MongoDB a developer can store and process dynamically generated attributes.

MongoDB key characteristics and use cases

In this section, we will analyze MongoDB's characteristics as a database. Understanding the features that MongoDB provides can help developers and architects evaluate the requirement at hand and how MongoDB can help fulfill it. Also, we will go through some common use cases from MongoDB Inc's experience that have delivered the best results for its users.

Key characteristics

MongoDB has grown to a general purpose NoSQL database, offering the best of both RDBMS and NoSQL worlds. Some of the key characteristics are:

- It's a general purpose database. In contrast with other NoSQL databases that are built for purpose (for example, graph databases), MongoDB can serve heterogeneous loads and multiple purposes within an application.
- Flexible schema design. Document oriented approaches with non-defined attributes that can be modified on the fly is a key contrast between MongoDB and relational databases.
- It's built with high availability from the ground up. In our era of five nines in availability, this has to be a given. Coupled with automatic failover on detection of a server failure, this can help achieve high uptime.
- Feature rich. Offering the full range of SQL equivalent operators along with features such as MapReduce, aggregation framework, TTL/capped collections, and secondary indexing, MongoDB can fit many use cases, no matter how diverse the requirements are.
- Scalability and load balancing. It's built to scale, both vertically but most importantly horizontally. Using sharding, an architect can share load between different instances and achieve both read and write scalability. Data balancing happens automatically and transparently to the user by the shard balancer.

- Aggregation framework. Having an extract transform load framework built in the database means that a developer can perform most of the ETL logic before the data leaves the database, eliminating in many cases the need for complex data pipelines.
- Native replication. Data will get replicated across a replica set without complicated setup.
- Security features. Both authentication and authorization are taken into account so that an architect can secure her MongoDB instances.
- JSON (BSON, Binary JSON) objects for storing and transmitting documents. JSON is widely used across the web for frontend and API communication and as such it's easier when the database is using the same protocol.
- MapReduce. Even though the MapReduce engine isn't as advanced as it is in dedicated frameworks, it is nonetheless a great tool for building data pipelines.
- Querying and geospatial information in 2D and 3D. This may not be critical for many applications, but if it is for your use case then it's really convenient to be able to use the same database for geospatial calculations along with data storage.

What is the use case for MongoDB?

MongoDB being a hugely popular NoSQL database means that there are several use cases where it has succeeded in supporting quality applications with a great time to market delivery time.

Many of its most successful use cases center around the following areas:

- Integration of siloed data providing a single view of them
- Internet of Things
- Mobile applications
- Real-time analytics
- Personalization
- Catalog management
- Content management

All these success stories share some common characteristics. We will try and break these down in order of relative importance.

Schema flexibility is most probably the most important one. Being able to store documents inside a collection that can have different properties can help both during development phase but also in ingesting data from heterogeneous sources that may or may not have the same properties. In contrast with an RDBMS where columns need to be predefined and having sparse data can be penalized, in MongoDB this is the norm and it's a feature that most use cases share. Having the ability to deep nest attributes into documents, add arrays of values into attributes and all the while being able to search and index these fields helps application developers exploit the schema-less nature of MongoDB.

Scaling and sharding are the most common patterns for MongoDB use cases. Easily scaling using built-in sharding and using replica sets for data replication and offloading primary servers from read load can help developers store data effectively.

Many use cases also use MongoDB as a way of archiving data. Used as a pure data store and not having the need to define schemas, it's fairly easy to dump data into MongoDB, only to be analyzed at a later date by business analysts either using the shell or some of the numerous BI tools that can integrate easily with MongoDB. Breaking data down further based on time caps or document count can help serve these datasets from RAM, the use case where MongoDB is most effective.

On this point, keeping datasets in RAM is more often another common pattern. MongoDB uses MMAP storage (called **MMAPv1**) in most versions up to the most recent, which delegates data mapping to the underlying operating system. This means that most GNU/Linux based systems working with collections that can be stored in RAM will dramatically increase performance. This is less of an issue with the introduction of pluggable storage engines like WiredTiger, more on that in `Chapter 8`, *Storage Engines*.

Capped collections are also a feature used in many use cases. Capped collections can restrict documents in a collection by count or by overall size of the collection. In the latter case, we need to have an estimate of size per document to calculate how many documents will fit in our target size. Capped collections are a quick and dirty solution to answer requests like *"Give me the last hour's overview of the logs."* without any need for maintenance and running async background jobs to clean our collection. Oftentimes, these may be used to quickly build and operate a queuing system. Instead of deploying and maintaining a dedicated queuing system like ActiveMQ, a developer can use a collection to store messages and then use native tailable cursors provided by MongoDB to iterate through results as they pile up and feed an external system.

Low operational overhead is also a common pattern in use cases. Developers working in agile teams can operate and maintain clusters of MongoDB servers without the need for a dedicated DBA. MongoDB Management Service can greatly help in reducing administrative overhead, whereas MongoDB Atlas, the hosted solution by MongoDB Inc., means that developers don't need to deal with operational headaches.

In terms of business sectors using MongoDB, there is a huge variety coming from almost all industries. Where there seems to be a greater penetration though, is in cases that have to deal with lots of data with a relatively low business value in each single data point. Fields like IoT can benefit the most by exploiting availability over consistency design, storing lots of data from sensors in a cost efficient way. Financial services on the other hand, many times have absolutely stringent consistency requirements aligned with proper ACID characteristics that make MongoDB more of a challenge to adapt. Transactions carrying financial data can be a few bytes but have an impact of millions of dollars, hence all the safety nets around transmitting this type of information correctly.

Location-based data is also a field where MongoDB has thrived. Foursquare being one of the most prominent early clients, MongoDB offers quite a rich set of features around 2D and 3D geolocation data, offering features like searching by distance, geofencing, and intersection between geographical areas.

Overall, the rich feature set is the common pattern across different use cases. By providing features that can be used in many different industries and applications, MongoDB can be a unified solution for all business needs, offering users the ability to minimize operational overhead and at the same time iterate quickly in product development.

MongoDB criticism

MongoDB has had its fair share of criticism throughout the years. The web-scale proposition has been met with skepticism by many developers. The counter argument is that scale is not needed most of the time and we should focus on other design considerations. While this may be true on several occasions, it's a false dichotomy and in an ideal world we would have both. MongoDB is as close as it can get to combining scalability with features and ease of use/time to market.

MongoDB's schema-less nature is also a big point of debate and argument. Schema-less can be really beneficial in many use cases as it allows for heterogeneous data to be dumped into the database without complex cleansing or ending up with lots of empty columns or blocks of text stuffed into a single column. On the other hand, this is a double-edged sword as a developer may end up with many documents in a collection that have loose semantics in their fields and it becomes really hard to extract these semantics at the code level. What we can have in the end if schema design is not optimal, is a plain datastore rather than a database.

Lack of proper ACID guarantees is a recurring complaint from the relational world. Indeed, if a developer needs access to more than one document at a time it's not easy to guarantee RDBMS properties as there are no transactions. Having no transactions in the RDBMS sense also means that complex writes will need to have application level logic to rollback. If you need to update three documents in two collections to mark an application level transaction complete and the third document doesn't get updated for whatever reason, the application will need to undo the previous two writes, something that may not be exactly trivial.

Defaults that favored setting up MongoDB but not operating it in a production environment are also frowned upon. For years, the default write behavior was **write and forget**, sending a write wouldn't wait for an acknowledgement before attempting the next write, resulting in insane write speeds with poor behavior in case of failure. Authentication is also an afterthought, leaving thousands of MongoDB databases in the public internet prey to whoever wants to read the stored data. Even though these were conscious design decisions, they are decisions that have affected developers' perception of MongoDB.

There are of course good points to be made from criticism. There are use cases where a non relational, unsupporting transactions database will not be a good choice. Any application that depends on transactions and places ACID properties higher than anything else is probably a great use case for a traditional RDBMS but not for a NoSQL database.

MongoDB configuration and best practices

Without diving too deep into why, in this section we present some best practices around operations, schema design, durability, replication, sharding, and security. More information as to why and how to implement these best practices will be presented in the respective chapters and as always with best practices, these have to be taken with a pinch of salt.

Operational best practices

MongoDB as a database is built with developers in mind and developed during the web era so does not require as much operational overhead as traditional RDBMSs. That being said, there are some best practices that need to be followed to be proactive and achieve high availability goals.

In order of importance (somewhat), here they are:

1. **Turn journaling on by default**: Journaling uses a write ahead log to be able to recover in case a mongo server gets shut down abruptly. With MMAPv1 storage engine, journaling should be always on. With WiredTiger storage engine, journaling and checkpointing are used together to ensure data durability. In any case, it's a good practice to use journaling and fine tune the size of journals and frequency of checkpoints to avoid risk of data loss. In MMAPv1, the journal is flushed to disk every 100 ms by default. If MongoDB is waiting for the journal before acknowledging the write operation, the journal is flushed to disk every 30 ms.

2. **Your working set should fit in memory**: Again, especially when using MMAPv1 the working set is best being less than the RAM of the underlying machine or VM. MMAPv1 uses memory mapped files from the underlying operating system which can benefit greatly if there isn't much swap happening between RAM and disk. WiredTiger on the other hand is much more efficient at using memory but still benefits greatly from the same principles. The working set is at maximum the datasize plus index size as reported by db.stats().

3. **Mind the location of your data files**: Data files can be mounted anywhere using the --dbpath command line option. It is really important to make sure data files are stored in partitions with sufficient disk space, preferably XFS or at least Ext4.

4. **Keep yourself updated with versions**: Odd major numbered versions are the stable ones. So, 3.2 is stable whereas 3.3 is not. In this example 3.3 is the development version that will eventually materialize into stable version 3.4 . It's a good practice to always update to the latest security updated version (3.4.3 at the time of writing) and consider updating as soon as the next stable version comes out (3.6 at this example).

5. **Use Mongo MMS to graphically monitor your service**: MongoDB Inc's free monitoring service is a great tool to get an overview of a MongoDB cluster, notifications, and alerts and be proactive about potential issues.

6. **Scale up if your metrics show heavy use**: Actually not really heavy usage. Key metrics of >65% in CPU, RAM, or if you are starting to notice disk swapping should be an alert to start thinking about scaling, either vertically by using bigger machines or horizontally by sharding.

7. **Be careful when sharding**: Sharding is like a strong commitment to your shard key. If you make the wrong decision it may be really difficult operationally to go back. When designing for sharding, architects need to take a long and deep consideration of current workloads both in reads and also writes plus what the expected data access patterns are.

8. **Use an application driver maintained by the MongoDB team**: These drivers are supported and in general get updated faster than their equivalents. If MongoDB does not support the language you are using yet, please open a ticket in MongoDB's JIRA tracking system.

9. **Schedule regular backups**: No matter if you are using standalone servers, replica sets, or sharding, a regular backup policy should also be used as a second level guard against data loss. XFS is a great choice as a filesystem as it can perform snapshot backups.

10. **Manual backups should be avoided**: Regular automated backups should be used when possible. If we need to resort to a manual backup then we can use a hidden member in a replica set to take the backup from. We have to make sure that we are using `db.fsyncwithlock` at this member to get the maximum consistency at this node, along with journaling turned on. If this volume is on AWS, we can get away with taking an EBS snapshot straight away.

11. **Enable database access control**: Never, ever put a database in a production system without access control. Access control should both be implemented at a node level by a proper firewall that only allows access to specific application servers to the database and also in DB level by using the built-in roles, or defining custom defined ones. This has to be initialized at startup time by using the `--auth` command-line parameter and configured using the `admin` collection.

12. **Test your deployment using real data**: MongoDB being a schema-less document oriented database means that you may have documents with varying fields. This means that it's even more important than with an RDBMS to test using data that resembles production data as closely as possible. A document with an extra field of an unexpected value can make the difference between an application working smoothly or crashing at runtime. Try to deploy a staging server using production level data or at least fake your production data in staging using an appropriate library like Faker for Ruby.

Schema design best practices

MongoDB is schema-less and you have to design your collections and indexes to accommodate for this fact:

- **Index early and often**: Identify common query patterns using MMS, Compass GUI, or logs and index for these early and using as many indexes as possible at the beginning of a project.
- **Eliminate unnecessary indexes**: A bit counter-intuitive to the preceding suggestion, monitor your database for changing query patterns and drop the indexes that aren't being used. An index will consume RAM and I/O as it needs to be stored and updated alongside with documents in the database. Using an aggregation pipeline and `$indexStats` a developer can identify indexes that are seldom being used and eliminate them.
- **Use a compound index rather than index intersection**: Querying with multiple predicates (A and B , C or D and E and so on) will most of the time work better with a single compound index than with multiple simple indexes. Also, a compound index will have its data ordered by field and we can use this to our advantage when querying. An index on fields A,B,C will be used in queries for A, (A,B), (A,B,C) but not in querying for (B,C) or (C) .
- **Low selectivity indexes**: Indexing a field on gender for example will statistically still return half of our documents back, whereas an index on last name will only return a handful of documents with the same last name.
- **Use of regular expressions**: Again, since indexes are ordered by value, searching using a regular expression with leading wildcards (that is, `/.*BASE/`) won't be able to use the index. Searching with trailing wildcards (that is, `/DATA.*/`) can be efficient as long as there are enough case sensitive characters in the expression.
- **Avoid negation in queries**: Indexes are indexing values, not the absence of them. Using NOT in queries can result in full table scans instead of using the index.
- **Use partial indexes**: If we need to index a subset of the documents in a collection, partial indexes can help us minimize the index set and improve performance. A partial index will include a condition on the filter that we use in the desired query.
- **Use document validation**: Use document validation to monitor for new attributes being inserted to your documents and decide what to do with them. With document validation set to warn, we can keep a log of documents that were inserted with arbitrary attributes that we didn't expect during the design phase and decide if this is a bug or a feature of our design.

- **Use MongoDB Compass**: MongoDB's free visualization tool is great to get a quick overview of our data and how it grows across time.
- **Respect the maximum document size of 16 MB**: The maximum document size for MongoDB is 16 MB. This is a fairly generous limit but it is one that should not be violated under any circumstance. Allowing documents to grow unbounded should not be an option and as efficient as it may be to embed documents, we should always keep in mind that this should be under control.
- **Use the appropriate storage engine**: MongoDB has introduced several new storage engines since version 3.2. The in-memory storage engine should be used for real-time workloads, whereas the encrypted storage engine should be the engine of choice when there are strict requirements around data security.

Best practices for write durability

Writing durability can be fine tuned in MongoDB and according to our application design it should be as strict as possible without affecting our performance goals.

Fine tune data flush to disk interval: In the WiredTiger storage engine, the default is to flush data to disk every 60 seconds after the last checkpoint, or after 2 GB of data has been written. This can be changed using the `--wiredTigerCheckpointDelaySecs` command-line option.

In MMAPv1, data files are flushed to disk every 60 seconds. This can be changed using the `--syncDelay` command-line option:

- With WiredTiger, use the XFS filesystem for multi-disk consistent snapshots
- Turn off atime and diratime in data volumes
- Make sure you have enough swap space, usually double your memory size
- Use a NOOP scheduler if running in virtualized environments
- Raise file descriptor limits to the tens of thousands
- Disable transparent huge pages, enable standard 4K VM pages instead
- Write safety should be at least journaled
- SSD read ahead default should be set to 16 blocks, HDD should be 32 blocks
- Turn NUMA off in BIOS
- Use RAID 10

- Synchronize time between hosts using NTP especially in sharded environments
- Only use 64-bit builds for production; 32-bit builds are outdated and can only support up to 2 GB of memory

Best practices for replication

Replica sets are MongoDB's mechanism to provide redundancy, high availability, and higher read throughput under the right conditions. Replication in MongoDB is easy to configure and light in operational terms:

- **Always use replica sets**: Even if your dataset is at the moment small and you don't expect it to grow exponentially, you never know when that might happen. Also, having a replica set of at least three servers helps design for redundancy, separating work loads between real time and analytics (using the secondaries) and having data redundancy built from day one.
- **Use a replica set to your advantage**: A replica set is not just for data replication. We can and should in most cases use the primary server for writes and preference reads from one of the secondaries to offload the primary server. This can be done by setting read preference for reads, together with the correct write concern to ensure writes propagate as needed.
- **Use an odd number of replicas in a MongoDB replica set**: If a server does down or loses connectivity with the rest of them (network partitioning), the rest have to vote as to which one will be elected as the primary server. If we have an odd number of replica set members, we can guarantee that each subset of servers knows if they belong to the majority or the minority of the replica set members. If we can't have an odd number of replicas, we need to have one extra host set as an arbiter with the sole purpose of voting in the election process. Even a micro instance in EC2 could serve this purpose.

Best practices for sharding

Sharding is MongoDB's solution for horizontal scaling. In Chapter 8, *Storage Engines*, we will cover how to use it in more detail, here are some best practices based on the underlying data architecture:

- **Think about query routing**: Based on different shard keys and techniques, the mongos query router may direct the query to some or all of the members of a shard. It's important to take our queries into account when designing sharding so that we don't end up with our queries hitting all of our shards.
- **Use tag aware sharding**: Tags can provide more fine-grained distribution of data across our shards. Using the right set of tags for each shard, we can ensure that subsets of data get stored in a specific set of shards. This can be useful for data proximity between application servers, MongoDB shards, and the users.

Best practices for security

Security is always a multi-layered approach and these few recommendations do not form an exhaustive list, rather just the bare basics that need to be done in any MongoDB database:

- HTTP status interface should be disabled.
- REST API should be disabled.
- JSON API should be disabled.
- Connect to MongoDB using SSL.
- Audit system activity.
- Use a dedicated system user to access MongoDB with appropriate system level access
- Disable server-side scripting if not needed. This will affect MapReduce, built-in `db.group()` commands, and `$where` operations. If these are not used in your codebase, it is better to disable server-side scripting at startup using the `--noscripting` parameter.

Best practices for AWS

When using MongoDB, we can use our own servers in a datacenter, a MongoDB hosted solution like MongoDB Atlas, or get instances from Amazon using EC2. EC2 instances are virtualized and share resources in a transparent way with collocated VMs in the same physical host. So there are some more considerations to take into account if going down that route:

- Use EBS optimized EC2 instances.
- Get EBS volumes with provisioned IOPS (I/O operations per second) for consistent performance.

- Use EBS snapshotting for backup and restore.
- Use different Availability Zones for High Availability and different regions for Disaster Recovery.
  Different availability zones within each region that Amazon provides guarantee that our data will be highly available. Different regions should only be used for Disaster Recovery in case a catastrophic event ever takes out an entire region. A region can be EU-West-2 for London, whereas an availability zone is a subdivision within a region; currently two availability zones are available for London.
- Deploy global, access local.
- For truly global applications with users from different time zones, we should have application servers in different regions access data that is closest to them using the right read preference configuration in each server.

Reference documentation

Reading a book is great, reading this book is even greater, but continuous learning is the only way to keep up to date with MongoDB. These are the places you should go for updates and development/operational reference.

MongoDB documentation

Online documentation available at: `https://docs.mongodb.com/manual/` is the starting point for every developer, new or seasoned.

The JIRA tracker is a great place to take a look at fixed bugs and features coming up next: `https://jira.mongodb.org/browse/SERVER/`.

Packt references

Some other great books on MongoDB are:

- *MongoDB for Java developers*, by Francesco Marchioni
- *MongoDB Data Modeling*, by Wilson da Rocha França
- Any book by Kristina Chodorow

Further reading

The MongoDB user group (`https://groups.google.com/forum/#!forum/mongodb-user`) has a great archive of user questions about features, and long-standing bugs. It's a place to go when something doesn't work as expected.

Online forums (Stack Overflow, reddit, among others) are always a source of knowledge with the trap that something may have been posted a few years ago and may not apply anymore. Always check before trying.

And finally, MongoDB university is a great place to keep your skills up to date and learn about the latest features and additions: `https://university.mongodb.com/`.

Summary

In this chapter, we went on a journey through web, SQL, and NoSQL technologies from their inception to their current state. We identified how MongoDB has been shaping the world of NoSQL databases for the past years and how it is positioned against other SQL and NoSQL solutions.

We explored MongoDB's key characteristics and how MongoDB has been used in production deployments. We identified best practices for designing, deploying, and operating MongoDB.

Finally, we learned how to learn by going through documentation and online resources to stay up to date with latest features and developments.

In the next chapter, we will go deeper into schema design and data modeling and how to connect to MongoDB both using the official drivers and also using an **Object Document Mapper (ODM)**, a variation of object-relational mappers for NoSQL databases.

2
Schema Design and Data Modeling

The second chapter of our book will focus on schema design for schema-less databases such as MongoDB. This may sound counterintuitive; in fact there are considerations that we should take into account when developing for MongoDB.

The main points of this chapter are:

- Schema considerations for NoSQL
- Data types supported by MongoDB
- Comparison between different data types
- How to model our data for atomic operations
- Modeling relationships between collections:
    - One to one
    - One to many
    - Many to many
- How to prepare data for text searches in MongoDB
- Ruby:
    - How to connect using the Ruby mongo driver
    - How to connect using Ruby's most widely used ODM, Mongoid
    - Mongoid model inheritance management
- Python:
    - How to connect using the Python mongo driver
    - How to connect using Python's ODM, PyMODM
    - PyMODM model inheritance management

- PHP:
  - Sample code using annotations-driven code
  - How to connect using the MongoDB PHP driver
  - How to connect using PHP's ODM, Doctrine
  - Model inheritance management using Doctrine

Relational schema design

In relational databases, we design with the goal of avoiding anomalies and redundancy. Anomalies can happen when we have the same information stored in multiple columns; we update one of them but not the rest and we end up with conflicting information for the same column of information. An anomaly can also happen when we cannot delete a row without losing information that we need, possibly in other rows referenced by it. Data redundancy can happen when our data is not in a normal form, but has duplicate data across different tables, which can lead to data inconsistency and is difficult to maintain.

In relational databases, we use normal forms to normalize our data. Starting from the basic **1NF (first normal form)**, onto the **2NF**, **3NF**, and **BCNF**, we model our data taking functional dependencies into account and, if we follow the rules, we can end up with many more tables than domain model objects.

In practice, relational database modeling is often driven by the structure of the data that we have. In web applications following some sort of MVC model pattern, we will model our database according to our models, which are modeled after the UML diagram conventions. Abstractions such the ORM for Django or the Active Record for Rails help application developers abstract database structure to object models. Ultimately, many times we end up designing our database based on the structure of the available data. Thus, we are designing around the answers that we can have.

MongoDB schema design

In contrast to relational databases, in MongoDB we have to base our modeling on our application-specific data access patterns. Finding out the questions that our users will have is paramount to designing our entities. In contrast to an RDBMS, data duplication and denormalization are used far more frequently and with solid reason.

The document model that MongoDB uses means that every document can hold substantially more or less information than the next one, even within the same collection. Coupled with rich and detailed queries being possible in MongoDB in the embedded document level, this means that we are free to design our documents in any way that we want. When we know our data access patterns we can estimate which fields need to be embedded and which can be split out to different collections.

Read-write ratio

The read to write ratio is often an important design consideration for MongoDB modeling. When reading data, we want to avoid scatter and gather situations, where we have to hit several shards with random I/O requests to get the data our application needs.

When writing data, on the other hand, we want to spread out writes to as many servers as possible, to avoid overloading any single one of them. These goals appear to be conflicting on the surface but they can be combined once we know our access patterns, coupled with application design considerations, like using a replica set to read from secondary nodes.

Data modeling

In this section, we will discuss the data types MongoDB uses, how they map to data types that programming languages use, and how we can model data relationships in MongoDB using Ruby, Python, and PHP.

Data types

MongoDB uses BSON, a binary-encoded serialization for JSON documents. BSON extends on JSON data types offering for example, native date and binary data types.

BSON, compared to protocol buffers, allows for more flexible schemas that come at the cost of space efficiency. In general, BSON is space efficient, easy to traverse, and time-efficient in encoding/decoding operations.

Type	Number	Alias	Notes
Double	1	double	
String	2	string	
Object	3	object	

Array	4	`array`	
Binary data	5	`binData`	
ObjectId	7	`objectId`	
Boolean	8	`bool`	
Date	9	`date`	
Null	10	`null`	
Regular expression	11	`regex`	
JavaScript	13	`javascript`	
JavaScript (with scope)	15	`javascriptWithScope`	
32-bit integer	16	`int`	
Timestamp	17	`timestamp`	
64-bit integer	18	`long`	
Decimal128	19	`decimal`	New in version 3.4
Min key	-1	`minKey`	
Max key	127	`maxKey`	
Undefined	6	`undefined`	Deprecated
DBPointer	12	`dbPointer`	Deprecated
Symbol	14	`symbol`	Deprecated

MongoDB Documentation https://docs.mongodb.com/manual/reference/bson-types/

In MongoDB, we can have documents with different value types for a given field and distinguish among them in querying using the `$type` operator.

For example, if we have a balance field in GBP with 32-bit integers and double data types, if the balance has pennies in it or not, we can easily query for all accounts that have a rounded balance with any of the following queries:

```
db.account.find( { "balance" : { $type : 16 } } );
db.account.find( { "balance" : { $type : "integer" } } );
```

Comparing different data types

Due to the nature of MongoDB, it's perfectly acceptable to have different data type objects in the same field. This may happen by accident or on purpose (that is, null and actual values in a field)

The sorting order of different types of data is as follows from highest to lowest:

1. `MaxKey` (internal type).
2. Regular expression.
3. Timestamp.
4. Date.
5. Boolean.
6. `ObjectId`.
7. `BinData`.
8. Array.
9. Object.
10. Symbol, string.
11. Numbers (`ints`, `longs`, `doubles`).
12. Null.
13. `MinKey` (internal type).

Non-existent fields get sorted as if they have null in the respective field. Comparing arrays is a bit more complex. An ascending order of comparison (or <) will compare the smallest element of each array. A descending order of comparison (or >) will compare the largest element of each array.

For example, see the following scenario:

```
> db.types.find()
{ "_id" : ObjectId("5908d58455454e2de6519c49"), "a" : [ 1, 2, 3 ] }
{ "_id" : ObjectId("5908d59d55454e2de6519c4a"), "a" : [ 2, 5 ] }
```

In ascending order, this is as follows:

```
> db.types.find().sort({a:1})
{ "_id" : ObjectId("5908d58455454e2de6519c49"), "a" : [ 1, 2, 3 ] }
{ "_id" : ObjectId("5908d59d55454e2de6519c4a"), "a" : [ 2, 5 ] }
```

Whereas in descending order it is as follows:

```
> db.types.find().sort({a:-1})
{ "_id" : ObjectId("5908d59d55454e2de6519c4a"), "a" : [ 2, 5 ] }
{ "_id" : ObjectId("5908d58455454e2de6519c49"), "a" : [ 1, 2, 3 ] }
```

The same applies when comparing an array with a single number value, as illustrated in the following example.

Inserting a new document with an integer value of 4:

```
> db.types.insert({"a":4})
WriteResult({ "nInserted" : 1 })
```

Descending sort:

```
> db.types.find().sort({a:-1})
{ "_id" : ObjectId("5908d59d55454e2de6519c4a"), "a" : [ 2, 5 ] }
{ "_id" : ObjectId("5908d73c55454e2de6519c4c"), "a" : 4 }
{ "_id" : ObjectId("5908d58455454e2de6519c49"), "a" : [ 1, 2, 3 ] }
```

Ascending sort:

```
> db.types.find().sort({a:1})
{ "_id" : ObjectId("5908d58455454e2de6519c49"), "a" : [ 1, 2, 3 ] }
{ "_id" : ObjectId("5908d59d55454e2de6519c4a"), "a" : [ b, 5 ] }
{ "_id" : ObjectId("5908d73c55454e2de6519c4c"), "a" : 4 }
```

In each case, we highlighted the values being compared in bold.

Date type

Dates are stored as milliseconds with effect from January 1st, 1970 (epoch time). They are 64-bit signed integers, allowing for a range of 135 million years before and after 1970. A negative date value denotes a date before January 1st, 1970. The BSON specification refers to the Date type as *UTC datetime*.

Dates in MongoDB are stored in UTC. There isn't a *timestamp with timezone* datatype like in some relational databases. Applications that need to access and modify timestamps based on local time should store the timezone offset together with the date and offset dates on an application level.

In the MongoDB shell, this could be done this way using JavaScript:

```
var now = new Date();
db.page_views.save({date: now,
                    offset: now.getTimezoneOffset()});
```

And then applying the saved offset to reconstruct the original local time:

```
var record = db.page_views.findOne();
var localNow = new Date( record.date.getTime() - ( record.offset * 60000 )
);
```

ObjectId

ObjectId is a special data type for MongoDB. Every document has an _id field from cradle to grave. It is the primary key for each document in a collection and has to be unique. If we omit this field in a create statement, it will be assigned automatically with an ObjectId.

Messing with the ObjectId is not advisable but we can use it (with caution!) for our purposes.

ObjectId is:

- 12-bytes
- Ordered; sorting by _id will sort by creation time for each document
- Storing the creation time that can be accessed by .getTimeStamp() in the shell

The structure of an ObjectId:

- a 4-byte value representing the seconds since the Unix epoch
- a 3-byte machine identifier
- a 2-byte process id
- a 3-byte counter, starting with a random value

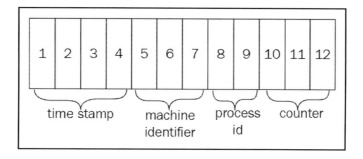

By their structure, `ObjectIds` will be unique for all purposes; however since these are generated on the client side, one should check the underlying library's source code to verify that implementation is according to specification.

Modeling data for atomic operations

MongoDB is relaxing many of the typical **ACID (Atomicity, Consistency, Isolation, Durability)** constraints found in RDBMSes. In the absence of transactions, it can be sometimes a pain to keep state consistent across operations, especially in event of failures.

Luckily, some operations are atomic at the document level:

- `update()`
- `findandmodify()`
- `remove()`

These are all atomic (all or nothing) for a single document.

This means that if we embed information in the same document, we can make sure that they are always in sync.

An example would be an inventory application, with a document per item in our inventory, where we would need to total available items left, how many have been placed in a shopping cart in sync, and summing up to the total available items.

With `total_available = 5`, `available_now = 3`, `shopping_cart_count = 2`, this could look like:

```
{available_now : 3, Shopping_cart_by: ["userA", "userB"] }
```

When someone places the item in his/her shopping cart, we can issue an atomic update, adding his/her userId in the `shopping_cart_by` field and decreasing the `available_now` field by 1 at the same time.

This operation will be guaranteed atomic at the document level. If we need to update multiple documents within the same collection, the update may update some of the documents but not all of them and still go through.

This pattern can help in some cases but unfortunately not with every case. In many cases, we need multiple updates being applied all or nothing across documents or even collections.

A typical example would be a bank transfer between two accounts. We want to subtract *x* GBP from user A, then add *x* to user B. If we fail to do either of the two steps, we should return to the original state for both balances.

The details of this pattern are outside the scope of this book, but roughly, the idea is to implement a hand-coded two phase commit protocol. This protocol should create a new transaction entry for each transfer with every possible state in this transaction such as initial, pending, applied, done, canceling, and canceled and, based on the state that each transaction is left at, apply the appropriate `rollback` function to it.

If you find yourself absolutely needing to implement transactions in a database that was built to avoid them, take a step back and rethink why you need to do that…

Write isolation

Sparingly, we could use `$isolated` to isolate writes to multiple documents from other writers or readers to these documents. In the previous example, we could use `$isolated` to update multiple documents and make sure that we update both balances before anyone else gets the chance to double-spend to drain the source account from its funds.

What this won't give us though, is atomicity, the all-or-nothing approach. So if the update only partially modifies both accounts, we still need to detect and unroll any modifications made in the pending state.

`$isolated` uses an exclusive lock in the entire collection no matter the storage engine used. This means a severe speed penalty when using it, especially for WiredTiger document level locking semantics.

`$isolated` does not work with sharded clusters, which may be an issue when we decide to go from replica sets to sharded deployment.

Read isolation and consistency

MongoDB read operations would be characterized as **read uncommitted** in a traditional RDBMS definition. What this means is that by default reads may get values that may not finally persist to the disk in the event, for example, of data loss or a replica set rollback operation.

In particular, when updating multiple documents with the default write behavior, lack of isolation may result in the following results:

- Reads may miss documents that were updated during the update operations
- Non-serializable operations
- Read operations are not point-in-time

These can be resolved by using the `$isolated` operator with a heavy performance penalty.

Queries with cursors that don't use `.snapshot()` may also in some cases get inconsistent results. This can happen if the query's result cursor fetches a document, this document receives an update while the query is still fetching results and because of insufficient padding, ends up in a different physical location on disk, ahead of the query's result cursor position. `.snapshot()` is a solution for this edge case, with the following limitations:

- It doesn't work with sharding
- It doesn't work with `sort()` or `hint()` to force an index to be used
- It still will not provide point-in-time read behavior

If our collection has mostly static data, we can use a unique index in the query field to simulate `snapshot()` and still be able to apply `sort()` to it.

All in all, we need to apply safeguards at the application level to make sure that we won't end up with unexpected results.

Starting from version 3.4, MongoDB offers a linearizable read concern. With linearizable read concern from a primary member of a replica set and a majority write concern, we can ensure that multiple threads can read and write a single document as if a single thread was performing these operations one after the other. This is considered a linearizable schedule in RDBMS and MongoDB calls it the real time order.

Modeling relationships

In the following sections, we will explain how we can translate relationships in Relational Database Management Systems theory into MongoDB's document-collection hierarchy. We will also examine how we can model our data for text search in MongoDB.

One-to-one

Coming from the relational DB world, we identify objects by their relationships. A one-to-one relationship could be a person with an address. Modeling it in a relational database would most probably require two tables: a person and an `address` table with a foreign key `person_id` in the `address` table.

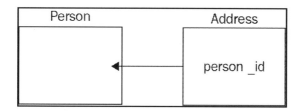

The perfect analogy in MongoDB would be two collections, person and address, looking like this:

```
> db.Person.findOne()
{
"_id" : ObjectId("590a530e3e37d79acac26a41"), "name" : "alex"
}
> db.Address.findOne()
{
"_id" : ObjectId("590a537f3e37d79acac26a42"),
"person_id" : ObjectId("590a530e3e37d79acac26a41"),
"address" : "N29DD"
}
```

Now we can use the same pattern as we do in a relational database to find a person from an address:

```
> db.Person.find({"_id":
db.Address.findOne({"address":"N29DD"}).person_id})
{
"_id" : ObjectId("590a530e3e37d79acac26a41"), "name" : "alex"
}
```

This pattern is well known and works in the relational world.

In MongoDB, we don't have to follow this pattern and there are more suitable ways to model these kinds of relationship.

A way in which we would typically model a one-one or one-few relationship in MongoDB would be through embedding. The same example would then become if the person has two addresses:

```
{ "_id" : ObjectId("590a55863e37d79acac26a43"), "name" : "alex", "address"
: [ "N29DD", "SW1E5ND" ] }
```

Using an embedded array we can have access to every address this user has. Embedding querying is rich and flexible so that we can store more information in each document:

```
{ "_id" : ObjectId("590a56743e37d79acac26a44"),
"name" : "alex",
"address" : [ { "description" : "home", "postcode" : "N29DD" },
{ "description" : "work", "postcode" : "SW1E5ND" } ] }
```

Advantages of this approach:

- No need for two queries across different collections
- Can exploit atomic updates to make sure that updates in the document will be all-or-nothing from the perspective of other readers of this document
- Can embed attributes in multiple nest levels creating complex structures

The most notable disadvantage is that the document maximum size is 16 MB so this approach cannot be used for an arbitrary, ever growing number of attributes. Storing hundreds of elements in embedded arrays will also degrade performance.

One-to-many, many-to-many

When the number of elements in the many side of the relationship can grow unbounded, it's better to use references.

References can come in two forms:

From the one-side of the relationship, store an array of many-sided-elements:

```
> db.Person.findOne()
{ "_id" : ObjectId("590a530e3e37d79acac26a41"), "name" : "alex", addresses:
[ ObjectID('590a56743e37d79acac26a44'),
ObjectID('590a56743e37d79acac26a46'),
ObjectID('590a56743e37d79acac26a54') ] }
```

This way we can get the array of addresses from the one-side and then query with `in` to get all the documents from the many-side:

```
> person = db.Person.findOne({"name":"mary"})
> addresses = db.Addresses.find({_id: {$in: person.addresses} })
```

Turning this one-many to many-many is as easy as storing this array in both ends of the relationship (`person` and `address` collections).

From the many-side of the relationship, store a reference to the one-side:

```
> db.Address.find()
{ "_id" : ObjectId("590a55863e37d79acac26a44"), "person":
ObjectId("590a530e3e37d79acac26a41"), "address" : [ "N29DD" ] }
{ "_id" : ObjectId("590a55863e37d79acac26a46"), "person":
ObjectId("590a530e3e37d79acac26a41"), "address" : [ "SW1E5ND" ] }
{ "_id" : ObjectId("590a55863e37d79acac26a54"), "person":
ObjectId("590a530e3e37d79acac26a41"), "address" : [ "N225QG" ] }
> person = db.Person.findOne({"name":"alex"})
> addresses = db.Addresses.find({"person": person._id})
```

As we can see, with both designs we need to make two queries to the database to fetch the information. The second approach has the advantage that it won't let any document grow unbounded so it can be used in cases where one-many is one-millions.

Modeling data for keyword searches

Searching for keywords in a document is a common operation for many applications. If this is a core operation, it makes sense to use a specialized store for search, such as Elasticsearch; however MongoDB can be used efficiently until scale dictates moving to a different solution.

The basic need for keyword search is to be able to search the entire document for keywords. For example, with a document in the `products` collection:

```
{ name : "Macbook Pro late 2016 15in" ,
  manufacturer : "Apple" ,
  price: 2000 ,
  keywords : [ "Macbook Pro late 2016 15in", "2000", "Apple", "macbook",
"laptop", "computer" ]
  }
```

We can create a multi-key index in the `keywords` field:

```
> db.products.createIndex( { keywords: 1 } )
```

Now we can search in the `keywords` field for any name, manufacturer, price fields, and also any of the custom keywords we set up. This is not an efficient or flexible approach as we need to keep keywords lists in sync, can't use stemming, and can't rank results (it's more like filtering than searching) with the only upside being implementation time.

Since version 2.4 , MongoDB has had a special text index type. This can be declared in one or multiple fields and supports stemming, tokenization, exact phrase (" "), negation (-), and weighting results.

Index declaration on three fields with custom weights:

```
db.products.createIndex({
    name: "text",
    manufacturer: "text",
   price: "text"
  },
 {
    weights: { name: 10,
      manufacturer: 5,
      price: 1 },
    name: "ProductIndex"
  })
```

In this example, name is 10 times more important that price but only two from a manufacturer.

A text index can also be declared with a wildcard, matching all fields that match the pattern:

```
db.collection.createIndex( { "$**": "text" } )
```

This can be useful when we have unstructured data and we may not know all the fields that they will come with. We can drop the index by name just like with any other index.

The greatest advantage though, other than all the features, is that all record keeping is done by the database.

Connecting to MongoDB

There are two ways to connect to MongoDB. The first is using the driver for your programming language. The second is by using an ODM layer to map your model objects to MongoDB in a transparent way. In this section, we will cover both ways using three of the most popular languages for web application development: Ruby, Python, and PHP.

Connecting using Ruby

Ruby was one of the first languages to have support from MongoDB with an official driver. The official mongo-ruby-driver on GitHub is the recommended way to connect to a MongoDB instance.

Installation is as simple as adding it to the Gemfile:

```
gem 'mongo', '~> 3.4'
```

 You need to install Ruby, then install RVM from https://rvm.io/rvm/ install and finally run gem install bundler for this.

And then in our class we can connect to a database:

```
require 'mongo'
client = Mongo::Client.new([ '127.0.0.1:27017' ], database: 'test')
```

This is the simplest example possible, connecting to a single database instance called test in our localhost. In most use cases we would at least have a replica set to connect to, as in the following snippet:

```
client_host = ['server1_hostname:server1_ip, server2_hostname:server2_ip']
 client_options = {
   database: 'YOUR_DATABASE_NAME',
   replica_set: 'REPLICA_SET_NAME',
   user: 'YOUR_USERNAME',
   password: 'YOUR_PASSWORD'
 }
client = Mongo::Client.new(client_host, client_options)
```

The client_host servers are seeding the client driver with servers to attempt to connect to. Once connected, the driver will determine the server that it has to connect to according to the primary/secondary read or write configuration.

The replica_set attribute needs to match the replica set name to be able to connect.

`user` and `password` are optional but highly recommended in any MongoDB instance. It's a good practice to enable authentication by default in the `mongod.conf` file and we will go over this in `Chapter 7.` *Monitoring, Backup, and Security.*

Connecting to a sharded cluster is similar to a replica set with the only difference being that, instead of supplying the server host/port, we need to connect to the mongo router, the mongos process.

Mongoid ODM

Using a low-level driver to connect to the MongoDB database is often not the most efficient route. All the flexibility that a low-level driver provides is offset against longer development times and code to glue our models with the database.

An **ODM (Object Document Mapper)** can be the answer to these problems. Just like ORMs, ODMs bridge the gap between our models and the database. In Rails, the most widely used MVC framework for Ruby, Mongoid, can be used to model our data in a similar way to Active Record.

Installing the gem is similar to the Mongo Ruby driver, by adding a single file in the Gemfile:

```
gem 'mongoid', '~> 6.1.0'
```

Depending on the version of Rails, we may need to add the following to `application.rb` as well:

```
config.generators do |g|
g.orm :mongoid
end
```

Connecting to the database is done through a config file, `mongoid.yml`. Configuration options are passed as key-value pairs with semantic indentation. Its structure is similar to the `database.yml` used for relational databases.

Some of the options that we can pass through the `mongoid.yml` file are:

Option Value	Description
Database	The database name.
Hosts	Our database hosts.
Write / w	The write concern (default is 1).

Auth_mech	Authentication mechanism. Valid options are: :scram, :mongodb_cr, :mongodb_x509, and :plain. The default option on 3.0 is :scram, whereas the default on 2.4 and 2.6 is :plain.
Auth_source	The authentication source for our authentication mechanism.
Min_pool_size/max_pool_size	Minimum and maximum pool size for connections.
SSL/ssl_cert/ssl_key/ ssl_key_pass_phrase/ssl_verify	A set of options regarding SSL connections to the database.
Include_root_in_json	Include the root model name in JSON serialization.
Include_type_for_serialization	Include the _type field when serializing MongoDB objects.
Use_activesupport_time_zone	Use activesupport's time zone when converting timestamps between server and client.

The next step is to modify our models to be stored in MongoDB. This is as simple as including one line of code in the model declaration:

```
class Person
  include Mongoid::Document
End
```

We can also use the following:

```
include Mongoid::Timestamps
```

We use it to generate created_at and updated_at fields in a similar way to Active Record. Data fields do not need to be declared by type in our models but it's a good practice to do so. The supported data types are:

- Array
- BigDecimal
- Boolean
- Date

- DateTime
- Float
- Hash
- Integer
- BSON::ObjectId
- BSON::Binary
- Range
- Regexp
- String
- Symbol
- Time
- TimeWithZone

If the types of fields are not defined, fields will be cast to the object and stored in the database. This is slightly faster but doesn't support all types. If we try to use BigDecimal, Date, DateTime, or Range we will get back an error.

Inheritance with Mongoid models

Here you can see an example of inheritance using Mongoid models:

```
class Canvas
  include Mongoid::Document
  field :name, type: String
  embeds_many :shapes
end

class Shape
  include Mongoid::Document
  field :x, type: Integer
  field :y, type: Integer
  embedded_in :canvas
end

class Circle < Shape
  field :radius, type: Float
end

class Rectangle < Shape
  field :width, type: Float
```

```
    field :height, type: Float
end
```

Now we have a `Canvas` class with many `Shape` objects embedded in it. Mongoid will automatically create a field, `_type` to distinguish between parent and child node fields. In scenarios where documents are inherited from their fields, relationships, validations, and scopes get copied down into their child documents, but not vice-versa.

`embeds_many` and `embedded_in` pair will create embedded subdocuments to store the relationships. If we want to store these via referencing to `ObjectId` we can do so by substituting these with `has_many and belongs_to`.

More examples on CRUD operations will follow in the next chapter.

Connecting using Python

A strong contender to Ruby and Rails is Python with Django. Similar to Mongoid there is MongoEngine and an official MongoDB low level driver, PyMongo.

Installing PyMongo can be done using `pip` or `easy_install`:

```
python -m pip install pymongo
python -m easy_install pymongo
```

Then in our class we can connect to a database:

```
>>> from pymongo import MongoClient
>>> client = MongoClient()
```

Connecting to a replica set needs a set of seed servers for the client to find out what the primary, secondary, or arbiter nodes in the set are:

```
client =
pymongo.MongoClient('mongodb://user:passwd@node1:p1,node2:p2/?replicaSet=rs
name')
```

Using the connection string URL we can pass a username/password and `replicaSet` name all in a single string. Some of the most interesting options for the connection string URL are presented in the next section.

Connecting to a shard requires the server host and IP for the mongo router, which is the mongos process.

PyMODM ODM

Similar to Ruby's Mongoid, PyMODM is an ODM for Python that follows closely on Django's built-in ORM. Installing it can be done via pip:

```
pip install pymodm
```

Then we need to edit `settings.py` and replace the database engine with a dummy database:

```
DATABASES = {
    'default': {
        'ENGINE': 'django.db.backends.dummy'
    }
}
```

And add our connection string anywhere in `settings.py`:

```
from pymodm import connect
connect("mongodb://localhost:27017/myDatabase", alias="MyApplication")
```

Here we have to use a connection string that has the following structure:

```
mongodb://[username:password@]host1[:port1][,host2[:port2],...[,hostN[:port
N]]][/[database][?options]]
```

Options have to be pairs of name=value with an `&amp;` between each pair. Some interesting pairs are:

Name	Description
`minPoolSize`/`maxPoolSize`	Minimum and maximum pool size for connections.
`w`	Write concern option.
`wtimeoutMS`	Timeout for write concern operations.
`Journal`	Journal options.
`readPreference`	Read preference to be used for replica sets. Available options are: `primary`, `primaryPreferred`, `secondary`, `secondaryPreferred`, `nearest`.
`maxStalenessSeconds`	Specifies, in seconds, how stale (data lagging behind master) a secondary can be before the client stops using it for read operations.
`SSL`	Using SSL to connect to the database.

authSource	Used in conjunction with username, specifies the database associated with the user's credentials. When we use external authentication mechanisms this should be `$external` for LDAP or Kerberos.

authMechanism	• Authentication mechanism can be used for connections. Available options for MongoDB are:
	  ○ SCRAM-SHA-1
	  ○ MONGODB-CR
	  ○ MONGODB-X509
	• MongoDB enterprise (paid version) offers two more options:
	  ○ GSSAPI (Kerberos)
	  ○ PLAIN (LDAP SASL)

Model classes need to inherit from MongoModel. A sample class will look like this:

```
from pymodm import MongoModel, fields
class User(MongoModel):
    email = fields.EmailField(primary_key=True)
    first_name = fields.CharField()
    last_name = fields.CharField()
```

This has a User class with first_name, last_name, and email fields where email is the primary field.

Inheritance with PyMODM models

Handling one-one and one-many relationships in MongoDB can be done using references or embedding. This example shows both ways: references for the model user and embedding for the comment model:

```
from pymodm import EmbeddedMongoModel, MongoModel, fields

class Comment(EmbeddedMongoModel):
    author = fields.ReferenceField(User)
    content = fields.CharField()

class Post(MongoModel):
    title = fields.CharField()
    author = fields.ReferenceField(User)
    revised_on = fields.DateTimeField()
    content = fields.CharField()
    comments = fields.EmbeddedDocumentListField(Comment)
```

Similar to Mongoid for Ruby, we can define relationships as being embedded or referenced, depending on our design decision.

Connecting using PHP

The MongoDB PHP driver was rewritten from scratch two years ago to support the PHP 5, PHP 7, and HHVM architectures. The current architecture is shown in the following diagram:

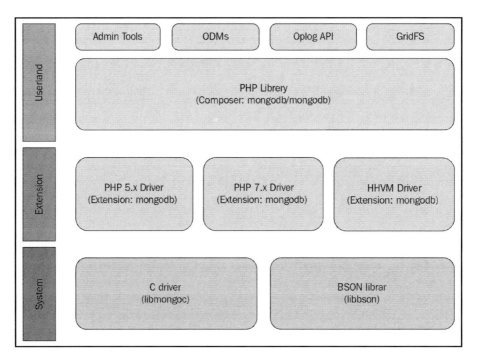

Currently we have official drivers for all three architectures with full support for the underlying functionality.

Installation is a two-step process. First we need to install the MongoDB extension. This extension is dependent on the version of PHP (or HHVM) that we have installed and can be done using brew in Mac. For example with PHP 7.0:

```
brew install php70-mongodb
```

Then, using composer (a widely used dependency manager for PHP):

```
composer require mongodb/mongodb
```

Connecting to the database can then be done by using the connection string URI or by passing an array of options.

Using the connection string URI we have:

```
$client = new MongoDB\Client($uri = 'mongodb://127.0.0.1/', array
$uriOptions = [], array $driverOptions = [])
```

For example, to connect to a replica set using SSL authentication:

```
$client = new
MongoDB\Client('mongodb://myUsername:myPassword@rs1.example.com,rs2.example
.com/?ssl=true&amp;replicaSet=myReplicaSet&amp;authSource=admin');
```

Or we can use the `$uriOptions` parameter to pass in parameters without using the connection string URL, like this:

```
$client = new MongoDB\Client(
    'mongodb://rs1.example.com,rs2.example.com/'
    [
        'username' => 'myUsername',
        'password' => 'myPassword',
        'ssl' => true,
        'replicaSet' => 'myReplicaSet',
        'authSource' => 'admin',
    ],
);
```

The set of `$uriOptions` and the connection string URL options available are analogous to the ones used for Ruby and Python.

Doctrine ODM

Laravel is one of the most widely used MVC frameworks for PHP, similar in architecture to Django and Rails from the Python and Ruby worlds respectively. We will follow through configuring our models using a stack of Laravel, Doctrine, and MongoDB. This section assumes that Doctrine is installed and working with Laravel 5.x.

Doctrine entities are **POPO (Plain Old PHP Objects)** that, unlike Eloquent, Laravel's default ORM doesn't need to inherit from the `Model` class. Doctrine uses the Data Mapper pattern, whereas Eloquent uses Active Record. Skipping the `get()` `set()` methods, a simple class would look like:

```
use Doctrine\ORM\Mapping AS ORM;
use Doctrine\Common\Collections\ArrayCollection;
/**
 * @ORM\Entity
 * @ORM\Table(name="scientist")
 */
class Scientist
{
    /**
     * @ORM\Id
     * @ORM\GeneratedValue
     * @ORM\Column(type="integer")
     */
    protected $id;
    /**
     * @ORM\Column(type="string")
     */
    protected $firstname;
    /**
     * @ORM\Column(type="string")
     */
    protected $lastname;
    /**
     * @ORM\OneToMany(targetEntity="Theory", mappedBy="scientist",
cascade={"persist"})
     * @var ArrayCollection|Theory[]
     */
    protected $theories;
    /**
     * @param $firstname
     * @param $lastname
     */
    public function __construct($firstname, $lastname)
    {
        $this->firstname = $firstname;
        $this->lastname  = $lastname;
        $this->theories = new ArrayCollection;
    }
...
    public function addTheory(Theory $theory)
    {
        if(!$this->theories->contains($theory)) {
```

```
            $theory->setScientist($this);
            $this->theories->add($theory);
        }
    }
```

This POPO-based model used annotations to define field types that need to be persisted in MongoDB. For example, `@ORM\Column(type="string")` defines a field in MongoDB with the string type `firstname` and `lastname` as the attribute names, in the respective lines.

There is a whole set of annotations available here `http://doctrine-orm.readthedocs.io/en/latest/reference/annotations-reference.html`. If we want to separate the POPO structure from annotations, we can also define them using YAML or XML instead of inlining them with annotations in our POPO model classes.

Inheritance with Doctrine

Modeling one-one and one-many relationships can be done via annotations, YAML, or XML. Using annotations, we can define multiple embedded subdocuments within our document:

```
/** @Document */
class User
{
    // ...
    /** @EmbedMany(targetDocument="Phonenumber") */
    private $phonenumbers = array();
    // ...
}
/** @EmbeddedDocument */
class Phonenumber
{
    // ...
}
```

Here a `User` document embeds many `PhoneNumbers`. `@EmbedOne()` will embed one subdocument to be used for modeling one-one relationships.

Referencing is similar to embedding:

```
/** @Document */
class User
{
    // ...
    /**
     * @ReferenceMany(targetDocument="Account")
```

```
    */
    private $accounts = array();
    // ...
}
/** @Document */
class Account
{
    // ...
}
```

`@ReferenceMany()` and `@ReferenceOne()` are used to model one-many and one-one relationships via referencing into a separate collection.

Summary

In this chapter, we learned about schema design for relational databases and MongoDB and how we can achieve the same goal starting from a different starting point.

In MongoDB, we have to think about read/write ratios, the questions that our users will have in the most common cases, as well as cardinality among relationships.

We learned about atomic operations and how we can construct our queries so that we can have ACID properties without the overhead of transactions.

We also learned about MongoDB data types, how they can be compared, and some special data types such as the `ObjectId` that can be used both by the database and for our advantage.

Starting from modeling simple one-one relationships, we went through one-many and also many-many relationship modeling, without the need for an intermediate table, like we would do in a relational database, either using references or embedded documents.

We learned how to model data for keyword searches, one of the features that most applications need to support in a web context.

Finally, we explored different use cases for using MongoDB with three of the most popular web programming languages. We saw examples using Ruby with the official driver and Mongoid ODM. Then we explored how to connect using Python with the official driver and PyMODM ODM, and lastly we worked through an example using PHP with the official driver and Doctrine ODM.

With all these languages (and many others), there are both official drivers offering support and full access functionality to the underlying database operations and also **object data modeling** frameworks for ease of modeling our data and rapid development.

In the next chapter, we will dive deeper into the MongoDB shell and the operations we can achieve using it. We will also master using the drivers for CRUD operations on our documents.

3
MongoDB CRUD Operations

In this chapter, we will learn how to use the mongo shell for database administration operations. Starting with simple **CRUD** (**create**, **read**, **update**, **delete**) operations, we will master scripting from the shell. We will also learn how to write MapReduce scripts from the shell and contrast them to the aggregation framework, which we will dive deeper into in `Chapter 5`, *Aggregation*. Finally, we will explore authentication and authorization using the MongoDB community and its paid counterpart, the Enterprise Edition.

CRUD using the shell

The mongo shell is equivalent to the administration console used by relational databases. Connecting to the mongo shell is as easy as typing the following:

```
$ mongo
```

Type it on the command line for standalone servers or replica sets. Inside the shell, we can view available databases simply by typing the following:

```
$ db
```

And connect to a database by typing the following:

```
> use <database_name>
```

The mongo shell can be used for querying and updating data in our databases. Finding documents from a collection named `books` is as easy as the following:

```
> db.books.find()
{ "_id" : ObjectId("592033f6141daf984112d07c"), "title" : "mastering
mongoDB", "isbn" : "101" }
```

And inserting this document in the `books` collection can be done via the following:

```
> db.books.insert({title: 'mastering mongoDB', isbn: '101'})
WriteResult({ "nInserted" : 1 })
```

The result we get back from MongoDB informs us that the write succeeded and inserted one new document in the database.

Deleting this document has similar syntax and results:

```
> db.books.remove({isbn: '101'})
WriteResult({ "nRemoved" : 1 })
```

Try to update this same document:

```
> db.books.update({isbn:'101'}, {price: 30})
WriteResult({ "nMatched" : 1, "nUpserted" : 0, "nModified" : 1 })
> db.books.find()
{ "_id" : ObjectId("592034c7141daf984112d07d"), "price" : 30 }
```

Here, we notice a couple of things:

- First, the JSON-like formatted field in the `update` command is our query to search for documents to update.
- The `WriteResult` object notifies us that the query matched one document and notified one document.
- Most importantly, the contents of this document were entirely replaced by the contents of the second JSON-like formatted field. We lost information on the title and ISBN!

By default, the `update` command in MongoDB will replace the contents of our document with the document we specify in the second argument. If we want to update the document and add new fields to it we need to use the `$set` operator like this:

```
> db.books.update({isbn:'101'}, {$set: {price: 30}})
WriteResult({ "nMatched" : 1, "nUpserted" : 0, "nModified" : 1 })
```

Now our document matches what we would expect:

```
> db.books.find()
{ "_id" : ObjectId("592035f6141daf984112d07f"), "title" : "mastering
mongoDB", "isbn" : "101", "price" : 30 }
```

However, deleting a document can be done in several ways, the most simple of which is by its unique `ObjectId`:

```
> db.books.remove("592035f6141daf984112d07f")
WriteResult({ "nRemoved" : 1 })
> db.books.find()
>
```

We can see here that when there are no results, the mongo shell will not return anything other than the shell prompt itself >.

Scripting for the mongo shell

Administering the database using built-in commands is helpful but is not the main reason for using the shell. The true power of the mongo shell comes from the fact that it is a JavaScript shell.

We can declare and assign variables in the shell:

```
> var title = 'MongoDB in a nutshell'
> title
MongoDB in a nutshell
> db.books.insert({title: title, isbn: 102})
WriteResult({ "nInserted" : 1 })
> db.books.find()
{ "_id" : ObjectId("59203874141daf984112d080"), "title" : "MongoDB in a
nutshell", "isbn" : 102 }
```

In the previous example, we declared a new title variable as `MongoDB in a nutshell` and used the variable to insert a new document into our `books` collection, as shown.

As it's a JavaScript shell, we can use it for functions and scripts that generate complex results from our database.

```
> queryBooksByIsbn = function(isbn) { return db.books.find({isbn: isbn})}
```

With this one-liner we are creating a new function named `queryBooksByIsbn` that takes a single argument, the `isbn` value. With the data that we have in our collection we can use our new function and get back books by ISBN:

```
> queryBooksByIsbn("101")
{ "_id" : ObjectId("592035f6141daf984112d07f"), "title" : "mastering
mongoDB", "isbn" : "101", "price" : 30 }
```

Using the shell, we can write and test these scripts. Once we are satisfied we can store them in `.js` files and invoke them directly from the command line:

```
$ mongo <script_name>.js
```

Some useful notes about the default behavior of these scripts:

- Write operations will use a default write concern of 1, which is global for MongoDB as of the current version. Write concern 1 will request an ack that the write operation has propagated to the standalone `mongod` or the primary in a replica set.
- To get results from operations from a script back to standard output, we must use either JavaScript's built-in `print()` function or the mongo-specific `printjson()` function, which prints out results formatted in JSON.

Differences between scripting for the mongo shell and using it directly

When writing scripts for the mongo shell we cannot use the shell helpers. MongoDB's commands like `use <database_name>`, `show collections`, and other helpers are built into the shell and so are not available from the JavaScript context where our scripts will get executed. Fortunately, there are equivalents to them that are available from the JavaScript execution context, as shown in the following table:

Shell helpers	JavaScript equivalents
`show dbs, show databases`	`db.adminCommand('listDatabases')`
`use <database_name>`	`db = db.getSiblingDB('<database_name>')`
`show collections`	`db.getCollectionNames()`
`show users`	`db.getUsers()`
`show roles`	`db.getRoles({showBuiltinRoles: true})`

show log <logname>	db.adminCommand({ 'getLog' : '<logname>' })
show logs	db.adminCommand({ 'getLog' : '*' })

it	cursor = db.collection.find()
	if (cursor.hasNext()){
	  cursor.next();
	}

In the previous table, `it` is the iteration cursor that the mongo shell returns when we query and get back too many results to show in one batch.

Using the mongo shell, we can script almost anything that we would from a client, meaning that we have a really powerful tool for prototyping and getting quick insights into our data.

Batch inserts using the shell

When using the shell, many times we want to insert a large number of documents programmatically. The most straightforward implementation, since we have a JavaScript shell, is to iterate through a loop, generating each document along the way and performing a write operation in every iteration in the loop like this:

```
> authorMongoFactory = function() {for(loop=0;loop<1000;loop++)
{db.books.insert({name: "MongoDB factory book" + loop})}}
function () {for(loop=0;loop<1000;loop++) {db.books.insert({name: "MongoDB
factory book" + loop})}}
```

In this simple example, we create an `authorMongoFactory()` method for an author who writes 1,000 books on MongoDB with a slightly different name for each one:

```
> authorMongoFactory()
```

This will result in 1,000 writes being issued to the database. This, while convenient, is significantly harder for the database to handle.

Instead, using a bulk write, we can issue a single database insert command with the 1,000 documents that we have prepared beforehand:

```
> fastAuthorMongoFactory = function() {
var bulk = db.books.initializeUnorderedBulkOp();
for(loop=0;loop<1000;loop++) {bulk.insert({name: "MongoDB factory book" +
loop})}
bulk.execute();
}
```

The end result is the same as before, with 1,000 documents following this structure in our `books` collection:

```
> db.books.find()
{ "_id" : ObjectId("59204251141daf984112d851"), "name" : "MongoDB factory
book0" }
{ "_id" : ObjectId("59204251141daf984112d852"), "name" : "MongoDB factory
book1" }
{ "_id" : ObjectId("59204251141daf984112d853"), "name" : "MongoDB factory
book2" }
...
{ "_id" : ObjectId("59204251141daf984112d853"), "name" : "MongoDB factory
book999" }
```

The difference from the user's perspective lies in speed of execution and reduced strain on the database.

In the preceding example, we used `initializeUnorderedBulkOp()` for the bulk operation builder setup. The reason we did that is because we don't care about the order of insertions being the same as the order in which we add them to our bulk variable with the `bulk.insert()` command.

This makes sense when we can make sure that all operations are unrelated to each other or idempotent.

If we care about having the same order of insertions we can use `initializeOrderedBulkOp()`, changing the second line of our function to this:

```
var bulk = db.books.initializeOrderedBulkOp();
```

Batch operations using the mongo shell

In the case of inserts, we can generally expect that the order of operations doesn't matter.

Bulk, however, can be used with many more operations than just inserts. In the following example, we have a single book with isbn : 101 and the name Mastering MongoDB in a bookOrders collection with the number of available copies to purchase in the available field, with 99 books available for purchase:

```
> db.bookOrders.find()
{ "_id" : ObjectId("59204793141daf984112dc3c"), "isbn" : 101, "name" :
"Mastering MongoDB", "available" : 99 }
```

With the following series of operations in a single bulk operation we are adding 1 book to the inventory and then ordering 100 books, for a final total of 0 copies available:

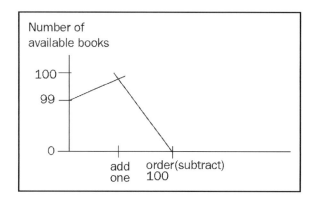

x axis is "inventory orders from/to our warehouse"

```
> var bulk = db.bookOrders.initializeOrderedBulkOp();
> bulk.find({isbn: 101}).updateOne({$inc: {available : 1}});
> bulk.find({isbn: 101}).updateOne({$inc: {available : -100}});
> bulk.execute();
```

Because we are using initializeOrderedBulkOp() we can make sure that we are adding one book before ordering 100 so that we are never out of stock. On the contrary, if we were using initializeUnorderedBulkOp() then we wouldn't have such a guarantee and we might end up with the 100-book order coming in before the addition of the new book, resulting in an application error as we don't have that many books to fulfill the order.

When executing through an ordered list of operations, MongoDB will split the operations into batches of 1,000 and group these by operation. For example, if we have 1,002 inserts, then 998 updates, then 1,004 deletes, and finally 5 inserts we will end up with the following:

```
[1000 inserts]
[2 inserts]
[998 updates]
[1000 deletes]
[4 deletes]
[5 inserts]
```

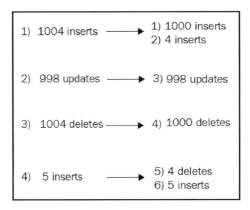

Diagram with the series of inserts

This doesn't affect the series of operations, but implicitly means that our operations will leave the database in batches of 1,000. This behavior is not guaranteed to stay in future versions (!).

If we want to inspect the execution of a `bulk.execute()` command we can issue `bulk.getOperations()` right after we `execute()`.

 Since version 3.2 MongoDB has offered an alternative command for bulk writes, `BulkWrite()`.

`BulkWrite` arguments are the series of operations we want to execute, `WriteConcern` (default is again 1), and if these should go in order (they will be ordered by default):

```
> db.collection.bulkWrite(
  [ <operation 1>, <operation 2>, ... ],
  {
      writeConcern : <document>,
```

```
        ordered : <boolean>
    }
)
```

Operations are the same ones supported by `Bulk`:

- `insertOne`
- `updateOne`
- `updateMany`
- `deleteOne`
- `deleteMany`
- `replaceOne`

`updateOne`, `deleteOne`, and `replaceOne` have matching filters; if they match more than one document, they will only operate on the first one. It's important to design these queries so that they don't match more than one documents or else behavior will be undefined.

Administration

Using MongoDB should most of the time feel and be transparent to the developer. Since there are no schemas, there is no need for migrations and generally developers find themselves spending less time on administrative tasks in the database world.

That being said, there are several tasks that an experienced MongoDB developer or architect can perform to keep MongoDB up to speed and performing as well as it can.

At the process level, there is the `shutDown` command to shut down the MongoDB server.

At the database level we have the following:

- `dropDatabase`
- `listCollections`
- `copyDB` or `clone` to clone a remote database locally
- `repairDatabase` when our database is not in a consistent state due to an unclean shutdown

Whereas at the collection level there are the following:

- `drop` to drop a collection
- `create` to create a collection
- `renameCollection` to rename a collection
- `cloneCollection` to clone a remote collection to our local DB
- `cloneCollectionAsCapped` to clone a collection into a new capped collection
- `convertToCapped` to convert a collection to a capped one

At the index level we can use the following:

- `createIndexes`
- `listIndexes`
- `dropIndexes`
- `reIndex`

We will also go through a few other commands that are more important from an administration standpoint.

fsync

MongoDB normally writes all operations to the disk every 60 seconds. `fsync` will force data to persist to disk immediately and synchronously.

If we want to take a backup of our databases we need to apply a lock as well. Locking will block all writes and some reads while `fsync` is operating.

In almost all cases, it's better to use journaling and refer to our techniques for backup and restore in `Chapter 7`, *Monitoring, Backup, and Security*, for maximum availability and performance.

compact

MongoDB documents take up a specified amount of space on disk. If we perform an update that increases the size of a document this may end up being moved out of sequence to the end of the storage block, creating a hole in storage, resulting in increased execution times for this update, and possibly missing it from running queries. The `compact` operation will defragment space resulting in less space being used.

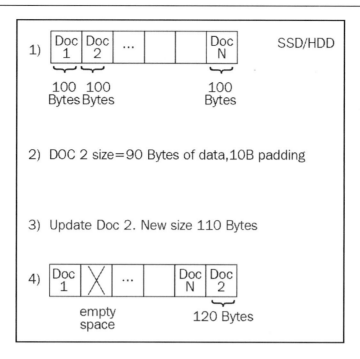

compact can also take a paddingFactor argument as follows:

```
> db.runCommand ( { compact: '<collection>', paddingFactor: 2.0 } )
```

paddingFactor is preallocated space in each document that ranges from 1.0 (no padding, the default value) to 4.0 for calculated padding of 300 bytes for each 100 bytes of document space needed when we initially insert it.

Adding padding can help alleviate the problem of updates moving documents around, at the expense of more disk space being needed for each document when created.

currentOp/killOp

db.currentOp() will show us the current running operation in the database and will attempt to kill it. We need to run the use admin command before running killOp(). Needless to say, using killOp() against internal MongoDB operations is not recommended or advised as the database may end up in an undefined state:

```
> db.runCommand( { "killOp": 1, "op": <operationId> } )
```

collMod

`collMod` is used to pass flags to a collection modifying the underlying database's behavior.

Since version 3.2, the most interesting set of flags that we can pass to a collection is document validation.

Document validation can specify a set of rules to be applied to new updates and inserts into a collection. This means that current documents will get checked if they get modified.

We can only apply validations to documents that are already valid if we set `validationLevel` to `moderate`. By specifying `validationAction` we can log documents that are invalid by setting it to `warn` or prevent updates from happening altogether by setting it to `error`.

For example, with the previous example of `BookOrders` we can set a validator on the `isbn` and `name` fields being present for every insert or update like this:

```
> db.runCommand( { collMod: "bookOrders",
"validator" : {
        "$and" : [
            {
                "isbn" : {
                    "$exists" : true
                }
            },
            {
                "name" : {
                    "$exists" : true
                }
            }
        ]
    }
})
```

Here, we get back:

```
{ "ok" : 1 }
```

Then if we try to insert a new document with only the `isbn` field being present, we get an error:

```
> db.bookOrders.insert({isbn: 102})
WriteResult({
"nInserted" : 0,
"writeError" : {
"code" : 121,
```

```
"errmsg" : "Document failed validation"
}
})
>
```

We get an error because our validation failed. Managing validation from the shell is really useful as we can write scripts to manage them and also make sure that everything is in place.

touch

The `touch` command will load data and/or index data from storage to memory. This is typically useful if our script will subsequently use this data, speeding up execution:

```
> db.runCommand({ touch: "bookOrders", data: true/false, index: true/false
})
```

This command should be used with caution in production systems, as loading data and indexes into memory will displace existing data from it.

MapReduce in the mongo shell

One of the most interesting features, which has been underappreciated and not widely supported throughout MongoDB history, is the ability to write MapReduce natively using the shell.

MapReduce is a data processing method for getting aggregation results from large sets of data. The main advantage is that it is inherently parallelizable as evidenced by frameworks such as Hadoop.

MapReduce is really useful when used to implement a data pipeline. Multiple MapReduce commands can be chained to produce different results. An example would be aggregating data by different reporting periods (hour, day, week, month, year) where we use the output of each more granular reporting period to produce a less granular report.

A simple example of MapReduce in our examples would be as follows, given that our input books collection is as follows:

```
> db.books.find()
{ "_id" : ObjectId("592149c4aabac953a3a1e31e"), "isbn" : "101", "name" :
"Mastering MongoDB", "price" : 30 }
{ "_id" : ObjectId("59214bc1aabac954263b24e0"), "isbn" : "102", "name" :
"MongoDB in 7 years", "price" : 50 }
```

```
{ "_id" : ObjectId("59214bc1aabac954263b24e1"), "isbn" : "103", "name" :
"MongoDB for experts", "price" : 40 }
```

And our map and reduce functions are defined as follows:

```
> var mapper = function() {
                     emit(this.id, 1);
              };
```

In this mapper, we simply output a key of the id of each document with a value of 1:

```
> var reducer = function(id, count) {
                     return Array.sum(count);
              };
```

In the reducer, we sum across all values (where each one has a value of 1):

```
> db.books.mapReduce(mapper, reducer, { out:"books_count" });
{
"result" : "books_count",
"timeMillis" : 16613,
"counts" : {
"input" : 3,
"emit" : 3,
"reduce" : 1,
"output" : 1
},
"ok" : 1
}
> db.books_count.find()
{ "_id" : null, "value" : 3 }
>
```

Our final output is a document with no ID, since we didn't output any value for id, and a value of 6, since there are six documents in the input dataset.

Using MapReduce, MongoDB will apply map to each input document, emitting key-value pairs at the end of the map phase. Then each reducer will get key-value pairs with the same key as input, processing all multiple values. The reducer's output will be a single key-value pair for each key.

Optionally, we can use a finalize function to further process the results of the mapper and reducer. MapReduce functions use JavaScript and run within the mongod process. MapReduce can output inline as a single document, subject to the 16 MB document size limit, or as multiple documents in an output collection. Input and output collections can be sharded.

MapReduce concurrency

MapReduce operations will place several short-lived locks that should not affect operations. However, at the end of the reduce phase, if we are outputting data to an existing collection, then output actions such as `merge`, `reduce`, and `replace` will take an exclusive global write lock for the whole server, blocking all other writes in the `db` instance. If we want to avoid that we should invoke MapReduce in the following way:

```
> db.collection.mapReduce(
                     mapper,
                     reducer,
                     {
                        out: { merge/reduce: bookOrders, nonAtomic: true
}
                     })
```

We can apply `nonAtomic` only to `merge` or `reduce` actions. `replace` will just replace the contents of documents in `bookOrders`, which would not take much time anyway.

With the `merge` action, the new result is merged with the existing result if the output collection already exists. If an existing document has the same key as the new result, then it will overwrite that existing document.

With the `reduce` action, the new result is processed together with the existing result if the output collection already exists. If an existing document has the same key as the new result, it will apply the `reduce` function to both the new and the existing documents and overwrite the existing document with the result.

Although MapReduce has been present since the early versions of MongoDB, it hasn't evolved as much as the rest of the database, resulting in its usage being less than that of specialized MapReduce frameworks such as Hadoop, which we will learn more about in `Chapter 9`, *Harnessing Big Data with MongoDB*.

Incremental MapReduce

Incremental MapReduce is a pattern where we use MapReduce to aggregate to previously calculated values. An example would be counting non-distinct users in a collection for different reporting periods (that is, hour, day, month) without the need to recalculate the result every hour.

To set up our data for incremental MapReduce we need to do the following:

- Output our reduce data to a different collection
- At the end of every hour, query *only* for the data that got into the collection in the last hour
- With the output of our reduce data, merge our results with the calculated results from the previous hour

Following up on the previous example, let's assume that we have a published field in each of the documents, with our input dataset being:

```
> db.books.find()
{ "_id" : ObjectId("592149c4aabac953a3a1e31e"), "isbn" : "101", "name" :
"Mastering MongoDB", "price" : 30, "published" :
ISODate("2017-06-25T00:00:00Z") }
{ "_id" : ObjectId("59214bc1aabac954263b24e0"), "isbn" : "102", "name" :
"MongoDB in 7 years", "price" : 50, "published" :
ISODate("2017-06-26T00:00:00Z") }
```

Using our previous example of counting books we would get the following:

```
var mapper = function() {
                        emit(this.id, 1);
                };
var reducer = function(id, count) {
                        return Array.sum(count);
                };
> db.books.mapReduce(mapper, reducer, { out: "books_count" })
{
"result" : "books_count",
"timeMillis" : 16700,
"counts" : {
"input" : 2,
"emit" : 2,
"reduce" : 1,
"output" : 1
},
"ok" : 1
}
> db.books_count.find()
{ "_id" : null, "value" : 2 }
```

Now we get a third book in our `mongo_books` collection with a document:

```
{ "_id" : ObjectId("59214bc1aabac954263b24e1"), "isbn" : "103", "name" :
"MongoDB for experts", "price" : 40, "published" :
ISODate("2017-07-01T00:00:00Z") }
> db.books.mapReduce( mapper, reducer, { query: { published: { $gte:
ISODate('2017-07-01 00:00:00') } }, out: { reduce: "books_count" } } )
> db.books_count.find()
{ "_id" : null, "value" : 3 }
```

What happened here, is that by querying for documents in July 2017 we only got the new document out of the query and then used its value to reduce the value with the already calculated value of 2 in our `books_count` document, adding 1 to the final sum of three documents.

This example, as contrived as it is, shows a powerful attribute of MapReduce: the ability to re-reduce results to incrementally calculate aggregations over time.

Troubleshooting MapReduce

Throughout the years, one of the major shortcomings of MapReduce frameworks has been the inherent difficulty in troubleshooting as opposed to simpler non-distributed patterns. Most of the time, the most effective tool is debugging using log statements to verify that output values match our expected values. In the mongo shell, this being a JavaScript shell, this is as simple as outputting using the `console.log()` function.

Diving deeper into MapReduce in MongoDB we can debug both in the map and the reduce phase by overloading the output values.

Debugging the mapper phase, we can overload the `emit()` function to test what the output key values are:

```
> var emit = function(key, value) {
  print("debugging mapper's emit");
  print("key: " + key + "  value: " + tojson(value));
}
```

We can then call it manually on a single document to verify that we get back the key-value pair that we would expect:

```
> var myDoc = db.orders.findOne( { _id:
ObjectId("50a8240b927d5d8b5891743c") } );
> mapper.apply(myDoc);
```

The reducer function is somewhat more complicated. A MapReduce reducer function must meet the following criteria:

- It must be idempotent
- The order of values coming from the `mapper` function should not matter for the reducer's result
- The `reduce` function must return the same type of result as the `mapper` function

We will dissect these following requirements to understand what they really mean:

- **It must be idempotent**: MapReduce by design may call the reducer multiple times for the same key with multiple values from the mapper phase. It also doesn't need to reduce single instances of a key as it's just added to the set. The final value should be the same no matter the order of execution. This can be verified by writing our own "verifier" function forcing the reducer to re-reduce or by executing the reducer many, many times:

  ```
  reduce( key, [ reduce(key, valuesArray) ] ) == reduce( key,
  valuesArray )
  ```

- **It must be commutative**: Again, because multiple invocations of the reducer may happen for the same key, if it has multiple values, the following should hold:

  ```
  reduce(key, [ C, reduce(key, [ A, B ]) ] ) == reduce( key, [ C,
  A, B ] )
  ```

- **The order of values coming from the mapper function should not matter for the reducer's result**: We can test that the order of values from the mapper doesn't change the output for the reducer by passing in documents to the mapper in a different order and verifying that we get the same results out:

  ```
  reduce( key, [ A, B ] ) == reduce( key, [ B, A ] )
  ```

- **The reduce function must return the same type of result as the mapper function**: Hand-in-hand with the first requirement, the type of object that the reduce function returns should be the same as the output of the `mapper` function.

Aggregation framework

Since version 2.2, MongoDB has provided a better way to work with aggregation, one that has been supported, adopted, and enhanced regularly ever since. The aggregation framework is modeled after data processing pipelines.

In data processing pipelines there are two main operations: filters that operate like queries, filtering documents, and document transformations that transform documents to get them ready for the next stage.

SQL to aggregation

An aggregation pipeline can replace and augment querying operations in the shell. A common pattern for development is:

- Verify that we have the correct data structures and get quick results using a series of queries in the shell
- Prototype pipeline results using the aggregation framework
- Refine and refactor if/when needed either by ETL processes to get data into a dedicated data warehouse or by more extensive usage of the application layer to get the insights that we need

In the following table, we can see how SQL commands map to the aggregation framework operators:

SQL	Aggregation framework
WHERE / HAVING	$match
GROUP BY	$group
SELECT	$project
ORDER BY	$sort
LIMIT	$limit
sum() / count()	$sum
join	$lookup

Aggregation versus MapReduce

In MongoDB, we can essentially get data out of our database using three methods: querying, the aggregation framework, and MapReduce. All three of them can be chained to each other and many times it is useful to do so; however it's important to understand when we should use aggregation and when MapReduce may be a better alternative.

 We can use both aggregation and MapReduce with sharded databases.

Aggregation is based on the concept of a pipeline. As such, it's important to be able to model our data from input to final output, in a series of transformations and processing that can get us there. It's also mostly useful when our intermediate results can be used on their own, or feed parallel pipelines. Our operations are limited by the operators that we have available from MongoDB so it's important to make sure that we can calculate all the results we need using available commands.

MapReduce on the other hand, can be used to construct pipelines by chaining the output of one MapReduce job to the input of the next one via an intermediate collection but this is not its primary purpose.

MapReduce's most common use case is to periodically calculate aggregations for large datasets. Having MongoDB's querying in place we can incrementally calculate these aggregations without the need to scan through the whole input table every time. In addition, its power comes from its flexibility as we can define mappers and reducers in JavaScript with the full flexibility of the language when calculating intermediate results. Not having the operators that the aggregation framework provides us, we have to implement them on our own.

In many cases, the answer is not either/or. We can (and should) use the aggregation framework to construct our ETL pipeline and resort to MapReduce for the parts that are not yet supported sufficiently by it.

A complete use case with aggregation and MapReduce is provided in Chapter 5, *Aggregation*.

Securing the shell

MongoDB is a database developed with ease of development in mind. As such, security at the database level was not baked in from the beginning and it was up to the developers and administrators to secure the MongoDB host from access outside the application server.

Unfortunately, this means that, as far as back as 2015, 39,890 databases were found open to the internet, with no security access configured. Many of them were production databases, one belonging to a French telecom operator and containing more than 8 million records from its customers.

Nowadays, there is no excuse for leaving any MongoDB server with the default authentication off settings, at all stages of development from local server deployment to production.

Authentication and authorization

Authentication and authorization are closely connected and sometimes confused. Authentication is about verifying the identity of a user to the database. An example of authentication is SSL, where the web server is verifying its identity, that it is who it claims to be, to the user.

Authorization is about determining what actions a user can take on a resource. In the next paragraphs, we will discuss authentication and authorization with these definitions in mind.

Authorization with MongoDB

MongoDB's most basic authorization relies on the username/password method. By default, MongoDB will not start with authorization enabled. To enable it, we need to start our server with the `--auth` parameter:

```
$ mongod --auth
```

To set up authorization, we need to start our server without authorization to set up a user. Setting up an `admin` user is as simple as follows:

```
> use admin
> db.createUser(
  {
    user: <adminUser>,
    pwd: <password>,
    roles: [ { role: <adminRole>, db: "admin" } ]
  }
)
```

Here, `<adminUser>` is the name of the user we want to create, `<password>` is the password, and `<adminRole>` can be any of the following values ordered from more powerful to least:

- root
- dbAdminAnyDatabase
- userAdminAnyDatabase
- readWriteAnyDatabase
- readAnyDatabase
- dbOwner
- dbAdmin
- userAdmin
- readWrite
- read

Of these roles, `root` is the superuser allowed access to everything. This is not recommended to be used, except for special circumstances.

All the `AnyDatabase` roles provide access to all databases, of which `dbAdminAnyDatabase` combines the `userAdminAnyDatabase` and `readWriteAnyDatabase` scopes, being an admin again, in all databases.

The rest of the roles are defined in the database that we want them to apply, by changing the roles subdocument of the preceding `db.createUser()`. For example, to create a `dbAdmin` for our `mongo_book` database , we would use the following:

```
> db.createUser(
  {
    user: <adminUser>,
    pwd: <password>,
    roles: [ { role: "dbAdmin", db: "mongo_book" } ]
  }
)
```

Cluster administration has even more roles, which we will cover in more depth in `Chapter 10`, *Replication*.

Finally, when we restart our database with the `--auth` flag set, we can use either the command line or the connection string (from any driver) to connect as `admin` and create new users with predefined or custom defined roles:

```
mongodb://[username:password@]host1[:port1][,host2[:port2],...[,hostN[:port
N]]][/[database][?options]]
```

Security tips for MongoDB

Common software system security precautions apply with MongoDB. We will outline some of them here and how to enable them.

Encrypting communication using TLS/SSL

Communication between the `mongod` or `mongos` server and the client mongo shell or applications should be encrypted. This is supported in most MongoDB distributions from 3.0 and onwards but we need to take care that we download the proper version with SSL support.

After that, we need to get a signed certificate from a trusted certificate authority or sign our own. Using self-signed certificates is fine for pre-production systems but in production it will mean that mongo servers won't be able to verify our identity, leaving us susceptible to man-in-the-middle attacks; thus using a proper certificate is highly recommended.

To start our MongoDB server with SSL we need the following:

```
$ mongod --sslMode requireSSL --sslPEMKeyFile <pem> --sslCAFile <ca>
```

Where <pem> is our .pem signed certificate file and <ca> is the .pem root certificate from the certificate authority that contains the root certificate chain.

These options can also be defined in our configuration file mongod.conf or mongos.conf in a YAML file format:

```
net:
  ssl:
      mode: requireSSL
      PEMKeyFile: /etc/ssl/mongodb.pem
      CAFile: /etc/ssl/ca.pem
      disabledProtocols: TLS1_0,TLS1_1,TLS1_2
```

Here, we specified a PEMKeyFile, a CAFile, and also that we won't allow the server to start with certificates that follow the TLS1_0, TLS1_1 or TLS1_2 versions. These are the available versions for disabledProtocols at this time.

Encrypting data

Using WiredTiger is highly recommended for encrypting data at rest as it supports it natively from version 3.2.

For users of the community version, this can be achieved in the storage selection of their choice, for example in AWS using EBS-encrypted storage volumes.

 This feature is available only for MongoDB Enterprise Edition.

Limiting network exposure

The oldest security method to secure any server is to disallow it from accepting connections from unknown sources. In MongoDB, this is done in a configuration file with a simple line:

```
net:
  bindIp: <string>
```

Her, <string> is a comma-separated list of IPs that the MongoDB server will accept connections from.

Firewalls and VPNs

Together with limiting network exposure on the server side, we can use firewalls to prevent access to our network from the outside internet. VPNs can also provide tunneled traffic between our servers but shouldn't be used as our sole security mechanism regardless.

Auditing

No matter how secure any system is, we need to keep a close eye on it from an auditing perspective to make sure that we detect possible breaches and stop them as soon as possible.

 This feature is available only for MongoDB Enterprise Edition.

For users of the community version, we have to set up auditing manually by logging changes to documents and collections in the application layer, possibly in a different database altogether. This will be addressed in the next chapter, which covers advanced querying using client drivers.

Use secure configuration options

It goes without saying that sane configuration options should be used. We must use one of the following:

1. MapReduce.
2. mongo shell group operation or a group operation from our client driver.
3. $where JavaScript server evaluation.

If we don't, we should disable server-side scripting by using the `--noscripting` option on the command line when we start our server.

Number 2 in the previous list can be a tricky one as many drivers may use MongoDB's `group()` command when we issue group commands in the driver; however, given the limitations that `group()` has in terms of performance and output documents, we should rethink our design to use the aggregation framework or application side aggregations.

The web interface also has to be disabled, by not using any of the following commands:

- `net.http.enabled`
- `net.http.JSONPEnabled`
- `net.http.RESTInterfaceEnabled`

On the contrary, `wireObjectCheck` needs to remain enabled, as it is by default, as this ensures that all documents stored by the `mongod` instance are valid BSON.

Authentication with MongoDB

By default, MongoDB uses SCRAM-SHA-1 as the default challenge and response authentication mechanism. This is an SHA-1 username/password-based mechanism for authentication. All drivers and the mongo shell itself have built-in methods to support it.

 This has changed since version 3.0 . In older versions the less secure MONGODB-CR was used.

Enterprise Edition

MongoDB's Enterprise Edition is a paid subscription product offering more features around security and administration.

Kerberos authentication

MongoDB Enterprise Edition also offers Kerberos authentication. Kerberos, named after the character Kerberos (or Cerberus) from Greek mythology, the ferocious three-headed guard dog of the underworld, Hades, focuses on mutual authentication between client-server protecting against eavesdropping and replay attacks.

Kerberos is widely used in Windows systems, through integration with Microsoft's Active Directory. To install Kerberos, we need to start `mongod` without Kerberos set up and then connect to the `$external` database (not the admin that we normally use for admin authorization) and create a user with a Kerberos role and permissions:

```
use $external
db.createUser(
  {
    user: "mongo_book_user@packt.net",
    roles: [ { role: "read", db: "mongo_book" } ]
  }
)
```

In the preceding example, we are authorizing the `mongo_book_user@packt.net` user to read our `mongo_book` database, just like we would do with a user using our admin system.

After that, we need to start our server with Kerberos support by passing in the `authenticationMechanisms` parameter:

```
--setParameter authenticationMechanisms=GSSAPI
```

And now we can connect from our server or command line:

```
$ mongo.exe --host <mongoserver> --authenticationMechanism=GSSAPI --authenticationDatabase='$external' --username mongo_book_user@packt.net
```

LDAP authentication

Similar to Kerberos authentication, we can also use LDAP in MongoDB Enterprise Edition only.

Setting up a user has to be done in the `$external` database and must match the name of the authentication LDAP name. The name may need to pass through a transformation and this may cause a mismatch between the LDAP name and the user entry in the `$external` database. Setting up LDAP authentication is beyond the scope of this book but the important thing to consider is that any changes in the LDAP server may need changes in the MongoDB server; they won't happen automatically.

Summary

In this chapter, we scratched the tip of the iceberg with CRUD operations. Starting from the mongo shell, we learned how to insert, delete, read, and modify documents. We also discussed the differences between one-off inserts and inserting in batches for performance.

Following that, we discussed administration tasks and how to perform them in the mongo shell. MapReduce and its successor, aggregation framework, were also discussed in this chapter: how they compare, how to use them, and how we can translate SQL queries to aggregation framework pipeline commands.

Finally, we discussed security and authentication with MongoDB. Securing our database is of paramount importance; we will learn more about this in Chapter 7, *Monitoring, Backup, and Security*.

In the next chapter, we will dive deeper into CRUD using three of the most popular languages for web development: Ruby, Python, and PHP.

4
Advanced Querying

In the previous chapter, we showed how to use the shell for scripting, administration, and developing in a secure way. In this chapter, we will dive deeper into using MongoDB with drivers and popular frameworks from Ruby, Python, and PHP.

We will also show best practices for using these languages and the variety of comparison and update operators that MongoDB supports on a database level and which are accessible through Ruby, Python, and PHP.

The frameworks that we will use for each language are:

- **Ruby**: mongo-ruby-driver and Mongoid
- **Python**: mongo-python-driver and PyMODM
- **PHP**: mongo-php-driver and Doctrine</li>

MongoDB CRUD operations

In this section we will cover CRUD operations using Ruby, Python, and PHP with the official MongoDB driver and some popular frameworks for each language respectively.

CRUD using the Ruby driver

In the previous chapter, we covered how to connect to MongoDB from Ruby, Python, and PHP using the drivers and ODM. In this chapter, we will explore create, read, update, and delete operations using the official drivers and the most commonly used **Object Document Mapper (ODM)** frameworks.

Creating documents

Using the process described in Chapter 2, *Schema Design and Data Modeling*, we assume that we have an @collection instance variable pointing to our books collection in a mongo_book database in the 127.0.0.1:27017 default database:

```
@collection = Mongo::Client.new([ '127.0.0.1:27017' ], :database =>
'mongo_book').database[:books]
```

Inserting a single document with our definition:

```
document = { isbn: '101', name: 'Mastering MongoDB', price: 30}
```

Can be done with a single line of code as follows:

```
result = @collection.insert_one(document)
```

The resulting object is a Mongo::Operation::Result class with content similar to what we had in the shell:

```
{"n"=>1, "ok"=>1.0}
```

Here, n is the number of affected documents; 1 means we inserted one object and ok means 1 (true).

Creating multiple documents in one step is similar to this. For two documents with isbn 102 and 103 and using insert_many instead of insert_one, we have:

```
documents = [ { isbn: '102', name: 'MongoDB in 7 years', price: 50 },
              { isbn: '103', name: 'MongoDB for experts', price: 40 } ]
result = @collection.insert_many(documents)
```

The resulting object is now a Mongo::BulkWrite::Result class, meaning that the BulkWrite interface was used for improved performance.

The main difference is that now we have an attribute, inserted_ids, which will return ObjectId of the inserted objects from the BSON::ObjectId class.

Read

Finding documents is done in the same way as creating them, at the collection level:

```
@collection.find( { isbn: '101' } )
```

Multiple search criteria can be chained and are equivalent to an AND operator in SQL:

```
@collection.find( { isbn: '101', name: 'Mastering MongoDB' } )
```

The mongo-ruby-driver provides several query options to enhance queries, the most widely used of which are listed in this table:

Option	Description
allow_partial_results	This is for use with sharded clusters. If a shard is down, it allows the query to return results from the shards that are up, potentially only getting a portion of the results.
batch_size(Integer)	Can change the batch size that the cursor will fetch from MongoDB. This is done on each GETMORE operation (for example, typing it on the mongo shell)
comment(String)	With this command we can add a comment in our query for documentation reasons.
hint(Hash)	We can force usage of an index using hint().
limit(Integer)	We can limit the result set to the number of documents specified by Integer.
max_scan(Integer)	We can limit the number of documents that will be scanned. This will return incomplete results and is useful if we are performing operations that we want to guarantee that they won't take a long time, such as, for example, if we connect to our production database.
no_cursor_timeout	If we don't specify this parameter, MongoDB will close any inactive cursor after 600 seconds. With this parameter our cursor will never be closed.
projection(Hash)	We can use this parameter to fetch or exclude specific attributes from our results. Will reduce data transfer over the wire. An example would be: client[:books].find.projection(:price => 1)
read(Hash)	We can specify a read preference to be applied only for this query: client[:books].find.read(:mode => :secondary_preferred)

show_disk_loc(Boolean)	We should use this option if for some reason we want to find the actual location of our results on disk
skip(Integer)	To skip the specified number of documents. Useful for pagination of results.
snapshot	To execute our query in snapshot mode. This is useful when we want more stringent consistency.
sort(Hash)	We can use this to sort our results. For example: client[:books].find.sort(:name => -1)

On top of the query options, mongo-ruby-driver provides some helper functions that can be chained at the method call level:

- .count: Total count for the preceding query
- .distinct(:field_name): Distinguish the results of the preceding query by :field_name

Find() returns a cursor containing the result set, which we can iterate using .each in Ruby like every other object:

```
result = @collection.find({ isbn: '101' })
result.each do |doc|
  puts doc.inspect
end
```

The output is as follows for our books collection:

```
{"_id"=>BSON::ObjectId('592149c4aabac953a3a1e31e'), "isbn"=>"101",
"name"=>"Mastering MongoDB", "price"=>30.0, "published"=>2017-06-25
00:00:00 UTC}
```

Chaining operations in find()

find(), by default, uses an AND operator to match multiple fields. If we want to use an OR operator, our query needs to be like this:

```
result = @collection.find('$or' => [{ isbn: '101' }, { isbn: '102' }]).to_a
puts result
{"_id"=>BSON::ObjectId('592149c4aabac953a3a1e31e'), "isbn"=>"101",
"name"=>"Mastering MongoDB", "price"=>30.0, "published"=>2017-06-25
00:00:00 UTC}{"_id"=>BSON::ObjectId('59214bc1aabac954263b24e0'),
"isbn"=>"102", "name"=>"MongoDB in 7 years", "price"=>50.0,
"published"=>2017-06-26 00:00:00 UTC}
```

We can also use $and instead of $or in the previous example:

```
result = @collection.find('$and' => [{ isbn: '101' }, { isbn: '102'
}]).to_a
puts result
```

This, of course, will return no results since no document can have both isbn 101 and 102.

An interesting and hard bug to find is if we define the same key multiple times, like this:

```
result = @collection.find({ isbn: '101', isbn: '102' })
puts result

{"_id"=>BSON::ObjectId('59214bc1aabac954263b24e0'), "isbn"=>"102",
"name"=>"MongoDB in 7 years", "price"=>50.0, "published"=>2017-06-26
00:00:00 UTC}
```

Whereas the opposite order will cause the document with isbn 101 to be returned:

```
result = @collection.find({ isbn: '102', isbn: '101' })
puts result
{"_id"=>BSON::ObjectId('592149c4aabac953a3a1e31e'), "isbn"=>"101",
"name"=>"Mastering MongoDB", "price"=>30.0, "published"=>2017-06-25
00:00:00 UTC}
```

 This is because, in Ruby hashes, by default all duplicated keys except for the last one are silently ignored. This may not happen in the simplistic form shown in the preceding example, but is prone to happen if we create keys programmatically.

Nested operations

Accessing embedded documents in mongo-ruby-driver is as simple as using the dot notation:

```
result = @collection.find({'meta.authors': 'alex giamas'}).to_a
puts result
"_id"=>BSON::ObjectId('593c24443c8ca55b969c4c54'), "isbn"=>"201",
"name"=>"Mastering MongoDB, 2nd Edition", "meta"=>{"authors"=>"alex
giamas"}}
```

 We need to enclose the key name in quotes (' ') to access the embedded object, just as we need it for operations starting with $, such as '$set'.

Update

Updating documents using the mongo-ruby-driver is chained to finding them. Using our example collection `books`, we can do:

```
@collection.update_one( { 'isbn': 101}, { '$set' => { name: 'Mastering
MongoDB, 2nd Edition' } } )
```

This finds the document with `isbn 101` and changes its name to `Mastering MongoDB, 2nd Edition`.

Similar to `update_one`, we can use `update_many` to update multiple documents retrieved via the first parameter of the method.

 If we don't use the `$set` operator, the contents of the document will be replaced by the new document.

Assuming Ruby version >=2.2 , keys can be unquoted or quoted, but keys that start with `$` need to be quoted like this:

```
@collection.update( { isbn: '101'}, { "$set": { name: "Mastering MongoDB,
2nd edition" } } )
```

The resulting object of an update will contain information about the operation, including these methods:

- `ok?`: A Boolean value that shows whether the operation was successful or not
- `matched_count`: The number of documents matching the query
- `modified_count`: The number of documents affected (updated)
- `upserted_count`: The number of documents upserted if the operation includes `$set`
- `upserted_id`: The unique `ObjectId` of the upserted document if there is one

Updates that modify fields of a constant data size will be *in place*, meaning that they won't move the document from its physical location on disk. This includes, for example, operations such as `$inc` and `$set` on the `Integer` and `Date` fields.

Updates that can increase the size of a document may result in the document being moved from its physical location on disk to a new location at the end of the file. In this case, queries may miss or return the document multiple times. To avoid this, we can use `$snapshot: true` while querying.

Delete

Deleting documents works similarly to finding documents. We need to find documents and then apply the delete operation.

For example, with our `books` collection used before, we can issue:

```
@collection.find( { isbn: '101' } ).delete_one
```

This will delete a single document. In our case, since `isbn` is unique for every document, this is expected. If our `find()` clause had matched multiple documents, then `delete_one` would have deleted just the first one that `find()` returns, which may or may not be what we want.

> If we use `delete_one` with a query matching multiple documents, the results may be unexpected.

If we want to delete all documents matching our `find()` query, we have to use `delete_many`, like this:

```
@collection.find( { price: { $gte: 30 } ).delete_many
```

In the preceding example, we are deleting all books that have a price greater than or equal to 30.

Batch operations

We can use the `BulkWrite` API for batch operations. In our previous insert many documents example, this would be:

```
@collection.bulk_write([ { insertMany: documents
                        }],
                  ordered: true)
```

The `BulkWrite` API can take the following parameters:

- `insertOne`
- `updateOne`
- `updateMany`

- `replaceOne`
- `deleteOne`
- `deleteMany`

One version of these commands will `insert`/`update`/`replace`/`delete` a single document even if the filter that we specify matches more than one document. In this case, it's important to have a filter that matches a single document to avoid unexpected behaviors.

It's also possible, and a perfectly valid use case, to include several operations in the first argument of the `bulk_write` command. This allows us to issue commands in a sequence when we have operations that depend on each other and we want to batch them in a logical order according to our business logic. Any error will stop `ordered:true` batch writes and we will need to manually roll back our operations. A notable exception is `writeConcern` errors, for example requesting a majority of our replica set members to acknowledge our write. In this case, batch writes will go through and we can observe the errors in the `writeConcernErrors` result field.

```
old_book = @collection.findOne(name: 'MongoDB for experts')
new_book = { isbn: 201, name: 'MongoDB for experts, 2nd Edition', price: 55
}
@collection.bulk_write([ {deleteOne: old_book}, { insertOne: new_book
                 }],
              ordered: true)
```

In the previous example, we made sure that we deleted the original book before adding the new (and more expensive) edition of our `MongoDB for experts` book.

`BulkWrite` can batch up to 1,000 operations. If we have more than 1,000 underlying operations in our commands, these will be split into chunks of thousands. It is a good practice to try to keep our write operations to a single batch if we can, to avoid unexpected behavior.

CRUD in Mongoid

In this section, we will use Mongoid to perform `create`, `read`, `update`, and `delete` operations. All of the code is also available on GitHub at:

`https://github.com/agiamas/mastering-mongodb/tree/master/chapter_4`

Read

Back in Chapter 2, *Schema Design and Data Modeling,* we described how to install, connect, and set up models, including inheritance to Mongoid. Here we will go through the most common use cases of CRUD.

Finding documents is done using a DSL similar to Active Record:

```
Book.find('592149c4aabac953a3a1e31e')
```

This will find by ObjectId and return the document with isbn 101, as will the query by name attribute:

```
Book.where(name: 'Mastering MongoDB')
```

In a similar fashion to dynamically generated active record queries by attribute, we can use the helper:

```
Book.find_by(name: 'Mastering MongoDB')
```

This queries by attribute name, equivalent to the previous query.

We should enable QueryCache to avoid hitting the database for the same query multiple times, like this:

```
Mongoid::QueryCache.enabled = true
```

This can be added in any code block we want to enable or in the initializer for Mongoid.

Scoping queries

We can scope queries in Mongoid using class methods:

```
Class Book
...
  def self.premium
    where(price: {'$gt': 20'})
  end
End
```

Then use this:

```
Book.premium
```

It will query for books with price greater than 20.

Create, update, and delete

The Ruby interface for creating documents is similar to Active Record:

```
Book.where(isbn: 202, name: 'Mastering MongoDB, 3rd Edition').create
```

This will return an error if the creation fails.

We can use the bang version to force an exception to be raised if saving the document fails:

```
Book.where(isbn: 202, name: 'Mastering MongoDB, 3rd Edition').create!
```

The bulk write API is not supported as of Mongoid version 6.x . The workaround is to use mongo-ruby-driver API, which will not use the `mongoid.yml` configuration or custom validations; or you can use `insert_many([array_of_documents])`, which will insert the documents one by one.

To update documents, we can use `update` or `update_all`. `update` will update *only* the first document retrieved by the query part, whereas `update_all` will update all of them:

```
Book.where(isbn: 202).update(name: 'Mastering MongoDB, THIRD Edition')
Book.where(price: { '$gt': 20 }).update_all(price_range: 'premium')
```

Deleting a document is similar to creating it, providing delete to skip callbacks and `destroy` if we want to execute any available callbacks in the affected document.

`delete_all` and `destroy_all` are convenience methods for multiple documents.

> `destroy_all` should be avoided if possible as it will load all documents into the memory to execute callbacks and thus can be memory-intensive.

CRUD using the Python driver

PyMongo is the officially supported driver for Python by MongoDB. In this section, we will use PyMongo to `create`, `read`, `update`, and `delete` documents in MongoDB.

Create and delete

The Python driver provides methods for CRUD just like Ruby and PHP. Following on from Chapter 2, *Schema Design and Data Modeling*, and the books variable that points to our books collection, we can have:

```python
from pymongo import MongoClient
from pprint import pprint

>>> book = {
    'isbn': '301',
    'name': 'Python and MongoDB',
    'price': 60
}
>>> insert_result = books.insert_one(book)
>>> pprint(insert_result)

<pymongo.results.InsertOneResult object at 0x104bf3370>

>>> result = list(books.find())
>>> pprint(result)

[{u'_id': ObjectId('592149c4aabac953a3a1e31e'),
 u'isbn': u'101',
 u'name': u'Mastering MongoDB',
 u'price': 30.0,
 u'published': datetime.datetime(2017, 6, 25, 0, 0)},
{u'_id': ObjectId('59214bc1aabac954263b24e0'),
 u'isbn': u'102',
 u'name': u'MongoDB in 7 years',
 u'price': 50.0,
 u'published': datetime.datetime(2017, 6, 26, 0, 0)},
{u'_id': ObjectId('593c24443c8ca55b969c4c54'),
 u'isbn': u'201',
 u'meta': {u'authors': u'alex giamas'},
 u'name': u'Mastering MongoDB, 2nd Edition'},
{u'_id': ObjectId('594061a9aabac94b7c858d3d'),
 u'isbn': u'301',
 u'name': u'Python and MongoDB',
 u'price': 60}]
```

In the previous example, we used insert_one() to insert a single document, which we can define using the Python dictionary notation; we can then query it for all documents in the collection.

The resulting object for `insert_one` and `insert_many` has two fields of interest:

- `Acknowledged`: A Boolean that is `true` if the insert has succeeded and false if it hasn't or if write concern is 0 (fire and forget write)
- `inserted_id` for `insert_one`: The `ObjectId` of the written document and `inserted_ids` for `insert_many`: The array of `ObjectIds` of the written documents

We used the `pprint` library to pretty-print the `find()` results. The built-in way to iterate through the result set is by using this:

```
for document in results:
    print(document)
```

Deleting documents is similar to creating them. We can use `delete_one` to delete the first instance or `delete_many` to delete all instances of the matched query.

```
>>> result = books.delete_many({ "isbn": "101" })
>>> print(result.deleted_count)
1
```

The `deleted_count` tells us how many documents were deleted; in our case, it is 1 even though we used the `delete_many` method.

To delete all documents from a collection, we can pass in the empty document `{ }`.

To drop a collection, we can use `drop()`:

```
>>> books.delete_many({})
>>> books.drop()
```

Finding documents

To find documents based on top-level attributes, we can simply use a dictionary:

```
>>> books.find({"name": "Mastering MongoDB"})

[{u'_id': ObjectId('592149c4aabac953a3a1e31e'),
 u'isbn': u'101',
 u'name': u'Mastering MongoDB',
 u'price': 30.0,
 u'published': datetime.datetime(2017, 6, 25, 0, 0)}]
```

To find documents in an embedded document, we can use the dot notation. In the following example, we use `meta.authors` to access the `authors` embedded document inside the meta document:

```
>>> result = list(books.find({"meta.authors": {"$regex": "aLEx",
"$options": "i"}}))
>>> pprint(result)

[{u'_id': ObjectId('593c24443c8ca55b969c4c54'),
  u'isbn': u'201',
  u'meta': {u'authors': u'alex giamas'},
  u'name': u'Mastering MongoDB, 2nd Edition'}]
```

In this example, we used a regular expression to match aLEx, case-insensitive, in every document in which the string is mentioned in the `meta.authors` embedded document. PyMongo uses this notation for regular expression queries, called the `$regex` notation in MongoDB documentation. The second parameter is the options parameter for `$regex`, which we'll explain in great detail in the *Using regular expressions* section later in this chapter.

Comparison operators are also supported, a full list of which is given in the *Comparison operators* section later in this chapter:

```
>>> result = list(books.find({ "price": {  "$gt":40 } }))
>>> pprint(result)

[{u'_id': ObjectId('594061a9aabac94b7c858d3d'),
  u'isbn': u'301',
  u'name': u'Python and MongoDB',
  u'price': 60}]
```

Adding multiple dictionaries in our query results in a logical AND query:

```
>>> result = list(books.find({"name": "Mastering MongoDB", "isbn": "101"}))
>>> pprint(result)

[{u'_id': ObjectId('592149c4aabac953a3a1e31e'),
  u'isbn': u'101',
  u'name': u'Mastering MongoDB',
  u'price': 30.0,
  u'published': datetime.datetime(2017, 6, 25, 0, 0)}]
```

For books having both `isbn=101` and `name=Mastering MongoDB`, to use logical operators such as `$or` and $and we have to use this syntax:

```
>>> result = list(books.find({"$or": [{"isbn": "101"}, {"isbn": "102"}]}))
>>> pprint(result)

[{u'_id': ObjectId('592149c4aabac953a3a1e31e'),
  u'isbn': u'101',
  u'name': u'Mastering MongoDB',
  u'price': 30.0,
  u'published': datetime.datetime(2017, 6, 25, 0, 0)},
 {u'_id': ObjectId('59214bc1aabac954263b24e0'),
  u'isbn': u'102',
  u'name': u'MongoDB in 7 years',
  u'price': 50.0,
  u'published': datetime.datetime(2017, 6, 26, 0, 0)}]
```

For books having an `isbn` of 101 or 102, if we want to combine AND and OR operators we have to use the `$and` operator like this:

```
>>> result = list(books.find({"$or": [{"$and": [{"name": "Mastering
MongoDB", "isbn": "101"}]}, {"$and": [{"name": "MongoDB in 7 years",
"isbn": "102"}]}]}))
>>> pprint(result)
[{u'_id': ObjectId('592149c4aabac953a3a1e31e'),
  u'isbn': u'101',
  u'name': u'Mastering MongoDB',
  u'price': 30.0,
  u'published': datetime.datetime(2017, 6, 25, 0, 0)},
 {u'_id': ObjectId('59214bc1aabac954263b24e0'),
  u'isbn': u'102',
  u'name': u'MongoDB in 7 years',
  u'price': 50.0,
  u'published': datetime.datetime(2017, 6, 26, 0, 0)}]
```

For a result of OR between 2 queries.

- The first query is asking for documents that have `isbn=101` AND `name=Mastering MongoDB`
- The second query is asking for documents that have `isbn=102` AND `name=MongoDB in 7 years`
- The result is the union of these two datasets

Updating documents

```
>>> result = books.update_one({"isbn": "101"}, {"$set": {"price": 100}})
>>> print(result.matched_count)
1
>>> print(result.modified_count)
1
```

Similar to inserting documents, when updating we can use `update_one` or `update_many`:

- The first argument here is the filter document for matching the documents that will be updated
- The second argument is the operation to be applied to the matched documents
- The third (optional) argument is `upsert=false` (default) or `true`, used to create a new document if it's not found

Another interesting argument is the optional `bypass_document_validation=false` (default) or `true`. This will ignore validations (if there are any) for the documents in the collection.

The resulting object will have `matched_count` for the number of documents that matched the filter query and `modified_count` for the number of documents that were affected by the `update` part of the query.

In our example, we are setting `price=100` for the first book with `isbn=101` through the `$set` update operator. A list of all update operators is shown in the *Update operators* section later in this chapter.

If we don't use an update operator as the second argument, the contents of the matched document will be entirely replaced by the new document.

CRUD using PyMODM

PyMODM is a core ODM that provides simple and extensible functionality. It is developed and maintained by MongoDB's engineers, who get fast updates and support for the latest stable version of MongoDB available.

In Chapter 2, *Schema Design and Data Modeling*, we explored how to define different models and connect to MongoDB. CRUD when using PyMODM, as with every ODM, is simpler than when using the low-level drivers.

Creating documents

A new user object as defined in Chapter 2, *Schema Design and Data Modeling*, can be created with a single line:

```
>>> user = User('alexgiamas@packt.com', 'Alex', 'Giamas').save()
```

In this example, we used positional arguments in the same order they were defined in the user model to assign values to the user model attributes.

We can also use keyword arguments or a mix of both, like this:

```
>>> user = User(email='alexgiamas@packt.com', 'Alex',
last_name='Giamas').save()
```

Bulk saving can be done by passing in an array of users to bulk_create():

```
>>> users = [ user1, user2,...,userN]
>>>    User.bulk_create(users)
```

Updating documents

We can modify a document by directly accessing the attributes and calling save() again:

```
>>> user.first_name = 'Alexandros'
>>> user.save()
```

If we want to update one or more documents, we have to use raw() to filter out the documents that will be affected and chain update() to set the new values:

```
>>> User.objects.raw({'first_name': {'$exists': True}})
            .update({'$set': {'updated_at': datetime.datetime.now()}})
```

In the preceding example, we search for all User documents that have a first name and set a new field, updated_at, to the current timestamp. The result of the raw() method is QuerySet, a class used in PyMODM to handle queries and work with documents in bulk.

Deleting documents

Deleting an API is similar to updating—using `QuerySet` to find the affected documents and then chaining on a `.delete()` method to delete them:

```
>>> User.objects.raw({'first_name': {'$exists': True}}).delete()
```

`BulkWrite` API is still not supported at the time of writing this book (June 2017) and the relevant ticket, PYMODM-43, is open. Methods such as `bulk_create()` will, under the hood, issue multiple commands to the database.

Querying documents

Querying is done using `QuerySet` as described before in `update` and `delete` operations.

Some convenience methods available are:

- `all()`
- `count()`
- `first()`
- `exclude(*fields)` to exclude some fields from the result
- `only(*fields)` to include only some fields in the result (this can be chained for a union of fields)
- `limit(limit)`
- `order_by(ordering)`
- `reverse()` if we want to reverse the `order_by()` order
- `skip(number)`
- `values()` to return Python dict instances instead of model instances

By using `raw()`, we can use the same queries that we described in the PyMongo section before for querying and still exploit the flexibility and convenience methods provided by the ODM layer.

CRUD using the PHP driver

In PHP, there is a new driver called `mongo-php-library` that should be used instead of the deprecated MongoClient. The overall architecture was explained in `Chapter 2`, *Schema Design and Data Modeling*. Here, we will cover more details of the API and how we can perform CRUD operations using it.

Create and delete

```
$document = array( "isbn" => "401", "name" => "MongoDB and PHP" );
$result = $collection->insertOne($document);
var_dump($result);
```

This is the output:

```
MongoDB\InsertOneResult Object
(
    [writeResult:MongoDB\InsertOneResult:private] =>
MongoDB\Driver\WriteResult Object
        (
            [nInserted] => 1
            [nMatched] => 0
            [nModified] => 0
            [nRemoved] => 0
            [nUpserted] => 0
            [upsertedIds] => Array
                (
                )

            [writeErrors] => Array
                (
                )

            [writeConcernError] =>
            [writeConcern] => MongoDB\Driver\WriteConcern Object
                (
                )

        )

    [insertedId:MongoDB\InsertOneResult:private] => MongoDB\BSON\ObjectID
Object
        (
            [oid] => 5941ac50aabac9d16f6da142
        )

    [isAcknowledged:MongoDB\InsertOneResult:private] => 1
)
```

The rather lengthy output contains all the information that we may need. We can get the ObjectId of the document inserted; the number of inserted, matched, modified, removed, and upserted documents by fields prefixed with n; and information about writeError or writeConcernError.

There are also convenience methods in the `$result` object if we want to get the information:

- `$result->getInsertedCount()`: To get the number of inserted objects
- `$result->getInsertedId()`: To get the `ObjectId` of the inserted document

We can also use the `->insertMany()` method to insert many documents at once, like this:

```
$documentAlpha = array( "isbn" => "402", "name" => "MongoDB and PHP, 2nd
Edition" );
$documentBeta  = array( "isbn" => "403", "name" => "MongoDB and PHP,
revisited" );
$result = $collection->insertMany([$documentAlpha, $documentBeta]);

print_r($result);
```

The result is:

```
(
    [writeResult:MongoDB\InsertManyResult:private] =>
MongoDB\Driver\WriteResult Object
        (
            [nInserted] => 2
            [nMatched] => 0
            [nModified] => 0
            [nRemoved] => 0
            [nUpserted] => 0
            [upsertedIds] => Array
                (
                )

            [writeErrors] => Array
                (
                )

            [writeConcernError] =>
            [writeConcern] => MongoDB\Driver\WriteConcern Object
                (
                )

        )

    [insertedIds:MongoDB\InsertManyResult:private] => Array
        (
            [0] => MongoDB\BSON\ObjectID Object
                (
                    [oid] => 5941ae85aabac9d1d16c63a2
```

```
                )

        [1] => MongoDB\BSON\ObjectID Object
            (
                [oid] => 5941ae85aabac9d1d16c63a3
            )

    )

    [isAcknowledged:MongoDB\InsertManyResult:private] => 1

)
```

Again, `$result->getInsertedCount()` **will return 2, whereas**
`$result->getInsertedIds()` **will return an array with the two newly created**
`ObjectIds`:

```
array(2) {
  [0]=>
  object(MongoDB\BSON\ObjectID)#13 (1) {
    ["oid"]=>
    string(24) "5941ae85aabac9d1d16c63a2"
  }
  [1]=>
  object(MongoDB\BSON\ObjectID)#14 (1) {
    ["oid"]=>
    string(24) "5941ae85aabac9d1d16c63a3"
  }
}
```

Deleting documents is similar to inserting but with the `deleteOne()` and `deleteMany()`
methods; an example of `deleteMany()` is shown here:

```
$deleteQuery = array( "isbn" => "401");
$deleteResult = $collection->deleteMany($deleteQuery);
print_r($result);
print($deleteResult->getDeletedCount());
```

Here is the output:

```
MongoDB\DeleteResult Object
(
    [writeResult:MongoDB\DeleteResult:private] => MongoDB\Driver\WriteResult
Object
        (
            [nInserted] => 0
            [nMatched] => 0
            [nModified] => 0
            [nRemoved] => 2
```

```
            [nUpserted] => 0
            [upsertedIds] => Array
                (
                )

            [writeErrors] => Array
                (
                )

            [writeConcernError] =>
            [writeConcern] => MongoDB\Driver\WriteConcern Object
                (
                )

        )

    [isAcknowledged:MongoDB\DeleteResult:private] => 1
)
2
```

In this example, we used ->getDeletedCount() to get the number of affected documents, which is printed out in the last line of the output.

Bulk write

The new PHP driver supports the bulk write interface to minimize network calls to MongoDB:

```
$manager = new MongoDB\Driver\Manager('mongodb://localhost:27017');
$bulk = new MongoDB\Driver\BulkWrite(array("ordered" => true));
$bulk->insert(array( "isbn" => "401", "name" => "MongoDB and PHP" ));
$bulk->insert(array( "isbn" => "402", "name" => "MongoDB and PHP, 2nd
Edition" ));
$bulk->update(array("isbn" => "402"), array('$set' => array("price" =>
15)));
$bulk->insert(array( "isbn" => "403", "name" => "MongoDB and PHP,
revisited" ));


$result = $manager->executeBulkWrite('mongo_book.books', $bulk);
print_r($result);
```

The result is:

```
MongoDB\Driver\WriteResult Object
(
    [nInserted] => 3
```

```
[nMatched] => 1
[nModified] => 1
[nRemoved] => 0
[nUpserted] => 0
[upsertedIds] => Array
    (
    )

[writeErrors] => Array
    (
    )

[writeConcernError] =>
[writeConcern] => MongoDB\Driver\WriteConcern Object
    (
    )

)
```

In the preceding example, we executed two inserts, one `update`, and a third `insert` in an ordered fashion. The `WriteResult` object contains a total of three inserted documents and one modified document.

The main difference compared to simple create/delete queries is that `executeBulkWrite()` is a method of the `MongoDB\Driver\Manager` class, which we instantiate on the first line.

Read

Querying an interface is similar to inserting and deleting, with the `findOne()` and `find()` methods used to retrieve the first result or all results of a query:

```
$document = $collection->findOne( array("isbn" => "101") );
$cursor = $collection->find( array( "name" => new
MongoDB\BSON\Regex("mongo", "i") ) );
```

In the second example, we are using a regular expression to search for a key name with the value `mongo` (case-insensitive).

Embedded documents can be queried using the `.` notation, as with the other languages that we examined earlier in this chapter:

```
$cursor = $collection->find( array('meta.price' => 50) );
```

We do this to query for an embedded document `price` inside the meta key field.

Similarly to Ruby and Python, in PHP we can query using comparison operators, like this:

```
$cursor = $collection->find( array( 'price' => array('$gte'=> 60) ) );
```

A complete list of comparison operators supported in the PHP driver is available at the end of this chapter.

Querying with multiple key-value pairs is an implicit AND, whereas queries using $or, $in, $nin, or AND ($and) combined with $or can be achieved with nested queries:

```
$cursor = $collection->find( array( '$or' => array(
                                        array("price" => array( '$gte'
=> 60)),
                                        array("price" => array( '$lte'
=> 20))
                                )));
```

This finds documents that have price>=60 OR price<=20.

Update

Updating documents has a similar interface with the ->updateOne() OR ->updateMany() method.

The first parameter is the query used to find documents and the second one will update our documents.

We can use any of the update operators explained at the end of this chapter to update in place or specify a new document to completely replace the document in the query:

```
$result = $collection->updateOne(
  array( "isbn" => "401"),
    array( '$set' => array( "price" => 39 ) )
);
```

 We can use single quotes or double quotes for key names, but if we have special operators starting with $, we need to use single quotes. We can use array("key" => "value") or ["key" => "value"]. We prefer the more explicit array() notation in this book.

The ->getMatchedCount() and ->getModifiedCount() methods will return the number of documents matched in the query part or the ones modified from the query. If the new value is the same as the existing value of a document, it will not be counted as modified.

CRUD using Doctrine

Following on from our Doctrine example in `Chapter 2`, *Schema Design and Data Modeling,* we will work on these models for CRUD operations.

Create, update, and delete

Creating documents is a two-step process. First, we create our document and set the attribute values:

```
$book = new Book();
$book->setName('MongoDB with Doctrine');
$book->setPrice(45);
```

And then we ask Doctrine to save `$book` in the next `flush()` call:

```
$dm->persist($book);
```

We can force saving by manually calling `flush()`:

```
$dm->flush();
```

In this example, `$dm` is a `DocumentManager` object that we use to connect to our MongoDB instance like this:

```
$dm = DocumentManager::create(new Connection(), $config);
```

Updating a document is as easy as assigning values to the attributes:

```
$book->price = 39;
$book->persist($book);
```

This will save our book `MongoDB with Doctrine` with the new price of `39`.

Updating documents in place uses the `QueryBuilder` interface.

Doctrine provides several helper methods around atomic updates, as listed here:

- `set($name, $value, $atomic = true)`
- `setNewObj($newObj)`
- `inc($name, $value)`
- `unsetField($field)`
- `push($field, $value)`
- `pushAll($field, array $valueArray)`

- addToSet($field, $value)
- addManyToSet($field, array $values)
- popFirst($field)
- popLast($field)
- pull($field, $value)
- pullAll($field, array $valueArray)

update will, by default, update the first document found by the query. If we want to change multiple documents, we need to use ->updateMany():

```
$dm->createQueryBuilder('Book')
   ->updateMany()
   ->field('price')->set(69)
   ->field('name')->equals('MongoDB with Doctrine')
   ->getQuery()
   ->execute();
```

In the preceding example we are setting the price of the book with name='MongoDB with Doctrine' to be 69. The list of comparison operators in Doctrine is available in the next section on read operations.

We can chain multiple comparison operators, resulting in an AND query and also multiple helper methods, resulting in updates to several fields.

Deleting a document is similar to creating it:

```
$dm->remove($book);
```

Removing multiple documents is best done using the QueryBuilder, which we will explore further in the following section:

```
$qb = $dm->createQueryBuilder('Book');
$qb->remove()
   ->field('price')->equals(50)
   ->getQuery()
   ->execute();
```

Read

Doctrine provides a `QueryBuilder` interface to build queries for MongoDB. Given that we have defined our models as described in Chapter 2, *Schema Design and Data Modeling*, we can do this to obtain an instance of a `QueryBuilder` named $db, get a default find-all query, and execute it:

```
$qb = $dm->createQueryBuilder('Book');
$query = $qb->getQuery();
$books = $query->execute();
```

The `$books` variable now contains an iterable lazy data-loading cursor over our result set.

Using `$qb->eagerCursor(true);` over the `QueryBuilder` object will return an eager cursor, fetching all data from MongoDB as soon as we start iterating our results.

Some helper methods for querying are listed here:

- `->getSingleResult()`: Equivalent to `findOne()`.
- `->select('name')`: Returns only the values for the `'key'` attribute from our books collection. `ObjectId` will always be returned.
- `->hint('book_name_idx')`: Forces the query to use this index. We'll see more about indexes in Chapter 6, *Indexing*.
- `->distinct('name')`: Returns distinct results by name.
- `->limit(10)`: Returns the first 10 results.
- `->sort('name', 'desc')`: Sorts by name (`desc` or `asc`).

Doctrine uses the concept of hydration when fetching documents from MongoDB. Using an identity map, it will cache MongoDB results in memory and consult this map before hitting the database. Disabling hydration can be done per query by using `->hydration(false)` or globally using the configuration as explained in Chapter 2, *Schema Design and Data Modeling*.

We can also force Doctrine to refresh data in the identity map for a query from MongoDB using `->refresh()` on $qb.

The comparison operators that we can use with Doctrine are:

- `where($javascript)`
- `in($values)`
- `notIn($values)`
- `equals($value)`
- `notEqual($value)`
- `gt($value)`
- `gte($value)`
- `lt($value)`
- `lte($value)`
- `range($start, $end)`
- `size($size)`
- `exists($bool)`
- `type($type)`
- `all($values)`
- `mod($mod)`
- `addOr($expr)`
- `addAnd($expr)`
- `references($document)`
- `includesReferenceTo($document)`

For example, consider this query:

```
$qb = $dm->createQueryBuilder('Book')
            ->field('price')->lt(30);
```

It will return all books whose price is less than 30.

`addAnd()` may seem redundant since chaining multiple query expressions in Doctrine is implicitly an AND, but it is useful if we want to do AND ((A OR B), (C OR D)) where A, B, C, and D are standalone expressions.

To nest multiple OR operators with an external AND and in other equally complex cases, the nested ORs need to be evaluated as expressions using ->expr():

```
$expression = $qb->expr()->field('name')->equals('MongoDB with Doctrine')
```

$expression is a standalone expression that can be used with $qb->addOr($expression) and similarly with addAnd().

Best practices

Some best practices for using Doctrine with MongoDB are as follows:

- Don't use unnecessary cascading. It impacts performance.
- Don't use unnecessary life cycle events. It impacts performance.
- Don't use special characters such as non-ASCII ones in class, field, table, or column names as Doctrine is not Unicode-safe yet.
- Initialize collection references in the model's constructor.
- Constrain relationships between objects as much as possible. Avoid bidirectional associations between models and eliminate the ones that are not needed. This helps with performance, loose coupling, and produces simpler and easily maintainable code.

Comparison operators

The following is a list of all comparison operators that MongoDB supports:

Name	Description
$eq	Matches values that are equal to a specified value
$gt	Matches values that are greater than a specified value
$gte	Matches values that are greater than or equal to the specified value
$lt	Matches values that are less than the specified value
$lte	Matches values that are less than or equal to the specified value
$ne	Matches all values that are not equal to the specified value
$in	Matches any of the values specified in an array
$nin	Matches none of the values specified in an array

Update operators

Name	Description
$inc	Increments the value of the field by the specified amount.
$mul	Multiplies the value of the field by the specified amount.
$rename	Renames a field.
$setOnInsert	Sets the value of a field if an update results in an insert of a document. It has no effect on update operations and modify existing documents.
$set	Sets the value of a field in a document.
$unset	Removes the specified field from a document.
$min	Only updates the field if the specified value is less than the existing field value.
$max	Only updates the field if the specified value is greater than the existing field value.
$currentDate	Sets the value of a field to the current date, either as a date or as a timestamp.

Smart querying

There are several considerations in MongoDB querying that we have to take into account. Here are some best practices for using regular expressions, query results, and cursors, and also what we should take into account when deleting documents.

Using regular expressions

MongoDB offers a rich interface for querying using regular expressions. In its simplest form, we can use regular expressions in queries by modifying the query string:

```
> db.books.find({"name": /mongo/})
```

This is done to search for books in our `books` collection that contain the name `mongo`. It is the equivalent of a SQL `LIKE` query.

 MongoDB has used **PCRE (Perl Compatible Regular Expression)** version 8.39 with UTF-8 support.

We can also use some options when querying:

Option	Description
i	Case insensitivity.
m	For patterns that include anchors (that is, ^ for the start and $ for the end), match at the beginning or end of each line for strings with multiline values. Without this option, these anchors match at the beginning or end of the string. If the pattern contains no anchors or if the string value has no newline characters (for example, \n), the m option has no effect.

In our previous example, if we wanted to search for `mongo`, `Mongo`, `MONGO`, and any other case-insensitive variation, we would need to use the i option, as follows:

```
> db.books.find({"name": /mongo/i})
```

Alternatively, we can use `$regex` operator, which provides more flexibility.

The same queries using `$regex` would be written as:

```
> db.books.find({'name': { '$regex': /mongo/ } })
> db.books.find({'name': { '$regex': /mongo/i } })
```

By using the $regex operator, we can use the following two options too:

Option	Description
x	Extended capability to ignore all whitespace characters in the $regex pattern unless escaped or included in a character class. Additionally, it ignores characters in between (and including) an un-escaped hash/pound (#) character and the next new line so that you may include comments in complicated patterns. This only applies to data characters; whitespace characters may never appear within special character sequences in a pattern. The x option does not affect the handling of the VT character (that is, code 11).
s	Allows the dot character (that is, .) to match all characters, including newline characters.

Expanding matching documents using regex makes our queries slower to execute.

Indexes using regular expressions can only be used if our regular expression queries for the beginning of a string that is indexed, that is, regular expressions starting with ^ or \A . If we want to query only using a starts with regular expression, we should avoid writing lengthier regular expressions even if they would match the same strings.

For example:

```
> db.books.find({'name': { '$regex': /mongo/ } })
> db.books.find({'name': { '$regex': /^mongo.*/ } })
```

Both queries will match name values starting with mongo (case-sensitive), but the first one will be faster as it will stop matching as soon as it hits the sixth character in every name value.

Query results and cursors

MongoDB's lack of support for transactions means that several semantics that we take for granted in RDBMS work differently.

As explained before, updates can modify the size of a document. Modifying the size can result in MongoDB moving the document on disk to a new slot towards the end of the storage file.

When we have multiple threads querying and updating a single collection, we can end up with a document appearing multiple times in the result set.

This will happen in the following scenario:

- Thread A starts querying the collection and matches document A1
- Thread B updates document A1, increasing its size and forcing MongoDB to move it to a different physical location towards the end of the storage file
- Thread A is still querying the collection. It reaches the end of the collection and finds document A1 again with its new value

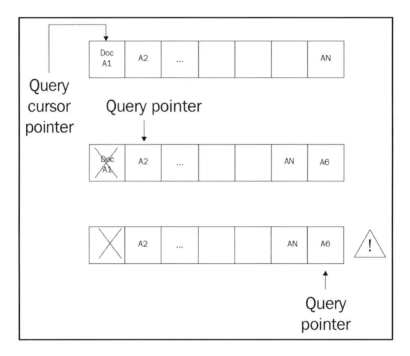

This is rare but can happen in production. If we can't safeguard from such a case in the application layer, we can use snapshot() to prevent it.

`snapshot()` is supported by official drivers and the shell by appending it into an operation that returns a cursor:

```
> db.books.find().snapshot()
```

`$snapshot` cannot be used with sharded collections. `$snapshot` has to be applied before the query returns the first document. Snapshot cannot be used together with `hint()` or `sort()` operators.

We can simulate the `snapshot()` behavior by querying using `hint({id :1})`, thus forcing the query engine to use the `id` index just like the `$snapshot` operator.

If our query runs on a unique index of a field whose values won't get modified during the duration of the query, we should use this to query to get the same query behavior. Even then, `snapshot()` cannot protect us from insertions or deletions happening in the middle of a query. The `$snapshot` operator will traverse the built-in index that every collection has on the id field, making it inherently slow. It should only be used as a last resort.

If we want to `update`, `insert`, or `delete` multiple documents without other threads seeing the results of our operation while it's happening, we can use the `$isolated` operator:

```
> db.books.remove( { price: { $gt: 30 }, $isolated: 1 } )
```

In this example, threads querying the `books` collection will see either all books with price greater than 30 or no books at all. The isolated operator will acquire an exclusive write lock in the collection for the whole duration of the query, no matter what the storage engine can support, contributing to contention in this collection.

Isolated operations are still not transactions. They don't provide `atomicity ( "all-or-nothing")`. So, if they fail midway, we need to manually roll back the operation to get our database into a consistent state.

Again, this should be a last resort and only used in cases where it's mission-critical to avoid multiple threads seeing inconsistent information at any time.

Storage considerations on delete

Deleting documents in MongoDB does not reclaim the disk space used by it. If we have 10 GB of disk space used by MongoDB and we delete all documents, we will still be using 10 GB. What happens under the hood is that MongoDB will mark these documents as deleted and may use the space to store new documents.

This results in our disk having space that is not used, yet not freed up for the operating system. If we want to claim it back, we can use `compact()` to reclaim unused space:

```
> db.books.compact()
```

Or alternatively, we can start the `mongod` server with the option `--repair`.

A better option is to enable compression, available from version 3.0 and only with the WiredTiger storage engine. We can use the snappy or zlib algorithm to compress our document size. This will, again, not prevent storage holes, but if we are tight on disk space, it is preferable to the heavy operational route of repair and compact.

Storage compression uses less disk space at the expense of CPU usage, but this trade-off is mostly worth it.

 Always take a backup before running operations that can result in catastrophic loss of data. Repair or compact will run in single thread, blocking the entire database from other operations. In production systems, always perform these on the slave first; then switch the master-slave roles and compact the ex-master, now-slave instance.

Summary

In this chapter we went through advanced querying concepts using Ruby, Python, and PHP both using the official drivers and an ODM.

Using Ruby and the Mongoid ODM, Python and the PyMODM ODM, and PHP and the Doctrine ODM, we went through code samples exploring how to `create`, `read`, `update`, and `delete` documents.

We also discussed batching operations for performance and best practices. We presented an exhaustive list of comparison and update operators that MongoDB uses.

Finally, we discussed smart querying, how cursors in querying work, what our storage performance considerations should be on delete, and how to use regular expressions.

In the next chapter we will learn about the aggregation framework, using a complete use case that involves processing transaction data from the Ethereum blockchain.

5
Aggregation

In Chapter 4, *Advanced Querying*, we went through querying using a variety of drivers and frameworks for Ruby, Python, and PHP. In this chapter, we will dive deeper into aggregation framework, where it can be useful, and the operators supported by MongoDB.

For this purpose, we will go through a complete example of aggregations to process transaction data from the Ethereum blockchain. The complete source code is available at:

https://github.com/agiamas/mastering-mongodb.

Why aggregation?

Aggregation framework was introduced by MongoDB in version 2.2 (2.1 in development branch). It serves as an alternative to both the MapReduce framework and also querying the database directly.

Using the aggregation framework, we can perform group by operations in the server. Thus we can project only the fields that are needed in the result set. Using the $match and $project operators, we can reduce the amount of data passed through the pipeline, resulting in faster data processing.

Self-joins, that is, joining data within the same collection, can also be performed using the aggregation framework as we will see in our use case.

When comparing the aggregation framework to the queries available via the shell or various other drivers, there is a use case for both.

For selection and projection queries, it's almost always better to use simple queries as the complexity of developing, testing, and deploying an aggregation framework operation cannot easily outweigh the simplicity of using built-in commands. Finding documents with (`db.books.find({price: 50}, {price: 1, name: 1})`) or without (`db.books.find({price: 50})`) projecting only some of the fields is simple and fast enough to not warrant usage of the aggregation framework.

On the other hand, if we want to perform group by and self-join operations using MongoDB, there might be a case for the aggregation framework. The most important limitation of the `group()` command in the MongoDB shell is that the result set has to fit in a document, thus meaning that it can't be more than 16 MB in size. In addition, the result of any `group()` command can't have more than 20,000 results. Finally, `group()` doesn't work with sharded input collections, which means that when our data size grows we have to rewrite our queries anyway.

In comparison to MapReduce, the aggregation framework is more limited in functionality and flexibility. In aggregation framework, we are limited by the available operators at hand. On the plus side, the API for aggregation framework is simpler to grasp and use than MapReduce. In terms of performance, aggregation framework was way faster than MapReduce in earlier versions of MongoDB but seems to be on a par with the most recent versions after the improvement in performance by MapReduce.

Finally, there is always the case of using the database as data storage and performing complex operations by the application. This can be quick to develop sometimes, but should be avoided as it will most likely incur memory, networking, and ultimately performance costs down the road.

In the next section, we will explain the available operators before using them in a real case.

Aggregation operators

In this section we will explain how to use aggregation operators. Aggregation operators are divided into two parts. Within each stage, we use **expression operators** to compare and process values. Between different stages, we use **aggregation stage operators** to define the data that will get passed on from one stage to the next as its as the format.

Aggregation stage operators

An aggregation pipeline is composed of different stages. These stages are declared in an array and executed sequentially, the output of every stage being the input of the next one.

The $out stage has to be the final stage in an aggregation pipeline, outputting data to an output collection by replacing or adding to the existing documents.

- $group: This is most commonly used to group by identifier expression and to apply the accumulator expression. It outputs one document per distinct group.
- $project: This is used for document transformation and outputs one document per input document.
- $match: This is used for filtering documents from input based on criteria.
- $lookup: This is used for filtering documents from input. Input can be documents from another collection in the same database selected by an outer left join.
- $out: This outputs the documents in this pipeline stage to an output collection by replacing or adding to the documents that already exist in the collection.
- $limit: This limits the number of documents passed on to the next aggregation phase based on criteria.
- $count: This returns a count of the number of documents at this stage of the pipeline.
- $skip: This skips a number of documents from passing on to the next stage of the pipeline.
- $sort: This sorts the documents based on criteria.
- $redact: As a combination of project and match, this will redact the selected fields from each document passing them on to the next stage of the pipeline.
- $unwind: This transforms an array of *n* elements to *n* documents each, with one element of the array passing them on to the next stage of the pipeline.
- $collStats: This returns statistics regarding the view or collection.
- $indexStats: This returns statistics regarding the indexes of the collection.
- $sample: This randomly selects a specified number of documents from input.
- $facet: This combines multiple aggregation pipelines within a single stage.
- $bucket: This splits documents into buckets based on selection criteria and bucket boundaries.

- $bucketAuto: This splits documents into buckets based on selection criteria and attempts to evenly distribute documents amongst buckets.
- $sortByCount: This groups incoming documents based on value of an expression and computes the count of documents in each bucket.
- $addFields: This adds new fields to documents and outputs the same number of documents as input, with the added fields.
- $replaceRoot: This replaces all existing fields of the input document (including the standard _id field) with the specified fields.
- $geoNear: This returns an ordered list of documents based on the proximity to a specified field. The output documents include a computed distance field.
- $graphLookup: This recursively searches in a collection and adds an array field with the results of the search in each output document.

Expression operators

Within every stage, we can define one or more expression operators to apply our intermediate calculations to.

Expression Boolean operators

Boolean operators are used to pass to the next stage of our aggregation pipeline a true or false value.

We can choose to pass along the originating (integer, string or whatever other type) value as well.

We can use the $and, $or, and $not operators the same way we would in any programming language.

Expression comparison operators

Comparison operators can be used in conjunction with Boolean operators to construct the expressions that we need to evaluate as true/false for the output of our pipeline's stage.

The most commonly used operators are listed here:

- $eq (equal)
- $ne (not equal)
- $gt (greater than)
- $gte (greater than or equal)
- $lt
- $lte

All the aforementioned mentioned operators return a Boolean value of true or false.

The only operator not returning a Boolean value is $cmp, which returns 0 if the two arguments are equivalent, 1 if the first value is greater than the second, and −1 if the second value is greater than the first.

Set expression and array operators

Set expressions perform set operations on arrays, treating arrays as sets. Set expressions ignores duplicate entries in each input array and the order of the elements.

If the set operation returns a set, the operation filters out duplicates in the result to output an array that contains only unique entries. The order of the elements in the output array is unspecified. If a set contains a nested array element, the set expression does not descend into the nested array but evaluates the array at top-level.

The available set operators are:

- $setEquals: This is true if the two sets have the same distinct elements
- $setIntersection: This returns the intersection (documents that appear in all) of all input sets
- $setUnion: This returns the union (documents that appear in at least one) of all input sets
- $setDifference: This returns the documents that appear in the first input set but not the second
- $setIsSubset: This is true if all documents in the first set appear in the second one, even if the two sets are identical
- $anyElementTrue: This is true if any of the elements in the set evaluate to true
- $allElementsTrue: This is true if all of the elements in the set evaluate to true

The available array operators are:

- `$arrayElemAt`: This returns the element at the array index position
- `$concatArrays`: This returns a concatenated array
- `$filter`: This returns a subset of the array based on specified criteria
- `$indexOfArray`: This returns the index of the array that fulfills the search criteria; if not, −1
- `$isArray`: This returns `true` if the input is an array; otherwise, `false`
- `$range`: This outputs an array containing a sequence of integers according to user-defined inputs
- `$reverseArray`: This returns an array with the elements in the opposite order
- `$reduce`: This reduces the elements of an array to a single value according to the specified input
- `$size`: This returns the number of items in the array
- `$slice`: This returns a subset of the array
- `$zip`: This returns a merged array
- `$in`: This returns `true` if the specified value is in the array; otherwise `false`

Expression date operators

Date operators are used to extract date information from date fields, when we want to calculate statistics based on day of week/month/year using the pipeline.

- `$dayOfYear` is used to get the day of year with a range of 1 to 366 for a leap year
- `$dayOfMonth` is used to get the day of month with a range of 1 to 31 inclusive
- `$dayOfWeek` is used with 1 being Sunday and 7 being Saturday (US style days)
- `$isoDayOfWeek` returns the weekday number in the ISODate 8601 format, with 1 being Monday and 7 being Sunday
- `$week` is the week number with 0 being the partial week at the beginning of each year to 53 for a year with a leap week
- `$isoWeek` returns week number in the ISODate 8601 format, 1 being the first week of the year that contains a Thursday and 53, a leap week if one exists
- `$year` / `$month` / `$hour` / `$minute` / `$milliSecond` return the relevant portion of the date in zero based numbering, except for `$month` which returns 1 through 12 inclusive.

- $isoWeekYear returns the year in the ISO 8601 format according to the date the last week in ISODate ends (that is, 2016/1/1 will still return 2015)
- $second returns 0 to 60 inclusive for leap seconds
- $dateToString converts a date input to a string

Expression string operators

Similar to date operators, string operators are used when we want to transform our data from one stage of the pipeline to the next one. Potential use cases include pre-processing text fields to extract relevant information to be used in later stages of our pipeline.

- $concat: This is used to concatenate strings.
- $split: This is used to split strings based on delimiter. If the delimiter is not found, the original string is returned.
- $strcasecmp: This is used in case-insensitive string comparison; 0 if strings are equal, 1 if the first string is great, otherwise −1.
- $toLower / $toUpper: This is used to convert string to all lowercase or all uppercase respectively.
- $indexOfBytes: This is used to return the Byte occurrence of the first occurrence of a substring in a string.
- $strLenBytes: This is the number of bytes in the input string.
- $substrBytes: This returns the specified bytes of the substring.

The equivalent methods for code points (a value in unicode, regardless of the underlying bytes in its representation) are:

- $indexOfCP
- $strLenCP
- $substrCP

Expression arithmetic operators

During each stage of the pipeline, we can apply one or more arithmetic operators to perform intermediate calculations.

- $abs, the absolute value.
- $add, can add numbers or a number to a date to get a new date.
- $ceil / $floor, ceiling and floor functions.
- $divide, to divide between two inputs.
- $exp, raises the natural number *e* to the specified exponential power.
- $pow, raises a number to the specified exponential power.
- $ln / $log / $log10. To calculate the natural log, the log on a custom base or a log base 10 respectively.
- $mod, the modular value.
- $multiply, to multiply between inputs.
- $sqrt, the square root of the input.
- $subtract, the result of subtracting the second value from the first. If both arguments are dates, returns the difference between them. If one argument is a date (has to be the first argument) and the other is a number, returns the resulting date.
- $trunc, to truncate the result.

Aggregation accumulators

Accumulators are probably the most widely used operators, allowing us to sum, average, get standard deviation statistics, and perform other operations in each member of our group.

- $sum is the sum of numerical values, ignores non-numerical values
- $avg is the average of numerical values, ignores non-numerical values
- $first / $last is the first and last value that passes through the pipeline stage, available in the group stage only
- $max / $min gets the maximum and minimum value that passes through the pipeline stage
- $push, will add a new element at the end of an input array, available in the group stage only

- `$addToSet`, will add an element (only if it does not exist) to an array treating it effectively as a set, available in the group stage only
- `$stdDevPop` / `$stdDevSamp` to get the population / sample standard deviation in the `$project` or `$match` stages

The aforementioned mentioned accumulators are available in the group or project pipeline phases except otherwise noted.

Conditional expressions

Expressions can be used to output different data to the next stage in our pipeline, based on Boolean truth tests.

```
$cond
```

This is a ternary operator that evaluates one expression, and depending on the result, returns the value of one of the other two expressions. It accepts either three expressions in an ordered list or three named parameters.

```
$ifNull
```

This returns either the non-null result of the first expression or the result of the second expression if the first expression results in a null result. Null result encompasses instances of undefined values or missing fields. It accepts two expressions as arguments. The result of the second expression can be null.

```
$switch
```

This evaluates a series of case expressions. When it finds an expression that evaluates to true, `$switch` executes a specified expression and breaks out of the control flow.

Other operators

There are some operators that are not as commonly used but can be useful in corner, use case-specific cases. The most important of them are listed in the following sections.

Text search

`$meta` This is used to access text search metadata.

Variable

$map This applies a subexpression to each element of an array and returns the array of resulting values in an order. It accepts named parameters.

$let This defines variables for use within the scope of a subexpression and returns the result of the subexpression. It accepts named parameters.

Literal

$literal This returns a value without parsing. It is used for values that the aggregation pipeline may interpret as an expression. For example, apply a $literal expression to a string that starts with $ to avoid parsing as a field path.

Parsing data type

$type, this returns the BSON data type of the field.

Limitations

The aggregation pipeline can output results in three distinct ways:

- Inline as a document containing the result set
- In a collection
- Returning a cursor to the result set

Inline results are subject to the BSON maximum document size of 16 MB, meaning that we should use this only if our final result is of fixed size. An example of this would be outputting the ObjectIds of the top five most ordered items from an e-commerce site.

A contrary example to that would be outputting the top 1,000 ordered items, along with the product information, including the description and other fields of variable size.

Outputting results into a collection is the preferred solution if we want to perform further processing of data. We can either output into a new collection or replace the contents of an existing collection. The aggregation output results will only be visible once the aggregation command succeeds, or else not visible at all.

> The output collection cannot be sharded or a capped collection (as of v3.4). If the aggregation output violates indexes (including the built-in index on the unique `ObjectId` per document) or document validation rules, aggregation will fail.

With all three options, every document output must not exceed the BSON maximum document size of 16 MB.

Each pipeline stage can have documents exceeding the 16 MB limit as these are handled by MongoDB internally. Each pipeline stage, however, can only use up to 100 MB of memory. If we expect more data in our stages, we should set `allowDiskUse:` to `true` to allow exceeding data to overflow to disk at the expense of performance.

`$graphLookup` does not support datasets over 100 MB and will ignore any setting on `allowDiskUse`.

Aggregation use case

In this rather lengthy section, we will use the aggregation framework to process data from the Ethereum blockchain.

Using our Python code from `https://github.com/agiamas/mastering-mongodb/tree/master/chapter_5`, we have extracted data from Ethereum and loaded it into our MongoDB database.

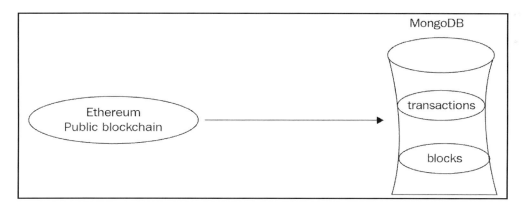

Our data resides in two collections, blocks and transactions.

A sample block document has the following fields:

- Number of transactions
- Number of contract internal transactions
- Block hash
- Parent block hash
- Mining difficulty
- Gas used
- Block height

```
> db.blocks.findOne()
{
"_id" : ObjectId("595368fbcedea89d3f4fb0ca"),
"number_transactions" : 28,
"timestamp" : NumberLong("1498324744877"),
"gas_used" : 4694483,
"number_internal_transactions" : 4,
"block_hash" :
"0x89d235c4e2e4e4978440f3cc1966f1ffb343b9b5cfec9e5cebc331fb810bded3
",
"difficulty" : NumberLong("882071747513072"),
"block_height" : 3923788
}
```

A sample transaction document has the following fields:

- Transaction hash
- Block height it belongs to
- From hash address
- To hash address
- Transaction value

- Transaction fee

```
> db.transactions.findOne()
{
"_id" : ObjectId("59535748cedea89997e8385a"),
"from" : "0x3c540be890df69eca5f0099bbedd5d667bd693f3",
"txfee" : 28594,
"timestamp" : ISODate("2017-06-06T11:23:10Z"),
"value" : 0,
"to" : "0x4b9e0d224dabcc96191cace2d367a8d8b75c9c81",
"txhash" :
"0xf205991d937bcb60955733e760356070319d95131a2d9643e3c48f2dfca39e77
",
"block" : 3923794
}
```

Sample data for our database is available on GitHub: `https://github.com/agiamas/mastering-mongodb`.

The code used to import this data into MongoDB is available here:

`https://github.com/agiamas/mastering-mongodb/tree/master/chapter_5`.

As curious developers in this novel blockchain technology, we want to analyze Ethereum transactions. We are especially keen to:

- Find the top 10 addresses that transactions originate from
- Find the top 10 addresses that transactions end in
- Find the average value per transaction, with statistics around deviation
- Find the average fee required per transaction, with statistics around deviation
- Find the time of day that the network is more active, by number of transactions or value of transactions
- Find the day of week that the network is more active, by number of transactions or value of transactions

We find the top 10 addresses that transactions originate from. To calculate this metric, we first count the number of occurrences with a 1 count for each one, group them by the value of the `from` field and output them into a new field called `count`.

Following that, we sort by the value of the `count` field in descending (-1) order and finally we limit the output to the first 10 documents that pass through the pipeline. These documents are the top 10 addresses that we are looking for.

Sample Python code is shown here:

```python
def top_ten_addresses_from(self):
    pipeline = [
        {"$group": {"_id": "$from", "count": {"$sum": 1}}},
        {"$sort": SON([("count", -1)])},
        {"$limit": 10},
    ]
    result = self.collection.aggregate(pipeline)
    for res in result:
        print(res)
```

```
{u'count': 38, u'_id': u'miningpoolhub_1'}
{u'count': 31, u'_id': u'Ethermine'}
{u'count': 30, u'_id': u'0x3c540be890df69eca5f0099bbedd5d667bd693f3'}
{u'count': 27, u'_id': u'0xb42b20ddbeabdc2a288be7ff847ff94fb48d2579'}
{u'count': 25, u'_id': u'ethfans.org'}
{u'count': 16, u'_id': u'Bittrex'}
{u'count': 8, u'_id': u'0x009735c1f7d06faaf9db5223c795e2d35080e826'}
{u'count': 8, u'_id': u'Oraclize'}
{u'count': 7, u'_id': u'0x1151314c646ce4e0efd76d1af4760ae66a9fe30f'}
{u'count': 7, u'_id': u'0x4d3ef0e8b49999de8fa4d531f07186cc3abe3d6e'}
```

Now we find the top 10 addresses that transactions end in. Similar to `from`, the calculation for the `to` addresses is exactly the same, only grouping by the `to` field instead of `from`:

```python
def top_ten_addresses_to(self):
    pipeline = [
        {"$group": {"_id": "$to", "count": {"$sum": 1}}},
        {"$sort": SON([("count", -1)])},
        {"$limit": 10},
    ]
    result = self.collection.aggregate(pipeline)
    for res in result:
        print(res)
```

```
{u'count': 33, u'_id': u'0x6090a6e47849629b7245dfa1ca21d94cd15878ef'}
{u'count': 30, u'_id': u'0x4b9e0d224dabcc96191cace2d367a8d8b75c9c81'}
{u'count': 25, u'_id': u'0x69ea6b31ef305d6b99bb2d4c9d99456fa108b02a'}
{u'count': 23, u'_id': u'0xe94b04a0fed112f3664e45adb2b8915693dd5ff3'}
{u'count': 22, u'_id': u'0x8d12a197cb00d4747a1fe03395095ce2a5cc6819'}
{u'count': 18, u'_id': u'0x91337a300e0361bddb2e377dd4e88ccb7796663d'}
{u'count': 13, u'_id': u'0x1c3f580daeaac2f540c998c8ae3e4b18440f7c45'}
{u'count': 12, u'_id': u'0xeef274b28bd40b717f5fea9b806d1203daad0807'}
{u'count': 9, u'_id': u'0x96fc4553a00c117c5b0bed950dd625d1c16dc894'}
{u'count': 9, u'_id': u'0xd43d09ec1bc5e57c8f3d0c64020d403b04c7f783'}
```

Let's find the average value per transaction, with statistics around deviation. In this example, we are using the $avg and $stdDevPop operators of the values of the value field to calculate statistics for this field. Using a simple $group operation, we output a single document with the id of our choice (here value) and the averageValues.

```
def average_value_per_transaction(self):
    pipeline = [
        {"$group": {"_id": "value", "averageValues": {"$avg": "$value"},
"stdDevValues": {"$stdDevPop": "$value"}}},
    ]
    result = self.collection.aggregate(pipeline)
    for res in result:
        print(res)
```

```
{u'averageValues': 5.227238976440972, u'_id': u'value', u'stdDevValues':
38.90322689649576}
```

Let's find the average fee required per transaction, with statistics around deviation. Average fees are similar to average values, replacing $value with $txfee:

```
def average_fee_per_transaction(self):
    pipeline = [
        {"$group": {"_id": "value", "averageFees": {"$avg": "$txfee"},
"stdDevValues": {"$stdDevPop": "$txfee"}}},
    ]
    result = self.collection.aggregate(pipeline)
    for res in result:
        print(res)
```

```
{u'_id': u'value', u'averageFees': 320842.0729166667, u'stdDevValues':
1798081.7305142984}
```

We find the time of day that the network is more active, by number of transactions or value of transactions.

To find out the most active hour for transactions, we use the $hour operator to extract the hour field from the ISODate() field in which we stored our datetime values and called timestamp.

```
def active_hour_of_day_transactions(self):
    pipeline = [
        {"$group": {"_id": {"$hour": "$timestamp"}, "transactions":
{"$sum": 1}}},
        {"$sort": SON([("transactions", -1)])},
        {"$limit": 1},
    ]
    result = self.collection.aggregate(pipeline)
```

```
            for res in result:
                print(res)

{u'_id': 11, u'transactions': 34}


    def active_hour_of_day_values(self):
        pipeline = [
            {"$group": {"_id": {"$hour": "$timestamp"},
"transaction_values": {"$sum": "$value"}}},
            {"$sort": SON([("transactions", -1)])},
            {"$limit": 1},
        ]
        result = self.collection.aggregate(pipeline)
        for res in result:
            print(res)

{u'transaction_values': 33.17773841, u'_id': 20}
```

Let's find the day of week that the network is more active, by number of transactions or value of transactions. Similar to the hour of day, we use the $dayOfWeek operator to extract the day of week from ISODate() objects. Days are numbered 1 for Sunday to 7 for Saturday, following the US convention.

```
    def active_day_of_week_transactions(self):
        pipeline = [
            {"$group": {"_id": {"$dayOfWeek": "$timestamp"}, "transactions":
{"$sum": 1}}},
            {"$sort": SON([("transactions", -1)])},
            {"$limit": 1},
        ]
        result = self.collection.aggregate(pipeline)
        for res in result:
            print(res)

{u'_id': 3, u'transactions': 92}


    def active_day_of_week_values(self):
        pipeline = [
            {"$group": {"_id": {"$dayOfWeek": "$timestamp"},
"transaction_values": {"$sum": "$value"}}},
            {"$sort": SON([("transactions", -1)])},
            {"$limit": 1},
        ]
```

```
result = self.collection.aggregate(pipeline)
for res in result:
    print(res)
```

```
{u'transaction_values': 547.62439312, u'_id': 2}
```

The aggregations that we calculated can be described in the figure here:

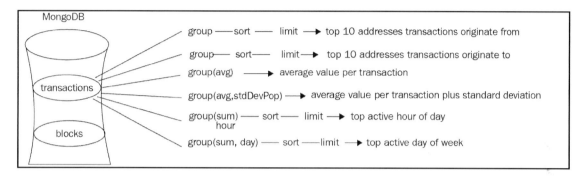

In terms of blocks, we would like to know:

- Average number of transactions per block, for both total overall transactions and also total contract internal transactions
- Average gas used per block
- Average difficulty per block and how it deviates

Average number of transactions per block, both in total and also in contract internal transactions. Averaging over the `number_transactions` field we can get the number of transactions per block as illustrated here:

```
def average_number_transactions_total_block(self):
    pipeline = [
        {"$group": {"_id": "average_transactions_per_block", "count":
{"$avg": "$number_transactions"}}},
    ]
    result = self.collection.aggregate(pipeline)
    for res in result:
        print(res)
```

```
{u'count': 39.458333333333336, u'_id': u'average_transactions_per_block'}
```

```
    def average_number_transactions_internal_block(self):
        pipeline = [
            {"$group": {"_id": "average_transactions_internal_per_block",
    "count": {"$avg": "$number_internal_transactions"}}},
        ]
        result = self.collection.aggregate(pipeline)
        for res in result:
            print(res)
```

```
{u'count': 8.0, u'_id': u'average_transactions_internal_per_block'}
```

Average gas used per block:

```
def average_gas_block(self):
    pipeline = [
        {"$group": {"_id": "average_gas_used_per_block",
                    "count": {"$avg": "$gas_used"}}},
    ]
    result = self.collection.aggregate(pipeline)
    for res in result:
        print(res)
```

```
{u'count': 2563647.9166666665, u'_id': u'average_gas_used_per_block'}
```

Average difficulty per block and how it deviates:

```
    def average_difficulty_block(self):
        pipeline = [
            {"$group": {"_id": "average_difficulty_per_block",
                        "count": {"$avg": "$difficulty"}, "stddev":
    {"$stdDevPop": "$difficulty"}}},
        ]
        result = self.collection.aggregate(pipeline)
        for res in result:
            print(res)
```

```
{u'count': 881676386932100.0, u'_id': u'average_difficulty_per_block',
u'stddev': 446694674991.6385}
```

Our aggregations are described in the following schema:

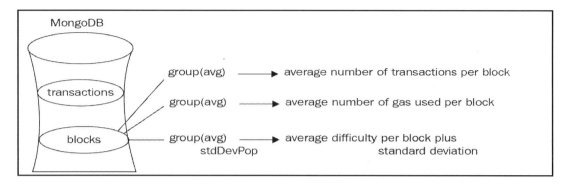

Now that we have basic statistics calculated, we want to up our game and identify more information about our transactions. Through our sophisticated machine learning algorithms, we have identified some of the transactions as either scam or **initial coin offering (ICO)** or maybe both.

In these documents, we have marked these attributes in an array called `tags` like this;

```
{
"_id" : ObjectId("59554977cedea8f696a416dd"),
"to" : "0x4b9e0d224dabcc96191cace2d367a8d8b75c9c81",
"txhash" :
"0xf205991d937bcb60955733e760356070319d95131a2d9643e3c48f2dfca39e77",
"from" : "0x3c540be890df69eca5f0099bbedd5d667bd693f3",
"block" : 3923794,
"txfee" : 28594,
"timestamp" : ISODate("2017-06-10T09:59:35Z"),
"tags" : [
"scam",
"ico"
],
"value" : 0
}
```

Now we want to get the transactions from June 2017, remove the _id field, and produce different documents according to the tags that we have identified. So, in the example of the aforementioned mentioned document, we would output two documents in our new collection `scam_ico_documents` for separate processing.

The way to do this via the aggregation framework is shown here:

```
def scam_or_ico_aggregation(self):
    pipeline = [
        {"$match": {"timestamp": {"$gte": datetime.datetime(2017,06,01),
"$lte": datetime.datetime(2017,07,01)}}},
        {"$project": {
            "to": 1,
            "txhash": 1,
            "from": 1,
            "block": 1,
            "txfee": 1,
            "tags": 1,
            "value": 1,
            "report_period": "June 2017",
            "_id": 0,
            }
        },
        {"$unwind": "$tags"},
        {"$out": "scam_ico_documents"}
    ]
    result = self.collection.aggregate(pipeline)
    for res in result:
        print(res)
```

Here we have four distinct steps in our aggregation framework pipeline:

1. Using $match, we only extract documents that have a field timestamp value of June 1st 2017.
2. Using project, we add a new `report_period` field with a value of June 2017 and remove the _id field by setting its value to 0. We keep the rest of the fields intact by using the value 1, as shown.
3. Using $unwind, we output one new document per tag in our $tags array.
4. Finally, using $out, we output all of our documents to a new `scam_ico_documents` collection.

Since we used the $out operator we will get no results in the command line. If we comment out {"$out": "scam_ico_documents"}, we get result documents that look like this:

```
{u'from': u'miningpoolhub_1', u'tags': u'scam', u'report_period': u'June
2017', u'value': 0.52415349, u'to':
u'0xdaf112bcbd38d231b1be4ae92a72a41aa2bb231d', u'txhash':
u'0xe11ea11df4190bf06cbdaf19ae88a707766b007b3d9f35270cde37ceccba9a5c',
u'txfee': 21.0, u'block': 3923785}
```

The final result in our database will look like this:

```
{
"_id" : ObjectId("5955533be9ec57bdb074074e"),
"to" : "0x4b9e0d224dabcc96191cace2d367a8d8b75c9c81",
"txhash" :
"0xf205991d937bcb60955733e760356070319d95131a2d9643e3c48f2dfca39e77",
"from" : "0x3c540be890df69eca5f0099bbedd5d667bd693f3",
"block" : 3923794,
"txfee" : 28594,
"tags" : "scam",
"value" : 0,
"report_period" : "June 2017"
}
```

Now that we have documents clearly separated in the scam_ico_documents collection, we can perform further analysis pretty easily. An example of this analysis would be to append more information on some of these scammers. Luckily, our data scientists have come up with some additional information, which we have extracted into a new collection scam_details, looking like this:

```
{
"_id" : ObjectId("5955510e14ae9238fe76d7f0"),
"scam_address" : "0x3c540be890df69eca5f0099bbedd5d667bd693f3",
Email_address": example@scammer.com"
}
```

We can now create a new aggregation pipeline job to join our scam_ico_documents with the scam_details collection and output these extended results in a new collection, scam_ico_documents_extended, like this:

```
def scam_add_information(self):
    client = MongoClient()
    db = client.mongo_book
    scam_collection = db.scam_ico_documents
    pipeline = [
        {"$lookup": {"from": "scam_details", "localField": "from",
"foreignField": "scam_address", "as": "scam_details_data"}},
```

```
            {"$match": {"scam_details_data": { "$ne": [] }}},
            {"$out": "scam_ico_documents_extended"}
        ]
    scam_collection.aggregate(pipeline)
```

Here we are using a three-step aggregation pipeline:

1. Use the `$lookup` command to join data from the `scam_details` collection and `scam_address` field with data from our local collection (`scam_ico_documents`) based on the value from the local collection attribute `from` being equal to the value in the `scam_details` collection `scam_address` field.
   If these are equal, the pipeline adds a new field to the document named `scam_details_data`.

2. Next, we only match the documents that have a `scam_details_data` field, the ones that matched with the lookup aggregation framework step.

3. Finally, we output these documents in a new collection called `scam_ico_documents_extended`.

These documents now look like this:

```
> db.scam_ico_documents_extended.findOne()
{
"_id" : ObjectId("5955533be9ec57bdb074074e"),
"to" : "0x4b9e0d224dabcc96191cace2d367a8d8b75c9c81",
"txhash" :
"0xf205991d937bcb60955733e760356070319d95131a2d9643e3c48f2dfca39e77",
"from" : "0x3c540be890df69eca5f0099bbedd5d667bd693f3",
"block" : 3923794,
"txfee" : 28594,
"tags" : "scam",
"value" : 0,
"report_period" : "June 2017",
"scam_details_data" : [
{
"_id" : ObjectId("5955510e14ae9238fe76d7f0"),
"scam_address" : "0x3c540be890df69eca5f0099bbedd5d667bd693f3",
email_address": example@scammer.com"
}]}
```

Using the aggregation framework, we have identified our data and can process it rapidly and efficiently.

The previous examples can be summed up in the following diagram:

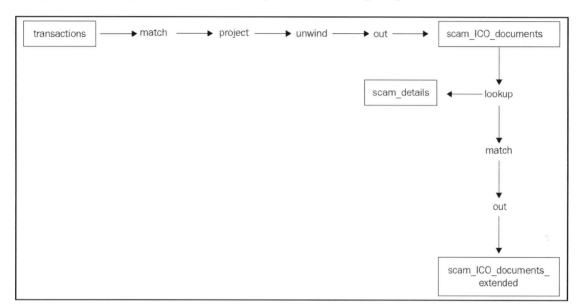

Summary

In this chapter, we dived deep into aggregation framework. We discussed why and when we should use aggregation as opposed to MapReduce and querying the database. We went through the vast array of options and functionality for aggregation.

We discussed aggregation stages and various operators such as Boolean operators, comparison operators, set operators, array operators, date operators, string operators, expression arithmetic operators, aggregation accumulators, conditional expressions and variables, and the literal and parsing data type operators

Using the Ethereum use case, we went through aggregation with working code and how to approach an engineering problem to solve it.

Finally, you learned about the limitation that the aggregation framework currently has and when to avoid it.

In the next chapter, we will switch gears to the topic of indexing and how to design and implement performant indexes for our read and write workloads.

6
Indexing

In this chapter, we will explore one of the most important properties of every database, indexing. Similar to book indexes, database indexes allow for quicker data retrieval. In the RDBMS world, indexes are widely used (and abused) to speed up data access.

In MongoDB, indexes play an integral part in schema and query design. MongoDB supports a wide array of indexes that we will learn about in this chapter:

- Single field
- Compound
- Multikey
- Geospatial
- Text
- Hashed
- Time to live
- Unique
- Partial
- Sparse
- Case-insensitive

In addition to learning about different types of index, we will show how to build and manage indexes for single-server deployments as well as complex sharded environments.

Finally, we will dive deeper into how MongoDB creates and organizes indexes with the goal of learning how to write more efficient indexes and evaluating the performance of our existing indexes.

Index internals

Indexes, in most cases, are essentially variations of the B-tree data structure. Invented by Rudolf Bayer and Ed McCreight in 1971 while working at Boeing research labs, the B-tree data structure allows for search, sequential access, inserts, and deletes to be performed in logarithmic time. The logarithmic time property stands for both the average case and the worst possible performance, which is a great property when applications cannot tolerate unexpected variations in performance behavior.

To further understand how important the **logarithmic time** part is, we have included a diagram as follows:

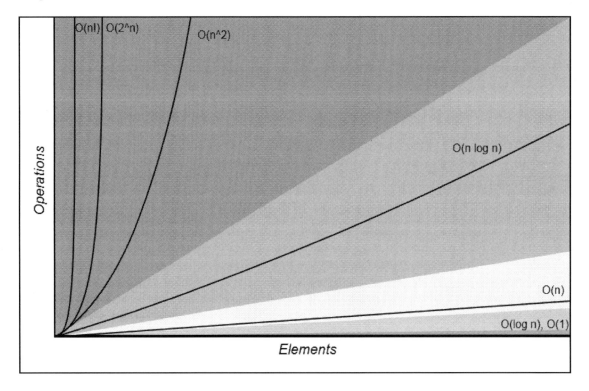

Source: http://bigocheatsheet.com/

In this diagram, we see logarithmic time performance as a flat line parallel to the *x* axis of the diagram. As the number of elements increases, constant time **O(n)** algorithms perform worse, whereas quadratic time algorithms **O(n^2)** go off the chart. For an algorithm that we rely on to get our data back to us as fast as possible, time performance is of the utmost importance.

Another interesting property of a B-tree is that it is self-balancing, meaning that it will self-adjust to always maintain these properties. Its precursor and closest relative is the binary search tree, a data structure that allows only two children for each parent node.

Schematically, a B-tree looks like this:

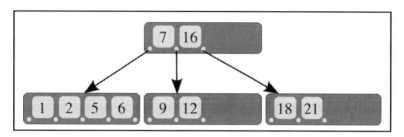

In the preceding diagram, we have a parent node with values **7,16** pointing to three child nodes.

If we want to search for the value **9**, knowing that it's greater than **7** and smaller than **16**, we'll be directed to the middle child node that contains the value straightaway.

Thanks to this structure, we are approximately halving our search space with every step, thus ending in a *log n* time complexity. Compared to sequentially scanning through every element, halving the number of elements with each and every step increases our gains exponentially as the number of elements we have to search through increases.

Index types

MongoDB offers a vast array of index types for different needs. In the following sections, we will identify the different types and the needs that each one of them fulfills.

Single field indexes

The most common and simple types of index are single-field indexes. An example of a single field/key index is the index on ObjectId (_id), which is generated by default in every MongoDB collection. The ObjectId index is also unique, preventing a second document from having the same ObjectId in a collection.

An index on a single field based on the `mongo_book` database that we used throughout the previous chapters is defined like this:

```
> db.books.createIndex( { price: 1 } )
```

Here we create an index on the field name, in ascending order of index creation. For descending order, the same index would be created like this:

```
> db.books.createIndex( { price: −1 } )
```

Ordering for index creation can be important if we expect our queries to be favoring values on the first documents stored in our index. However, due to the extremely efficient time complexity that indexes have, this will not be a consideration for most common use cases.

An index can be used for exact match queries or range queries on the field value. In the former case, the search can stop as soon as our pointer reaches the value after *O(logn)* time.

In range queries, due to the fact that we are storing values in order in our B-tree index, once we find the border value of our range query in a node of our B-tree, we know that all values in its children will be part of our result set, allowing us to conclude our search.

An example of this can be shown as follows:

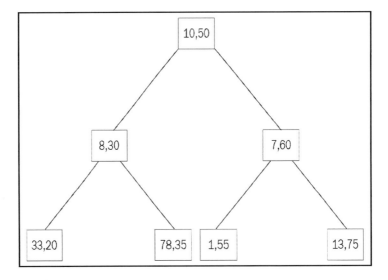

Indexing embedded fields

MongoDB as a document database supports embedding fields and whole documents in nested complex hierarchies inside the same document. Naturally, it also allows us to index these fields.

In our books collection example, we can have documents such as the following:

```
{
"_id" : ObjectId("5969ccb614ae9238fe76d7f1"),
"name" : "MongoDB Indexing Cookbook",
"isbn" : "1001",
"available" : 999,
"meta_data" : {
"page_count" : 256,
"average_customer_review" : 4.8
}
}
```

Here, the meta_data field is a document itself, with page_count and average_customer_review fields.

Again, we can create an index on page_count as follows:

```
db.books.createIndex( { "meta_data.page_count": 1 } )
```

This can answer queries on equality and range comparison around the meta_data.page_count field.

```
> db.books.find({"meta_data.page_count": { $gte: 200 } })
> db.books.find({"meta_data.page_count": 256 })
```

> To access embedded fields we use dot notation and need to include quotes ("") around the field's name

Indexing embedded documents

We can also index the embedded document as a whole in a similar way to indexing embedded fields:

```
> db.books.createIndex( { "meta_data": 1 } )
```

Here, we are indexing the whole document, expecting queries against its entirety like the following one:

```
> db.books.find({"meta_data": {"page_count":256,
"average_customer_review":4.8}})
```

The key difference is that when we index embedded fields we can perform range queries on them using the index, whereas when we index embedded documents we can only perform comparison queries using the index.

db.books.find({"meta_data.average_customer_review": { $gte: 4.8}, "meta_data.page_count": { $gte: 200 } }) will not use our meta_data index, whereas db.books.find({"meta_data": {"page_count":256, "average_customer_review":4.8}}) will use it.

Background indexes

Indexes can be created in the foreground, blocking all operations in the collection until they are built, or the background, allowing for concurrent operations. Building an index in the background is done by passing in the background: true parameter:

```
> db.books.createIndex( { price: 1 }, { background: true } )
```

Background indexes have some limitations that we will revisit in the last section of this chapter, *Building and managing indexes*.

Compound indexes

Compound indexes are a generalization of single-key indexes, allowing for multiple fields to be included in the same index. They are useful when we expect our queries to span multiple fields in our documents and also for consolidating our indexes when we start having too many of them in our collection.

Compound indexes can have as many as 31 fields. They cannot have a hashed index type.

A compound index is declared in a similar way to single indexes, by defining the fields we want to index and the order of indexing:

```
> db.books.createIndex({"name": 1, "isbn": 1})
```

Sorting using compound indexes

Order of indexing is useful for sorting results. In single field indexes, MongoDB can traverse the index both ways so it doesn't matter which order we define.

In multi-field indexes, though, ordering can determine whether we can use this index to sort or not. In our preceding example, a query matching the sorting direction of our index creation will use our index:

```
> db.books.find().sort( { "name": 1, "isbn": 1 } )
```

It will also use a `sort` query with all of the sort fields reversed:

```
> db.books.find().sort( { "name": -1, "isbn": -1 } )
```

In this query, since we negated both of the fields, MongoDB can use the same index, traversing it from the end to the start.

The other two sorting orders are as follows:

```
> db.books.find().sort( { "name": -1, "isbn": 1 } )
> db.books.find().sort( { "name": 1, "isbn": -1 } )
```

They cannot be traversed using the index as the sort order that we want is not present in our index's B-tree data structure.

Reusing compound indexes

An important attribute of compound indexes is that they can be used for multiple queries on prefixes of the fields indexed. This is useful when we want to consolidate indexes that over time pile up in our collections.

See the compound (multi-field) index we created previously:

```
> db.books.createIndex({"name": 1, "isbn": 1})
```

This can be used for queries on **name** or {name, isbn}:

```
> db.books.find({"name":"MongoDB Indexing"})
> db.books.find({"isbn": "1001", "name":"MongoDB Indexing"})
```

The order of fields in our query doesn't matter, MongoDB will rearrange fields to match our query.

However, the order of fields in our index does matter. A query just for the isbn field cannot use our index:

```
> db.books.find({"isbn": "1001"})
```

The underlying reason is that our field's values are stored in the index as secondary, tertiary, and so on indexes; each one is embedded inside the previous ones, just like a matryoshka, the Russian nesting doll. This means that, when we query on the first field of our multi-field index, we can use the outermost doll to find our pattern, whereas searching for the first two fields, we can match the pattern on the outermost doll and then dive into the inner one.

This concept is called **prefix indexing** and together with index intersection is the most powerful tool for index consolidation as we will see later in this chapter.

Multikey indexes

Indexing scalar (single) values is explained in the preceding sections. However, one of the advantages we get from using MongoDB is the ability to easily store vector values in the form of arrays.

In the relational world, storing arrays is generally frowned upon as it violates the normal forms. In a document-oriented database such as MongoDB, it is frequently part of our design as we can store and query easily on complex structs of data.

Indexing arrays of documents is achieved by using the multikey index. A multikey index can store both arrays of scalar values as well as arrays of nested documents.

Creating a multikey index is the same as creating a regular index:

```
> db.books.createIndex({"tags":1})
```

Our new index will be a multikey index, allowing us to find documents by any of the tags stored in our array:

```
> db.books.find({tags:"new"})
{
"_id" : ObjectId("5969f4bc14ae9238fe76d7f2"),
"name" : "MongoDB Multikeys Cheatsheet",
"isbn" : "1002",
"available" : 1,
"meta_data" : {
"page_count" : 128,
"average_customer_review" : 3.9
},
"tags" : [
"mongodb",
"index",
"cheatsheet",
"new"
]
}
```

We can also create compound indexes with a multikey index but we can have, at the most, one array in each and every index document. Given that in MongoDB we don't specify the type of each field, this means that creating an index with two or more fields having an array value will fail at creation time and trying to insert a document with two or more fields as arrays will fail at insertion time.

For example, a compound index on `tags, analytics_data` will fail to be created if we have the following document in our database:

```
{
"_id" : ObjectId("5969f71314ae9238fe76d7f3"),
"name": "Mastering parallel arrays indexing",
"tags" : [
"A",
"B"
],
"analytics_data" : [
"1001",
"1002"
]
}

> db.books.createIndex({tags:1, analytics_data:1})
{
"ok" : 0,
"errmsg" : "cannot index parallel arrays [analytics_data] [tags]",
```

```
    "code" : 171,
    "codeName" : "CannotIndexParallelArrays"
}
```

Consequently, if we create the index first on an empty collection and try to insert this document, the insert will fail with the following error:

```
> db.books.find({isbn:
"1001"}).hint("international_standard_book_number_index")
.explain()
{
        "queryPlanner" : {
                "plannerVersion" : 1,
                "namespace" : "mongo_book.books",
                "indexFilterSet" : false,
                "parsedQuery" : {
                        "isbn" : {
                                "$eq" : "1001"
                        }
                },
                "winningPlan" : {
                        "stage" : "FETCH",
                        "inputStage" : {
                                "stage" : "IXSCAN",
                                "keyPattern" : {
                                        "isbn" : 1
                                },
                                "indexName" :
"international_standard_book_numbe
r_index",
                                "isMultiKey" : false,
                                "multiKeyPaths" : {
                                        "isbn" : [ ]
                                },
                                "isUnique" : false,
                                "isSparse" : false,
                                "isPartial" : false,
                                "indexVersion" : 2,
                                "direction" : "forward",
                                "indexBounds" : {
                                        "isbn" : [
                                                "[\"1001\", \"1001\"]"
                                        ]
                                }
                        }
                },
                "rejectedPlans" : [ ]
        },
```

```
"serverInfo" : {
        "host" : "PPMUMCPU0142",
        "port" : 27017,
        "version" : "3.4.7",
        "gitVersion" : "cf38c1b8a0a8dca4a11737581beafef4fe120bcd"
},
"ok" : 1
```

Hashed indexes cannot be multikey indexes.

Another limitation we will likely run into when trying to fine-tune our database is that multikey indexes cannot entirely cover a query. Covering a query with the index means that we can get our result data entirely from the index without accessing the data in our database at all. This can result in dramatically increased performance as indexes are most likely to be stored in RAM.

Querying for multiple values in multikey indexes will result in a two-step process from the index's perspective.

In the first step, `index` will be used to retrieve the first value of the array and then a sequential scan will run through the rest of the elements in the array. For example:

```
> db.books.find({tags: [ "mongodb", "index", "cheatsheet", "new" ] })
```

This will first search for all entries in multikey index tags that have a `mongodb` value and then sequentially scan through them to find the ones that also have the `index`, `cheatsheet`, and `new` tags.

A multikey index cannot be used as a shard key. However, if the shard key is a prefix index of a multikey index, it can be used. More on this in `Chapter 11`, *Sharding*.

Special types of index

Apart from the generic indexes, MongoDB supports indexes for special use cases. In this section, we will identify and explore how to use them.

Text

Text indexes are special indexes on string value fields to support text searches. This book is based on version 3 of the text index functionality, available since version 3.2.

A text index can be specified similarly to a regular index, replacing the index sort order (–1, 1) with the word `text` shown as follows:

```
> db.books.createIndex({"name": "text"})
```

 Any collection can have at most one text index. This text index can support multiple fields, text or not. It cannot support other special types such as multikey or geospatial. Text indexes cannot be used for sorting results, even if they are only part of a compound index.

Since we only have one text index per collection, we need to choose the fields wisely. Reconstructing this text index can take quite some time and having only one of them per collection makes maintenance quite tricky, as we will see towards the end of this chapter.

Luckily, this index can also be a compound index:

```
> db.books.createIndex( { "available": 1, "meta_data.page_count": 1,
"$**": "text" } )
```

A compound index with text fields follows the same rules regarding sorting and prefix indexing as we explained earlier in this chapter. We can use this index to query on `available` or `available, meta_data.page_count` or sort if the sort order allows for traversing our index in any direction.

We can also blindly index as text each and every field in a document that contains strings:

```
> db.books.createIndex( { "$**": "text" } )
```

This can result in unbounded index size and should be avoided but it can be useful if we have unstructured data, coming for example straight from application logs where we don't know which fields may be useful or not and we want to be able to query as many of them as possible.

Text indexes will apply stemming (removing common suffixes such as plural s / es for English language words) and remove stop words (a, an, the, and so on) from the index.

Text indexing supports more than 20 languages, including Spanish, Chinese, Urdu, Persian, and Arabic. Text indexes require special configuration to index correctly in languages other than English.

- **Case insensitivity and diacritic insensitivity**: A text index is case- and diacritic-insensitive. Version 3 of the text index (the one that comes with version 3.4) supports common C, simple S, and the special T case foldings as described in Unicode Character Database 8.0 case folding. In addition to case insensitivity, version 3 of the text index supports diacritic insensitivity. This expands insensitivity to characters with accents both in small- and capital-letter form. For example e, è, é, ê, ë and their capital letter counterparts can all be the same in comparison when using a text index. In previous versions of the text index these were treated as different strings.

- **Tokenization delimiters:** Version 3 of the text index supports the tokenization delimiters defined as Dash, Hyphen, Pattern_Syntax, Quotation_Mark, Terminal_Punctuation, and White_Space as described in Unicode Character Database 8.0 case folding.

Hashed

A hash index contains hashed values of the indexed field:

```
> db.books.createIndex( { name: "hashed" } )
```

This will create a hashed index on the name of each book of our books collection.

A hashed index is ideal for equality matches but cannot work with range queries. If we want to perform range queries on fields, we can create a regular index (or a compound index containing the field) and also a hash index for equality matches. Hashed indexes are used internally by MongoDB for hashed-based sharding as we will discuss in Chapter 11, *Sharding*. Hashed indexes truncate floating point fields to integers. Floating points should be avoided for hashed fields wherever possible.

TTL

Time to live indexes are used to automatically delete documents after an expiration time. Their syntax is as follows:

```
> db.books.createIndex( { "created_at_date": 1 }, { expireAfterSeconds:
86400 } )
```

The `created_at_date` field values have to be either a date or an array of dates (the earliest one will be used). In this example, documents will get deleted one day (86,400 seconds) after the `created_at_date`.

If the field does not exist or the value is not a date, the document will not expire. In other words, a TTL index silently fails, not returning any error when it does.

Data gets removed by a background job running every 60 seconds. As a result, there is no explicit accuracy guarantee as to how much longer documents will persist past their expiration date.

A TTL index is a regular single field index. It can be used for queries like a regular index. A TTL index cannot be a compound index, operate on a capped collection, or use the `_id` field.

The `_id` field implicitly contains a timestamp of the created time for the document but is not a `Date` field.

If we want each document to expire at a different, custom date point we have to set `{expireAfterSeconds: 0}` and set the TTL index date field manually to the date on which we want the document to expire.

Partial

A partial index on a collection is an index that applies only to the documents that satisfy the `partialFilterExpression` query.

We'll use our familiar `books` collection:

```
> db.books.createIndex(
  { price: 1, name: 1 },
  { partialFilterExpression: { price: { $gt: 30 } } }
)
```

Using this, we can have an index just for the books that have a price greater than 30. The advantage of partial indexes is that they are more lightweight in creation and maintenance and use less storage.

The `partialFilterExpression` filter, supports the following operators:

- Equality expressions (that is, `field: value` or using the `$eq` operator)
- The `$exists: true` expression
- The `$gt`, `$gte`, `$lt`, and `$lte` expressions
- `$type` expressions
- The `$and` operator at the top-level only

Partial indexes will only be used if the query can be satisfied as a whole by the partial index.

If our query matches, or is more restrictive than, the `partialFilterExpression` filter then the partial index will be used. If the results may not be contained in the partial index then the index will be totally ignored.

The `partialFilterExpression` does not need to be part of the sparse index fields. The following index is a valid sparse index:
```
> db.books.createIndex({ name: 1 }, {
partialFilterExpression: { price: { $gt: 30 } } })
```

To use this partial index, however, we need to query for both name and price greater than 30 or more.

Prefer partial to sparse indexes. Sparse indexes offer a subset of the functionality offered by partial indexes. Partial indexes were introduced in MongoDB 3.2 so if you have sparse indexes from earlier versions it may be a good idea to upgrade them. The `_id` field cannot be part of a partial index. A shard key index cannot be a partial index. `partialFilterExpression` cannot be combined with the sparse option.

Sparse

A sparse index is similar to the partial index, preceding it by several years (it has been available since version 1.8).

A sparse index only indexes values that contain the following field:

```
> db.books.createIndex( { "price": 1 }, { sparse: true } )
```

It will create an index with only the documents that contain a `price` field.

Some indexes are always sparse due to their nature:

- 2d, 2dsphere (version 2)
- geoHaystack
- text

A sparse and unique index will allow multiple documents missing the index key. It will not allow documents with the same index field value. A sparse and compound index with geospatial indexes (2d, 2dsphere, geoHaystack) will index the document as long as it has the `geospatial` field.

A sparse and compound index with the `text` field will index the document as long as it has the `text` field. A sparse and compound index without any of the two preceding cases will index the document as long as it has at least one of the fields.

Avoid creating new sparse indexes in the latest versions of MongoDB; use partial indexes instead.

Unique

A unique index is similar to an RDBMS unique index, forbidding duplicate values for the indexed field. MongoDB creates a unique index by default on the `_id` field for every inserted document:

```
> db.books.createIndex( { "name": 1 }, { unique: true } )
```

This will create a unique index on a book's name.

A unique index can also be a compound embedded field or embedded document index.

In a compound index, the uniqueness is enforced across the combination of values in all fields of the index; for example, the following will not violate the unique index:

```
> db.books.createIndex( { "name": 1, "isbn": 1 }, { unique: true } )
> db.books.insert({"name": "Mastering MongoDB", "isbn": "101"})
> db.books.insert({"name": "Mastering MongoDB", "isbn": "102"})
```

This is because, even though the name is the same, our index is looking for the unique combination of {name, isbn} and the two entries differ on isbn.

Unique does not work with hashed indexes. Unique indexes cannot be created if the collection already contains duplicate values of the indexed field. A unique index will not prevent the same document from having multiple values.

If a document is missing the indexed field it will be inserted. If a second document is missing the indexed field, it will not be inserted. This is because MongoDB will store the missing field value as null, thus only allowing one document to be missing the field.

Indexes that are a combination of unique and partial will only apply unique after partial has been applied. This means that there may be several documents with duplicate values if they are not part of partial filtering.

Case-insensitive

Case sensitivity is a common use case for indexes. Up until version 3.4, this was dealt with at the application level by creating duplicate fields with all lowercase characters and indexing this field to simulate a case-insensitive index.

Using the collation parameter, we can create case-insensitive indexes and even collections that behave as case-insensitive.

Collation in general allows users to specify language-specific rules for string comparison. A possible (but not the only) usage is for case-insensitive indexes and queries.

Using our familiar books collection, we can create a case-insensitive index on a name like this:

```
> db.books.createIndex( { "name" : 1 },
                         { collation: {
                             locale : 'en',
                             strength : 1
                         }
                       } )
```

strength is one of the collation parameters, the defining parameter for case sensitivity comparisons. Strength levels follow the **International Components for Unicode (ICU)** comparison levels. The values it accepts are as follows:

Strength value	Description
1a	Primary level of comparison. Comparison based on string value, ignoring any other differences such as case and diacritics.
2	Secondary level of comparison. Comparison based on primary level and if this is equal then compare diacritics (that is, accents).
3 (default)	Tertiary level of comparison. Same as level 2, adding case and variants.
4	Quaternary level. Limited for specific use cases to consider punctuation when levels 1-3 ignore punctuation or for processing Japanese text.
5	Identical level. Limited for specific use case: a tie breaker.

Creating the index with collation is not enough to get back case-insensitive results. We need to specify collation in our query as well:

```
> db.books.find( { name: "Mastering MongoDB" } ).collation( { locale: 'en',
strength: 1 } )
```

If we specify the same level of collation in our query as our index, then the index will be used.

We could specify a different level of collation as follows:

```
> db.books.find( { name: "Mastering MongoDB" } ).collation( { locale: 'en',
strength: 2 } )
```

Here, we cannot use the index as our index has collation level *1* and our query looks for collation level *2*.

If we don't use any collation in our queries, we will get results defaulting to level *3*, that is, case-sensitive.

Indexes in collections that were created using a different collation from the default will automatically inherit this collation level.

If we create a collection with collation level *1* as follows:

```
> db.createCollection("case_sensitive_books", { collation: { locale:
'en_US', strength: 1 } } )
```

Then, the following index will also have collation `strength: 1`:

```
> db.case_sensitive_books.createIndex( { name: 1 } )
```

And default queries to this collection will be collation `strength: 1`, case-sensitive. If we want to override this in our queries we need to specify a different level of collation in our queries or ignore the strength part altogether. The following two queries will return case-insensitive, default collation level results in our `case_sensitive_books` collection:

```
> db.case_sensitive_books.find( { name: "Mastering MongoDB" } ).collation(
{ locale: 'en', strength: 3 } ) // default collation strength value
> db.case_sensitive_books.find( { name: "Mastering MongoDB" } ).collation(
{ locale: 'en'  } ) // no value for collation, will reset to global default
(3) instead of default for case_sensitive_books collection (1)
```

Collation is a pretty strong and relatively new concept in MongoDB and so we will keep exploring it throughout different chapters.

Geospatial

Geospatial indexes were introduced early on in MongoDB and the fact that FourSquare is one of the earliest customers and success stories for MongoDB (then 10gen Inc) is probably no coincidence.

There are three distinct types of geospatial index that we will explore in this chapter.

2d

A `2d` geospatial index stores geospatial data as points on a two-dimensional plane. It is mostly kept for legacy reasons for coordinate pairs created before MongoDB 2.2 and in most cases should not be used with the latest versions.

2dSphere

A `2dSphere` geospatial index supports queries calculating geometries in an earth-like plane. It is more accurate than the simplistic `2d` index and can support both GeoJSON objects and coordinate pairs as input.

Its current version since MongoDB 3.2 is version 3. It is a sparse index by default, only indexing documents that have a 2dSphere field value.

Assuming that we have a location field in our books collection, tracking the home address of the main author of each book, we could create an index on this field like this:

```
> db.books.createIndex( { "location" : "2dsphere" } )
```

The location field needs to be a GeoJSON object, for example like this one:

```
location : { type: "Point", coordinates: [ 51.5876, 0.1643 ] }
```

A 2dSphere index can also be part of a compound index, as the first field or not.

```
> db.books.createIndex( { name: 1, location : "2dsphere" } )
```

geoHaystack

geoHaystack indexes are useful when we need to search geographical-based results in a small area. Like searching for a needle in a haystack, with a geoHaystack index we can define buckets of geolocation points and get back all the results that belong in this area.

Creating a geoHaystack index:

```
> db.books.createIndex( { "location" : "geoHaystack" ,
                  "name": 1 } ,
              { bucketSize: 2 } )
```

This will create buckets of documents within 2 units of latitude or longitude from each document.

Here, with the preceding example location:

```
location : { type: "Point", coordinates: [ 51.5876, 0.1643 ] }
```

Based on the bucketSize: 2, every document with location [49.5876..53.5876, -2.1643..2.1643] will belong in the same bucket as our location.

A document can appear in multiple buckets. If we want to use spherical geometry, 2dSphere is a better solution. geoHaystack indexes are sparse by default.

If we need to calculate the nearest document to our location and this is outside our bucketSize (that is, greater than 2 units of latitude/longitude in our example), queries will be inefficient and possible inaccurate. Use a 2dSphere index for such queries.

Building and managing indexes

Indexes can be built using the MongoDB shell or any of the available drivers. By default, indexes are built in the foreground, blocking all other operations in the database. This is faster but often undesirable, especially in production instances.

We can also build indexes in the background by adding the `{background: true}` parameter in our index commands in the shell. Background indexes will only block the current connection/thread. We can open a new connection (that is, using `mongo` in the command line) to connect to the same database:

```
> db.books.createIndex( { name: 1 }, { background: true } )
```

Background index building can take significantly more time than foreground, especially if the indexes can't fit in available RAM.

Index early, revisit indexes regularly for consolidation. Queries won't see partial index results. Queries will start getting results from an index only after it is completely created.

Do not use main application code to create indexes as it can impose unpredicted delays. Instead, get a list of indexes from the application and mark these for creation during maintenance windows.

Forcing index usage

We can force MongoDB to use an index by applying the `hint()` parameter:

```
> db.books.createIndex( { isbn: 1 }, { background: true } )
{
"createdCollectionAutomatically" : false,
"numIndexesBefore" : 8,
"numIndexesAfter" : 9,
"ok" : 1
}
```

The output from `createIndex` notifies us that the index was created (`"ok" : 1`), no collection was created automatically as part of index creation (`"createdCollectionAutomatically" : false`), the number of indexes before this index creation was 8, and now there are 9 indexes in total for this collection.

If we now try to search a book by `isbn`, we can use the `explain()` command to see the `winningPlan` subdocument where we can find which query plan was used:

```
> db.books.find({isbn: "1001"}).explain()
...
"winningPlan" : {
"stage" : "FETCH",
"inputStage" : {
"stage" : "IXSCAN",
"keyPattern" : {
"isbn" : 1,
"name" : 1
},
"indexName" : "isbn_1_name_1",
...
```

This means that an index with `isbn:1` and `name:1` was used instead of our newly-created index. We can also view our index in the `rejectedPlans` subdocument of the output:

```
...
"rejectedPlans" : [
{
"stage" : "FETCH",
"inputStage" : {
"stage" : "IXSCAN",
"keyPattern" : {
"isbn" : 1
},
"indexName" : "isbn_1",
...
```

This is in fact right as MongoDB is trying to reuse an index that is more specific than a more generic one.

We may have stumbled though in cases where our `isbn_1` index is performing better than the `isbn_1_name_1` one.

We can force MongoDB to use our newly created index as follows:

```
> db.books.find({isbn:
"1001"}).hint("international_standard_book_number_index")
.explain()
{
...
                "winningPlan" : {
                        "stage" : "FETCH",
                        "inputStage" : {
```

```
                    "stage" : "IXSCAN",
                    "keyPattern" : {
                            "isbn" : 1
                    },
...
```

Now the `winningPlan` subdocument contains our index, `isbn_1`, and there are no `rejectedPlans` elements: it's an empty array in the result set.

We cannot use `hint()` with the special type of text indexes.

Hint and sparse indexes

Sparse indexes by design do not include some documents in the index based on the presence/absence of a field. Queries that may include documents that are not present in the index will not use a sparse index.

Using `hint()` with a sparse index may result in wrong counts since it is forcing MongoDB to use an index that may not include all results that we want.

Older versions of `2dsphere`, `2d`, `geoHaystack`, and text indexes are sparse by default. `hint()` should be used with caution and after careful consideration of its implications.

Building indexes on replica sets

In replica sets, if we issue a `createIndex()` command, secondaries will begin creating the index after the primary is finished creating it. Similarly, in sharded environments, primaries will start building indexes and secondaries will start after the primary for each shard is finished.

A recommended approach to building indexes in replica sets is:

- Stop one secondary from the replica set
- Restart it as a standalone server in a different port
- Build the index from the shell as a standalone index
- Restart the secondary in the replica set
- Allow the secondary to catch up with the primary

We need to have a large enough oplog in the primary to make sure that the secondary will be able to catch up once it's reconnected. This is a manual process, involving several steps for each primary/secondary server.

This approach can be repeated for each secondary server in the replica set. Then for the primary server we can do either of these things:

1. Build the index in the background.
2. Step down the primary using `rs.stepDown()` and repeat the preceding process with the server as a secondary now.

Using approach number 2, when the primary steps down there will be a brief period when our cluster won't be taking any writes. Our application shouldn't timeout during this (usually less than) 30-60 second period.

Building an index in the background in the primary will build it in the background for the secondaries too. This may impact writes in our servers during index creation but on the plus side has exactly zero manual steps. It is always a good idea to have a staging environment that mirrors production and dry run operations that affect the live cluster in staging to avoid surprises.

Managing indexes

In this section, we will learn how we can give human-friendly names to our indexes and special considerations and limitations that we have to keep in mind for indexing.

Naming indexes

By default, index names are assigned automatically by MongoDB based on the fields indexed and the direction of the index (1,-1). If we want to assign our own name, we can do so at creation time:

```
> db.books.createIndex( { isbn: 1 }, { name:
"international_standard_book_number_index" } )
```

Now we have a new index called `international_standard_book_number_index` instead of how MongoDB would have named it (`"isbn_1"`).

> We can view all indexes in our `books` collection by using `db.books.getIndexes()`. A fully qualified index name has to be <=128 characters. That also includes `database_name`, `collection_name`, and the dots separating them.

Special considerations

The following are a few limitations to keep in mind around indexing:

- Index entries have to be <1024 bytes. This is mostly an internal consideration but we can keep it in mind if we run into issues with indexing.
- A collection can have up to 64 indexes.
- A compound index can have up to 31 fields.
- Special indexes cannot be combined in queries. This includes special query operators that have to use special indexes such as `$text` for text indexes and `$near` for geospatial indexes. This is because MongoDB can use multiple indexes to fulfill a query but not in all cases. More about this issue in the *Index intersection* section.
- Multikey and geospatial indexes cannot cover a query. This means that index data alone will not be enough to fulfill the query and the underlying documents will need to be processed by MongoDB to get back the complete set of results.
- Indexes have a unique constraint on fields. We cannot create multiple indexes on the same fields, differing only in options. This is a limitation for sparse and partial indexes, as we cannot create multiple variations of these indexes differing only in the filtering query.

Using indexes efficiently

Creating indexes is a decision that should not be taken lightly. As easy as it is to create indexes via the shell, it can create problems down the line if we end up with too many or inadequately efficient indexes. In this section, we will learn how to measure the performance of existing indexes, some tips for improving performance, and how we can consolidate the number of indexes so that we can have better performing indexes.

Measuring performance

To optimize, one must understand first. The first step towards understanding the performance of our indexes is to learn how to use the `explain()` command. The `explain()` command when used in conjunction with a query will return the query plan that MongoDB would use for this query instead of the actual results.

It is invoked by chaining it at the end of our query as follows:

```
> db.books.find().explain()
```

It can take three options: `queryPlanner` (the default), `executionStats`, and `allPlansExecution`.

Let's use the most verbose output, `allPlansExecution`:

```
> db.books.find().explain("allPlansExecution")
```

Here, we can get information for both the winning query plan and also some partial information about query plans that were considered during the planning phase but rejected because the query planner considered them slower. The `explain()` command returns a rather verbose output anyway, allowing for deep insights into how the query plan works to return our results.

At a first glance, we need to focus on whether the indexes that we think should be used are being used, and if the number of scanned documents matches as far as possible the number of returned documents.

For the first one, we can inspect the `stage` field and look for `IXSCAN`, which means that an index was used. Then in the sibling `indexName` field we should see the name of our expected index.

For the second one, we need to compare `keysExamined` with `nReturned` fields. We ideally want our indexes to be as selective as possible with regard to our queries, meaning that to return 100 documents, these would be the 100 documents that our index examines.

Of course, this is a tradeoff as indexes increase in number and size in our collection. We can have a limited number of indexes per collection and we definitely have a limited amount of RAM to fit these indexes so we must balance the tradeoff between having the best available indexes and these indexes not fitting into our memory and getting slowed down.

Improving performance

Once we get comfortable with measuring the performance of our most common and important queries for our users, we can start trying to improve them.

The general idea is that we need indexes when we expect or already have repeatable queries that are starting to run slow. Indexes do not come for free, as they impose a performance penalty in creation and maintenance but they are more than worth it for frequent queries and can reduce the lock % in our database if designed correctly.

Recapping on our suggestions from previous section we want our indexes to:

- Fit in RAM
- Ensure selectivity
- Be used to sort our query results
- Be used in our most common and important queries

Fitting in RAM can be ensured by using getIndexes() in our collections and making sure we are not creating large indexes. Also, by inspecting the system level available RAM and if swap is being used.

Selectivity as mentioned previously is ensured by comparing nReturned with keysExamined in each IXSCAN phase of our queries. We want these two numbers to be as close as possible.

Ensuring that our indexes are used to sort our query results is a combination of using compound indexes (which will be used as a whole and also for any prefix-based query) and also declaring the direction of our indexes to be in accordance with our most common queries.

Finally, aligning indexes with our query needs is a matter of application usage patterns which can uncover which queries are used most of the time and then using explain() on these queries to identify the query plan that is being used each time.

Index intersection

Index intersection refers to the concept of using more than one index to fulfill a query. This was added fairly recently and is not perfect yet; however we can exploit it to consolidate our indexes.

> We can verify if index intersection happened in a query by using explain() on the query and witnessing an AND_SORTED or AND_HASH stage in the executed query plan.

Index intersection can happen when we use OR ($or) queries by using a different index for each OR clause. Index intersection can happen when we use AND queries and we have either complete indexes for each AND clause or index prefixes for some or all of the clauses.

For example, with a query on our books collection as follows:

```
> db.books.find({ "isbn":"101", "price": { $gt: 20 }})
```

Here, with two indexes, one on isbn and the other on price, MongoDB can use each index to get the related results and then intersect on the index results to get the result set.

With compound indexes, as we have learned previously in this chapter, we can use index prefixing to support queries that contain the first *1...n-1* fields of an *n*-field compound index.

What we cannot support with compound indexes is queries that are looking for fields in the compound index, missing one or more of the previously defined fields.

 Order matters in compound indexes.

To satisfy these queries we can create indexes on the individual fields, which will then use index intersection and fulfill our needs. The downside to this approach is that, as the number *n* of fields increases, the number of indexes we have to create grows exponentially, thus increasing our need for storage and memory.

Index intersection will not work with sort(). We can't use one index for querying and a different index for applying sort() to our results.

However, if we have an index that can fulfill both, a part or the whole of our query AND the sort() field, then this index will be used.

References

- http://bigocheatsheet.com/
- https://commons.wikimedia.org/
- https://docs.mongodb.com/manual/core/index-intersection/

Summary

In this chapter, we learned about indexing. Starting from the underlying pinnings of an index and index internals, we explored different index types available in MongoDB and how we can use them. These are single-field, compound, multikey, as well as some special types such as text, hashed, TTL, partial, parse, unique, case-insensitive, and geospatial.

In the next part of the chapter, we learned about how to build and manage indexes using the shell, a basic part of administration and database management, even for NoSQL databases. Finally, we discussed how to improve our indexes, both at a high level, and also how we can use index intersection in practice to consolidate the number of our indexes.

In the next chapter, we will discuss how we can monitor our MongoDB cluster and keep consistent backups. We will also learn about how we can handle security in MongoDB.

7
Monitoring, Backup, and Security

In this chapter, we will discuss operational aspects of MongoDB. Monitoring, backup, and security should not be an afterthought but rather a necessary process before deploying MongoDB in a production environment. In addition, monitoring can and should be used to troubleshoot and improve performance at the development stage.

Having a backup strategy that produces correct and consistent backups as well as making sure that our backup strategy will work in the unfortunate case that it is needed will be covered in this chapter. Finally, we will discuss security for MongoDB from many different aspects such as authentication, authorization, network level security, and how to audit our security design.

Monitoring

When designing a software system, we undertake many explicit and implicit assumptions. We always try to make the best decisions based on our knowledge but there may be some parameters that we didn't take into account or just underestimated.

Using monitoring, we can validate our assumptions, verify that our application performs as intended, and scales as expected. Good monitoring systems are also vital for detecting software bugs and help us detect early potential security incidents.

What should we monitor?

By far the most important metric to monitor in MongoDB is memory usage. MongoDB (and every database system for what it's worth) uses system memory extensively to increase performance. No matter if we use MMAPv1 or WiredTiger storage, used memory is the first thing we should keep our eyes on.

Understanding how computer memory works can help us evaluate metrics from our monitoring system. These are the most important concepts related to computer memory.

Page faults

RAM is expensive and fast. Hard disk drives or solid state drives are relatively cheaper and slower and also provide durability of our data in the case of system and power failure. All our data is stored on disk and when we perform a query, MongoDB will try and fetch data from memory. If data is not in memory then it will fetch data from disk and copy it to memory. This is a page fault event, because of the fact that data in memory is organized in pages.

As page faults happen, memory gets filled up and eventually some pages need to be cleared for more recent data to come into memory. This is called a **page eviction event**. We cannot completely avoid page faults unless we have a really static dataset but we want to try and minimize page faults. This can be achieved by holding our working set in memory.

Resident memory

Resident memory size is the total amount of memory that MongoDB owns in RAM. This is the base metric to monitor and should be less than 80% of available memory.

Virtual and mapped memory

When MongoDB asks for a memory address, the operating system will return a virtual address. This may or may not be an actual address in RAM, depending on where data resides. MongoDB will use this virtual address to request the underlying data. When we have journaling enabled (which should be almost always), MongoDB will keep another address on record for the journaled data. Virtual memory refers to the size of all data requested by MongoDB, including journaling.

Mapped memory excludes journaling references.

What all of this means is that over time, our mapped memory will be roughly equal to our working set and virtual memory will be around twice the amount of our mapped memory.

Working set

Working set is the data size that MongoDB uses. In the case of a transactional database, this will end up being the data size that MongoDB holds but there are cases where we may have collections that are not used at all and so will not contribute to our working set.

Monitoring memory usage in WiredTiger

Understanding memory usage in MMAPv1 is relatively straightforward. MMAPv1 is using the `mmap()` system call under the hood to pass on the responsibility of the memory page to the underlying operating system. This is why when we use MMAPv1 memory usage will grow unbounded as the operating system is trying to fit as much of our dataset into memory.

With WiredTiger on the other hand, we define internal cache memory usage on startup. By default, the internal cache will be, at the maximum, between half of our RAM in GB—1 GB or 256 MB.

On top of the internal cache, there is also memory that MongoDB can allocate for other operations like maintaining connections and data processing (in-memory sort, MapReduce, aggregation, and others).

MongoDB processes will also use the underlying operating system's filesystem cache just like in MMAPv1. Data in the filesystem cache is compressed.

We can view the settings for the WiredTiger cache via the mongo shell as follows:

```
> db.serverStatus().wiredTiger.cache
```

We can adjust its size using the `storage.wiredTiger.engineConfig.cacheSizeGB` parameter.

The generic recommendation is to leave WiredTiger internal cache size at its default. If our data has a high compression ratio, it may be worth reducing the internal cache size by 10-20% to free more memory for the filesystem cache.

Tracking page faults

The number of page faults can remain fairly stable and not affect performance significantly. However, once the number of page faults reaches a certain threshold, our system will be severely degraded, quickly. This is even more evident for HDDs but also affects SSD drives as well.

The way to ensure that we don't run into problems regarding page faults is to always have a staging environment that is identical in setup to our production. This environment can be used to stress test how many page faults our system can handle without deteriorating performance. Then, comparing the actual number of page faults in our production system with the maximum number of page faults that we calculated from our staging system we know how much leeway we have left.

Another way to view page faults is via the shell looking at the `extra_info` field of `serverStatus`'s output:

```
> db.adminCommand({"serverStatus" : 1})['extra_info']
{ "note" : "fields vary by platform", "page_faults" : 3465 }
```

As the note states, these fields may not be present in every platform.

Tracking B-tree misses

As we saw in the previous chapter, proper indexing is the best way to keep our MongoDB responsive and performant. B-tree misses refer to page faults that happen when we try to access a B-tree index. Indexes are usually used frequently and are relatively small compared to our working set and the memory available so they should be in memory at all times.

If we have an increasing number of B-tree misses, or the ratio of B-tree hits / B-tree misses decreases, it's a sign that our indexes have grown in size and/or are not optimally designed. B-tree misses can also be monitored via MongoDB Cloud Manager or in the shell.

In the shell we can use collection stats to locate it.

I/O wait

I/O wait refers to the time that the operating system waits for an I/O operation to complete. It has a strongly positive correlation with page faults. If we see I/O wait increasing over time, it's a strong indication that page faults will follow as well. We should aim to keep I/O wait less than 60-70% for a healthy operational cluster.

Read and write queues

Another way to look at I/O wait and page faults are read and write queues. When we have page faults and I/O wait, requests will inevitably start queuing for either reads or writes. Queues are the effect rather than the root cause so by the time queues start building up we know that we have a problem to solve.

Lock percentage

This is more of an issue with earlier versions of MongoDB and less of an issue when using the WiredTiger storage engine. Lock percentage shows the percentage of time that the database is locked up waiting for an operation that uses exclusive lock to release it. It should generally be low, 10-20% at most and is a cause for concern if it gets over 50% for any reason.

Background flushes

MongoDB will flush data to the disk every 1 minute by default. Background flush refers to the time it takes for the data to persist to disk. It should not be more than 1 second for every one minute period.

Modifying the flush interval may help with background flush time; by writing to disk more frequently there will be less data to write and this could, in some cases, make writes faster.

The fact that background flush time gets affected by the write load means that if our background flush time starts getting too high, we should consider sharding our database to increase write capacity.

Tracking free space

A common issue when using MMAPv1 (less frequent with WiredTiger), is free disk space. As with memory, we need to track disk space usage and be proactive rather than reactive with it. Keep monitoring disk space usage with proper alerts when it reaches 40, 60, or 80% of disk space, especially for datasets that grow quickly.

Disk space issues are often the ones that cause the most headaches to administrators, DevOps, and developers because of the time it takes to move data around.

 The `directoryperdb` option can help with data sizing as we can split up our storage into different physically mounted disks.

Monitoring replication

Replica sets use the **oplog (operations log)** to keep the synced state. Every operation gets applied on the primary server and then gets written in the primary server's oplog, which is a capped collection. Secondaries read this oplog asynchronously and apply the operations one by one.

If the primary server gets overloaded, then secondaries won't be able to read and apply operations fast enough, generating replication lag. Replication lag is counted as the time difference between the last operation applied on the primary and the last operation applied on the secondary as stored in the oplog capped collection.

For example, if the time is 4:30:00 pm and the secondary just applied an operation that was applied on our primary server at 4:25:00 pm, this means that the secondary is lagging 5 minutes behind our primary server.

In our production cluster, replication lag should be close to or equal to zero.

Oplog size

Every member in a replica size will have a copy of the oplog in `db.oplog.rs()`. The reason is that if the primary steps down, one of the secondaries will get elected and needs to have an up to date version of the oplog for the new secondaries to track.

The oplog size is configurable and we should set it as big as possible. Oplog size doesn't affect memory usage and can make or break the database in case of operational issues.

The reason is that if replication lag increases over time, we will eventually get to the point where secondaries will fall back so much behind the primary that they won't be able to read from the primary's oplog as the oldest entry in the primary's oplog will be later than the latest entry applied in our secondary server.

In general, oplog should be at least 1-2 days' worth of operations. Oplog should be longer than the time it takes for the initial sync for the same reason as detailed previously.

Working set calculations

The working set is the strongest indicator of our memory requirements. Ideally, we would like to have our entire dataset in memory but most of the times this is not feasible. The next best thing is having our working set in memory. The working set can be calculated directly or indirectly.

Directly, we had the `workingSet` flag in `serverStatus` that we can invoke as follows from the shell:

```
> db.adminCommand({"serverStatus" : 1, "workingSet" : 1})
```

Unfortunately, this was removed in version 3.0 and so we will focus on the indirect method of calculating `workingSet`.

Indirectly, our working set is the size of data we need to satisfy 95% or more of our user's requests. To calculate this, we need to identify from the logs, queries users make and which datasets they use. Adding to it 30-50% for index memory requirements we can arrive at the working set calculation.

Another indirect way of estimating working size is the number of page faults. If we don't have page faults, then our working set fits in memory. Through trial and error we can estimate the point at which page faults start to happen and so again, understand our leeway.

If we can't have the working set in memory, then we should have at least enough memory so that the indexes can fit in memory. We described in the previous chapter how we can calculate index memory requirements and we can use this calculation to size our RAM accordingly.

Monitoring tools

There are several options for monitoring. In this section, we will discuss how we can monitor using MongoDB's own or third-party tools.

Hosted tools

MongoDB Inc.'s own tool MongoDB Cloud Manager (formerly MMS) is a robust tool for monitoring all of the metrics described previously. MongoDB Cloud Manager has a limited free tier and 30-days trial period.

Another option to use MongoDB Cloud Manager is via MongoDB Atlas, MongoDB Inc's DBaaS offering. This also has a limited free tier and is available in all three major cloud providers (Amazon, Google, Microsoft).

Open source tools

All major open source tools like Nagios, Munin, Cacti, and others provide plugin support for MongoDB. Although it is beyond the scope of this book, operations and DevOps should be familiar with both setting up and understanding the metrics described previously to effectively troubleshoot MongoDB and preemptively resolve issues before they grow out of proportion.

`mongotop`, `mongostat`, and scripts in the mongo shell can also be used for ad hoc monitoring. One of the risks with such manual processes though is that any failure of the scripts may jeopardize our database. If there are well known and tested tools for your monitoring needs, please avoid writing your own.

Backups

Lee Child once famously said:

> *"Hope for the best, plan for the worst."*

This should be our approach when designing our backup strategy for MongoDB. There are several distinct failure events that can happen.

Backups should be the cornerstone of our disaster recovery strategy in case something happens. Some developers may rely on replication for disaster recovery as it seems that having three copies of our data is more than enough. In case one of the copies goes away, we can always rebuild the cluster from the other two copies.

This is indeed the case in the event of disks failing for example. Disk failure is one of the most common failures in a production cluster and will statistically happen once disks start reaching their **MTBF (mean time between failures)** time.

However, it is not the only failure event that can happen. Security incidents or purely human errors are just as likely to happen and should be part of our plan as well. Catastrophic failures by means of losing all replica set members at once by a fire, a flood, an earthquake, or a disgruntled employee are all events that should not lead to production data loss.

A useful interim option in the middle ground between replication and implementing proper backups can be setting up a delayed replica set member. This member can be several hours or days lagging behind the primary server, thus not being affected by malicious changes in the primary. The important detail to take into account is that the oplog needs to be configured such that it can hold several hours of delay and also that this solution is only interim as it doesn't take into account the full range of reasons why we need disaster recovery but can definitely help with a subset of them.

This is called **disaster recovery**. Disaster recovery is a class of failures that require backups to be taken not only regularly but also using a process that isolates them both geographically and in terms of access rules from our production data.

Backup options

Depending on our deployment strategy, we can choose different options for backups.

Cloud-based solutions

The most straightforward solution comes if we are using a cloud DBaaS solution. In the example of MongoDB Inc's own MongoDB Atlas, we can manage backups from the GUI.

If we host MongoDB in our own servers, we can then use MongoDB Inc's MongoDB Cloud Manager (former MMS tool). Cloud Manager is a SaaS that we can point to our own servers to monitor and backup our data. It uses the same oplog that replication uses and can backup both replica sets and sharded clusters.

If we don't want (or can't for security reasons) to point our servers to an external SaaS service, we can use Cloud Manager's functionality on-premises using MongoDB Ops Manager. To get MongoDB Ops Manager we need to get a subscription to the Enterprise Advanced Edition of MongoDB for our cluster.

Backups with file system snapshots

The most common backup method in the past and still one that is widely used is relying on the underlying file system point-in-time snapshots functionality to backup our data.

EBS on EC2 and Logical Volume Manager on Linux support point-in-time snapshots.

Taking a backup of a replica set:

> If we use WiredTiger with the latest version of MongoDB we can have volume level backups even if our data and journal files reside in different volumes.

To take a backup of a replica set, we need to have a consistent state of our database. This implies that we have all our writes either committed to disk or in our journal files.

If we use WiredTiger storage our snapshot will be consistent as of the latest checkpoint, which is either 2 GB of data or the last minute.

> Ensure that you store the snapshot in an offsite volume for disaster recovery purposes. We need to have enabled journaling to use point-in-time snapshots. It's good practice to enable journaling regardless.

Taking a backup of a sharded cluster

If we want to take a backup of an entire sharded cluster we need to stop the balancer before starting. The reason is that if there are chunks migrating between different shards at the time that we take our snapshot our database will be in an inconsistent state having either incomplete or duplicate data chunks that were in-flight at the time we took our snapshot.

Backups from an entire sharded cluster will be approximate-in-time. If we need point-in-time precision we need to stop all writes in our database, something that is generally not possible for production systems.

First we need to disable the balancer by connecting to our mongos through the mongo shell:

```
> use config
> sh.stopBalancer()
```

Then if we don't have journaling enabled in our secondaries or we have journal and data files in different volumes we need to lock our secondaries mongod instances for all shards and the config server replica set.

 We also need to have a sufficient oplog size in these servers to enable them to be able to catch up to the primaries once we unlock them, or else we will need to resync them from scratch.

Given that we don't need to lock our secondaries, the next step is to back up the config server. In Linux and using LVM, this would be similar to this:

```
$ lvcreate --size 100M --snapshot --name snap-14082017 /dev/vg0/mongodb
```

Then we need to repeat the same process for a single member from each replica set in each shard.

Finally, we need to restart the balancer using the same mongo shell that we used to stop it:

```
> sh.setBalancerState(true)
```

Without going into too much detail here, it's evident that taking a backup of a sharded cluster is a complicated and time consuming procedure that needs prior planning and extensive testing to make sure not only that it works with minimal disruption but that also our backups are usable and can be restored back to our cluster.

Backups using mongodump

mongodump is a command-line tool that can take out a backup of the data in our MongoDB cluster. As such, the downside is that on restore, all indexes need to be recreated which may be a time consuming operation.

The major downside the mongodump tool has is that to write data to disk it needs to bring data from internal MongoDB storage to memory first. This means that in the case of production clusters running under strain, mongodump will invalidate data residing in memory from the working set with data that would not be residing in memory under regular operations, degrading the performance of our cluster.

On the plus side, when we use mongodump we can continue taking writes in our cluster and if we have a replica set we can use the --oplog option to include in its output oplog entries that occur during the mongodump operation.

If we go with that option we need to use --oplogReplay when we use the mongorestore tool to restore our data back in the MongoDB cluster.

mongodump is a great tool for single server deployments but once we get to larger deployments we should consider using different and better planned approaches to back up our data.

Backups by copying raw files

If we don't want to use any of the preceding options outlined, our last resort is copying the raw files using cp/rsync or something equivalent. This is generally not recommended for the following reasons:

- We need to stop all writes before copying files
- Backup size will be larger since we need to copy indexes, and any underlying padding and fragmentation storage overhead
- We cannot get point-in-time recovery using this method for replica sets and copying data from sharded clusters in a consistent and predictable manner is extremely difficult

This should be avoided unless no other option really exists.

Backups using queueing

Another strategy used in practice is utilizing a queuing system intercepting our database and the frontend software system. Having something like an ActiveMQ queue before inserts/updates/deletes in our database means that we can safely send out data to different sinks, these being MongoDB servers or log files in a separate repository. This method, like the delayed replica set method, can be useful for a class of backup problems but can fail for some others.

 This is a useful interim solution but should not be used as a permanent one.

EC2 backup and restore

MongoDB Cloud Manager can automate taking backups from EC2 volumes and since our data is in the cloud, why not use the Cloud Manager anyway.

If we can't use it for some reason, then we can write a script to take backups using the following steps:

- Assuming that we have journaling enabled (and we really should) and we have already mapped `dbpath` containing data and journal files to a single EBS volume we need to first find the EBS block instances associated with the running instance using `ec2-describe-instances`.
- The next step is to find the logical volumes that the `dbpath` of our mongodb database is mapped to using `lvdisplay`.
- Once we identify the logical devices from the logical volumes, we can use `ec2-create-snapshot` to create new snapshots. We need to include each and every logical device that maps to our `dbpath` directory.

To verify that our backups work, we need to create new volumes based on the snapshots and mount the new volumes there. Finally the `mongod` process should be able to start mounting the new data and we should connect using mongo to verify these.

Incremental backups

Taking full backups every time may be viable for some deployments but as size reaches a certain threshold, full backups take too much time and space.

At this point, we want to take full backups every once in a while (maybe one per month for example) and incremental backups in between (for example nightly).

Both Ops Manager and Cloud Manager support incremental backups and if we get to this size it may be a good idea to use a tool to take our backups instead of rolling our own.

If, for one reason or another, we don't want or can't use these tools, we have the option of restoring via the oplog, as follows:

- Take a full backup with any method previously described
- Lock writes on the secondary server of our replica set
- Note the latest entry in oplog
- Export entries in oplog after the latest entry in oplog:

```
> mongodump --host <secondary> -d local -c oplog.rs -o /mnt/mongo-
oldway_backup
    --query '{ "ts" : { $gt :  Timestamp(1467999203, 391) } }'
```

- Unlock writes on the secondary server

To restore we can use the `oplog.rs` file we just exported and use `mongorestore` with the option `--oplogReplay`:

```
> mongorestore -h <primary> --port <port> --oplogReplay
<data_file_position>
```

 This method requires locking writes and may not work in future versions.

An even better solution is to use the LVM filesystem with incremental backups but this depends on the underlying LVM implementation that we may or may not be able to tweak.

Security

Security is a multifaceted goal in a MongoDB cluster. For the rest of this chapter we will examine different attack vectors and how we can protect against them. In addition to these best practices, developers and administrators must always use common sense so that security interferes only as much as needed with operational goals.

Authentication

Authentication refers to verifying the identity of a client. This prevents impersonating someone else in order to gain access to our data.

The simplest way to authenticate is using a username/password pair. This can be done via the shell in two ways:

```
> db.auth( <username>, <password> )
```

Passing in a comma separated username and password will assume default values for the rest of the fields:

```
> db.auth( {
  user: <username>,
  pwd: <password>,
  mechanism: <authentication mechanism>,
  digestPassword: <boolean>
} )
```

If we pass a document object we can define more parameters than username/password.

The (authentication) mechanism parameter can take several different values with the default being SCRAM-SHA-1. The parameter value MONGODB-CR is used for backwards compatibility with versions earlier than 3.0

MONGODB-X509 is used for TLS/SSL authentication. Users and internal replica set servers can be authenticated using SSL certificates, which are self-generated and signed, or come from a trusted third-party authority.

To configure X509 for internal authentication of replica set members we need to supply either one of the following parameters:

This for the configuration file:

```
security.clusterAuthMode / net.ssl.clusterFile
```

Or like this on the command line:

```
--clusterAuthMode and --sslClusterFile
> mongod --replSet <name> --sslMode requireSSL --clusterAuthMode x509 --
sslClusterFile <path to membership certificate and key PEM file> --
sslPEMKeyFile <path to SSL certificate and key PEM file> --sslCAFile <path
to root CA PEM file>
```

MongoDB Enterprise Edition, the paid offering from MongoDB Inc., adds two more options for authentication.

The first added option is GSSAPI (Kerberos). Kerberos is a mature and robust authentication system that can be used, among others, for Windows based Active Directory deployments.

The second added option is PLAIN (LDAP SASL). LDAP is just like Kerberos; a mature and robust authentication mechanism. The main consideration when using PLAIN authentication mechanism is that credentials are transmitted in plaintext over the wire. This means that we should secure the path between client and server via VPN or a TSL/SSL connection to avoid a man in the middle stealing our credentials.

Authorization

After we have configured authentication to verify that users are who they claim they are when connecting to our MongoDB server, we need to configure the rights that each one of them will have in our database.

This is the authorization aspect of permissions. MongoDB uses role-based access control to control permissions for different user classes.

Every role has permissions to perform some actions on a resource.

A resource can be a collection or a database or any collections or any databases.

The command's format is:

```
{ db: <database>, collection: <collection> }
```

If we specify "" (empty string) for either db or collection it means any db or collection.

For example:

```
{ db: "mongo_books", collection: "" }
```

This would apply our action in every collection in database mongo_books.

 If the database is not the admin database, then this will not include system collections. System collections such as <db>.system.profile, <db>.system.js, admin.system.users, and admin.system.roles need to be defined explicitly.

Similar to the preceding, we can define:

```
{ db: "", collection: "" }
```

We define this to apply our rule to all collections across all databases, except system collections of course.

We can also apply rules across an entire cluster as follows:

```
{ resource: { cluster : true }, actions: [ "addShard" ] }
```

The preceding example grants privileges for the addShard action (adding a new shard to our system) across the entire cluster. The cluster resource can only be used for actions that affect the entire cluster rather than a collection or database, as for example shutdown, replSetReconfig, appendOplogNote, resync, closeAllDatabases, and addShard.

What follows is an extensive list of cluster specific actions and some of the most widely used actions.

The list of most widely used actions are:

- find
- insert
- remove
- update
- bypassDocumentValidation
- viewRole / viewUser

- createRole / dropRole
- createUser / dropUser
- inprog
- killop
- replSetGetConfig / replSetConfigure / replSetStateChange / resync
- getShardMap / getShardVersion / listShards / moveChunk / removeShard / addShard
- dropDatabase / dropIndex / fsync / repairDatabase / shutDown
- serverStatus / top / validate

Cluster-specific actions are:

- unlock
- authSchemaUpgrade
- cleanupOrphaned
- cpuProfiler
- inprog
- invalidateUserCache
- killop
- appendOplogNote
- replSetConfigure
- replSetGetConfig
- replSetGetStatus
- replSetHeartbeat
- replSetStateChange
- resync
- addShard
- flushRouterConfig
- getShardMap
- listShards
- removeShard
- shardingState
- applicationMessage
- closeAllDatabases
- connPoolSync

- `fsync`
- `getParameter`
- `hostInfo`
- `logRotate`
- `setParameter`
- `shutdown`
- `touch`
- `connPoolStats`
- `cursorInfo`
- `diagLogging`
- `getCmdLineOpts`
- `getLog`
- `listDatabases`
- `netstat`
- `serverStatus`
- `top`

If this sounds too complicated that is because it is. The flexibility that MongoDB allows in configuring different actions on resources means that we need to study and understand the extensive lists as described previously.

Thankfully, some of the most common actions and resources are bundled in built-in roles.

We can use the built-in roles to establish the baseline of permissions that we will give to our users and then fine grain these based on the extensive list.

User roles

There are two different generic user roles that we can specify:

- `read`: A read-only role across non-system collections and the following system collections: `system.indexes`, `system.js`, and `system.namespaces` collections

- `readWrite`: A read and modify role across non-system collections and the `system.js` collection

Database administration roles

There are three database specific administration roles shown as follows:

- dbAdmin: The basic admin user role which can perform schema-related tasks, indexing, gathering statistics. A dbAdmin cannot perform user and role management.

- userAdmin: Create and modify roles and users. This is complementary to the dbAdmin role.

 A userAdmin can modify itself to become a superuser in the database or, if scoped to the admin database, the MongoDB cluster.

- dbOwner: Combining readWrite, dbAdmin, and userAdmin roles, this is the most powerful admin user role.

Cluster administration roles

These are the cluster wide administration roles available:

- hostManager: Monitor and manage servers in a cluster.

- clusterManager: Provides management and monitoring actions on the cluster. A user with this role can access the config and local databases, which are used in sharding and replication, respectively.

- clusterMonitor: Read-only access for monitoring tools provided by MongoDB such as MongoDB Cloud Manager and Ops Manager agent.

- clusterAdmin: Provides the greatest cluster-management access. This role combines the privileges granted by the clusterManager, clusterMonitor, and hostManager roles. Additionally, the role provides the dropDatabase action.

Backup restore roles

Role-based authorization roles can be defined in the backup restore granularity level as well:

- `backup`: Provides privileges needed to back up data. This role provides sufficient privileges to use the MongoDB Cloud Manager backup agent, Ops Manager backup agent, or to use `mongodump`.

- `restore`: Provides privileges needed to restore data with `mongorestore` without the `--oplogReplay` option or without `system.profile` collection data.

Roles across all databases

Similarly, here are the set of available roles across all databases:

- `readAnyDatabase`: Provides the same read-only permissions as read, except it applies to all but the local and config databases in the cluster. The role also provides the `listDatabases` action on the cluster as a whole.

- `readWriteAnyDatabase`: Provides the same read and write permissions as `readWrite`, except it applies to all but the local and config databases in the cluster. The role also provides the `listDatabases` action on the cluster as a whole.

- `userAdminAnyDatabase`: Provides the same access to user administration operations as `userAdmin`, except it applies to all but the local and config databases in the cluster.

  Since the `userAdminAnyDatabase` role allows users to grant any privilege to any user, including themselves, the role also indirectly provides superuser access.

- `dbAdminAnyDatabase`: Provides the same access to database administration operations as `dbAdmin`, except it applies to all but the local and config databases in the cluster. The role also provides the `listDatabases` action on the cluster as a whole.

Superuser

Finally, these are the superuser roles available:

- `root`: Provides access to the operations and all the resources of the `readWriteAnyDatabase`, `dbAdminAnyDatabase`, `userAdminAnyDatabase`, `clusterAdmin`, `restore`, and `backup` combined.

- `__internal`: Similar to root user, any `__internal` user can perform any action against any object across the server.

 Superuser roles should be avoided as they can have potentially destructive permissions across all databases on our server.

Network level security

Apart from MongoDB specific security measures, there are best practices established for network level security:

- Only allow communication between servers and only open the ports that are used for communicating between them.
- Always use TLS/SSL for communication between servers. This prevents man-in-the-middle attacks impersonating a client.
- Always use different sets of development, staging, and production environments and security credentials. Ideally, create different accounts for each environment and enable two-factor authentication in both staging and production environments.

Auditing security

No matter how much we plan our security measures, a second or third pair of eyes from someone outside our organization can give a different view of our security measures and uncover problems that we may not have thought of or underestimated. Don't hesitate to involve security experts / white hat hackers to do penetration testing in your servers.

Special cases

Medical or financial applications require added levels of security for data privacy reasons.

If we are building an application in the healthcare space, accessing users' personal identifiable information, we may need to get HIPAA certified.

If we are building an application interacting with payments and managing cardholder information, we may need to become PCI/DSS compliant.

The specifics of each certification are outside the scope of this book but it is important to know that MongoDB has use cases in these fields that fulfill the requirements and as such it can be the right tool with proper design beforehand.

Overview

Summing up on best practice recommendations around security we have:

- **Enforce authentication**: Always enable authentication in production environments.
- **Enable access control**: First create a system administrator, and then use this administrator to create more limited users. Give as few permissions as are needed for each user role.
- Define fine grained roles in access control, not giving more permissions than needed for each user.
- **Encrypt communication between clients and servers**: Always use TLS/SSL for communication between clients and servers in production environments. Always use TLS/SSL for communication between mongod and mongos or config servers as well.
- **Encrypt data at rest**: MongoDB Enterprise Edition offers the functionality to encrypt data when stored, using WiredTiger encryption at rest.

 Alternatively, we can encrypt data using filesystem, device, or physical encryption. In the cloud, often we get the option of encryption as well, as for example with EBS on Amazon EC2.

- **Limit network exposure**: MongoDB servers should only be connected to the application servers and any other servers that are needed for operations. Ports other than the ones that we set up for MongoDB communications should not be open to the outside world.

If we want to debug MongoDB usage it's important to have a proxy server with controlled access set up to communicate with our database.

- **Audit servers for unusual activity**: MongoDB Enterprise Edition offers a utility for auditing. Using it we can output events to the console, a JSON file, a BSON file, or the syslog. In any case, it's important to make sure that audit events are stored in a partition that is not available to the system's users.

- Use a dedicated operating system user to run MongoDB. Make sure that the dedicated operating system user can access MongoDB but doesn't have unnecessary permissions.

- Disable JavaScript server-side scripts if not needed.

MongoDB can use JavaScript for server-side scripts with the following commands: `mapReduce()`, `group()`, `$where`. If we don't need these commands we should disable server-side scripting using the `--noscripting` option on the command line.

Summary

In this chapter, we learned about three operational aspects of MongoDB, namely monitoring, backups, and security.

We discussed the metrics that we should monitor in MongoDB and how to monitor them. Following that, we discussed how to take backups and make sure that we can use them to restore our data. Finally, we learned about security with authentication and authorization concepts as well as network level security and how to audit it.

As important as it is to design, build, and extend our application as needed, it is equally important to make sure that we can have peace of mind during operations and are safeguarded from unexpected events, that being human error or malicious users, internal and external.

In the next chapter, we will learn about pluggable storage engines, a new concept that was introduced in v3.0 of MongoDB. Pluggable storage engines allow for different use cases to be served, especially in application domains that have specific and stringent requirements around data handling and privacy.

8
Storage Engines

MongoDB introduced the concept of pluggable storage engines in version 3.0. After the acquisition of WiredTiger, it introduced its storage engine first as optional, and then as the default storage engine for the current version of MongoDB. In this chapter, we will dive deeply into the concept of storage engines, why they matter, and how we can choose the best one according to our workload.

Pluggable storage engines

With MongoDB breaking out from the web application paradigm into domains with different requirements, storage has become an increasingly important consideration.

Using multiple storage engines can be seen as an alternative way to using different storage solutions and databases in our infrastructure stack. This way, we can reduce operational complexity and development time to market with the application layer being agnostic of the underlying storage layer.

MongoDB offers four different storage engines at the moment, which we will examine in further detail in the next sections.

WiredTiger

As of version 3.2, WiredTiger is the default storage engine and also the best choice for most workloads. By providing document-level locking, it overcomes one of the most significant drawbacks earlier versions of MongoDB had—lock contention under high load.

We will explore some of WiredTiger's benefits in the following sections.

Document-level locking

Locking is so important that we explain the performance implications that fine-grained locking has in further detail at the end of this section. Having document, level locking as opposed to MMAPv1 collection-level locking can make a huge difference in many real-world use cases and is one of the main reasons to choose WiredTiger over MMAPv1.

Snapshots and checkpoints

WiredTiger uses **multiversion concurrency control (MVCC)**.

MVCC is based upon the concept that the database keeps multiple versions of an object so that readers will be able to view consistent data that doesn't change during a read.

In a database, if we have multiple readers accessing data at the same time that writers are modifying the data, we can end up with a case that readers view an inconsistent view of this data. The simplest and easiest way to solve this problem is to block all readers until the writers are done modifying data.

This will of course cause severe performance degradation. MVCC solves this problem by providing a snapshot of the database for each reader. At the time that the read starts, each reader is guaranteed to view data as it was at this point in time.

Any changes made by writers will only be seen by readers after the write has completed, or in database terms, after the transaction is committed.

To achieve this goal, when a write is coming in, updated data will be kept in a separate location on disk and MongoDB will mark the affected document as obsolete. MVCC is said to provide point in time consistent views.

This is equivalent to a read committed isolation level in traditional RDBMS systems.

For every operation, WiredTiger will snapshot our data at the exact moment that it happens and provide a consistent view of application data to the application.

When we write data, WiredTiger will create a snapshot every 2 GB of journal data or 60 seconds, whichever comes first. WiredTiger relies on its built-in journal to recover any data after the latest checkpoint in case of failure.

 We can disable journaling using WiredTiger but if the server crashes, we will lose any data after the last checkpoint is written.

Journaling

As explained in the *Snapshots and checkpoints* section, journaling is the cornerstone of WiredTiger crash recovery protection.

WiredTiger compresses the journal using the snappy compression algorithm. We can use the following setting to set a different compression algorithm:

```
storage.wiredTiger.engineConfig.journalCompressor
```

We can also disable journaling for WiredTiger by setting the following to `false`:

```
storage.journal.enabled
```

 If we use a replica set, we may be able to recover our data from a secondary which will get elected as a primary and start taking writes in the event that our primary fails. It's recommended to always use journaling, unless we understand and can take the risk of suffering through the consequences of not using it.

Data compression

MongoDB uses the snappy compression algorithm by default to compress data and prefixes for indexes.

Index-prefixed compression means that identical index key prefixes are stored only once per page of memory.

Compression not only reduces our storage footprint but will increase I/O operations per second as less data needs to be stored and moved to and from disk. Using more aggressive compression can lead to performance gains if our workload is I/O bound and not CPU bound.

We can define zlib compression instead of snappy or no compression by setting the following parameter to `false`:

```
storage.wiredTiger.collectionConfig.blockCompressor
```

 Data compression uses less storage at the expense of CPU. zlib compression achieves better compression at the expense of higher CPU usage as opposed to the default snappy compression algorithm.

We can disable index prefixes compression by setting the following parameter to `false`:

```
storage.wiredTiger.indexConfig.prefixCompression
```

We can also configure storage per-index during creation using the following parameter:

```
{ <storage-engine-name>: <options> }
```

Memory usage

WiredTiger is significantly different to MMAPv1 in how it uses RAM. MMAPv1 is essentially using the underlying operating system's filesystem cache to page data from disk to memory and vice versa.

WiredTiger, on the contrary, introduces the new concept of the WiredTiger internal cache.

The WiredTiger internal cache is by default the larger of either:

- 50% of RAM minus 1 GB
- 256 MB

This means if our server has 8 GB RAM:

max(3GB , 256 MB) = WiredTiger will use 3GB of RAM

And if our server has 2,512 MB RAM:

max(256 MB, 256 MB) = WiredTiger will use 256 MB of RAM

Essentially, for any server that has less than 2,512 MB RAM, WiredTiger will use 256 MB for its internal cache.

We can change the size of the WiredTiger internal cache by setting the following:

```
storage.wiredTiger.engineConfig.cacheSizeGB
```

Or from the command line using the following:

```
--wiredTigerCacheSizeGB
```

Apart from the WiredTiger internal cache, which is uncompressed for higher performance, MongoDB also uses the filesystem cache, which is compressed, just like MMAPv1, and will end up using all available memory in most cases.

The WiredTiger internal cache can provide similar performance to in-memory storage and as such, it is important to grow it as much as possible.

We can achieve better performance when using WiredTiger with multi-core processors. This is also a big win compared to MMAPv1, which does not scale as well.

 We can, and should, use Docker or other containerization technologies to isolate mongod processes from each other and make sure that we know how much memory each process can and should use in a production environment. It is not recommended to increase the WiredTiger internal cache above its default value. The filesystem cache should not be less than 20% of total RAM.

readConcern

WiredTiger supports multiple readConcern levels. Just like writeConcern, which is supported by every storage engine in MongoDB, with readConcern we can customize how many servers in a replica set must acknowledge the query results for the document to be returned in the result set.

Available options for read concern are as follows:

- local: Default option. Will return most recent data from the server. Data may or may not have propagated to the other servers in a replica set and we run the risk of a rollback.
- linearizable:
  - Only applicable for reads from the primary
  - Only applicable in queries that return a single result
  - Data returns satisfies two conditions:
    - majority writeConcern
    - Data was acknowledged before the start of the read operation

In addition, if we have set writeConcernMajorityJournalDefault to true, we are guaranteed that data won't get rolled back.

If we have set `writeConcernMajorityJournalDefault` to `false`, MongoDB will not wait for `majority` writes to be durable before acknowledging the write. In this case, our data may be rolled back in the event of a loss of a member from the replica set.

- `majority`: Data returned has already been propagated and acknowledged from the majority of the servers before read has started

> We need to use `maxTimeMS` when using `linearizable` and `majority` read concern levels in case we can't establish `majority writeConcern` to avoid blocking forever waiting for the response. In this case, the operation will return a timeout error.

> `local` and `linearizable` read concerns are available for MMAPv1 as well.

WiredTiger collection-level options

When we create a new collection, we can pass in options to WiredTiger like this:

```
> db.createCollection(
  "mongo_books",
  { storageEngine: { wiredTiger: { configString: "<key>=<value>" } } }
)
```

This helps to create our `mongo_books` collection with a key-value pair from the available ones that WiredTiger exposes through its API. Some of the most widely used key-value pairs are the following:

Key	Value
`block_allocation`	Best or first
`allocation_size`	512 B through to 4 KB; default 4 KB
`block_compressor`	None, lz4, snappy, zlib, zstd, or custom compressor identifier string depending on configuration
`memory_page_max`	512 B through to 10 TB; default 5 MB
`os_cache_max`	Integer greater than 0; default 0

This is taken directly from the definition in the WiredTiger documents located at: `http://source.wiredtiger.com/mongodb-3.4/struct_w_t___s_e_s_s_i_o_n.html`.

```
int WT_SESSION::create()
```

Collection-level options allow for flexibility in configuring storage but should be used with extreme care and after careful testing in development/staging environments.

> Collection-level options will get propagated to secondaries if applied to a primary in a replica set. `block_compressor` can also be configured from the command line globally for the database using the `--wiredTigerCollectionBlockCompressor` option.

WiredTiger performance strategies

As discussed earlier in this chapter, WiredTiger uses an internal cache to optimize performance. On top of it, there is always the filesystem cache that the operating system (and MMAPv1) uses to fetch data from disk.

By default, we have 50% of RAM dedicated to the filesystem cache and 50% to the WiredTiger internal cache.

The filesystem cache will keep data compressed as it is stored on disk. The internal cache will decompress it:

- **Strategy 1**: Allocate 80% or more to the internal cache. This has the goal of fitting our working set in WiredTiger's internal cache.
- **Strategy 2**: Allocate 80% or more to the filesystem cache. Our goal here is to avoid using the internal cache as much as possible and rely on the filesystem cache for our needs.
- **Strategy 3**: Use an SSD as the underlying storage for fast seek time and keep defaults at 50-50% allocation.
- **Strategy 4**: Enable compression in our storage layer through MongoDB's configuration to save on storage and potentially improve our performance by having a smaller working set size.

Our workload will dictate whether we need to deviate from the default *Strategy 1* to any of the rest. In general, we should use SSDs wherever possible and with MongoDB's configurable storage, we can even use SSDs for some of the nodes where we need the best performance and keep HDDs for analytics workloads.

WiredTiger B-tree versus LSM indexes

B-tree is the most common data structure for indexes across different database systems. WiredTiger offers the option to use a Log-Structured Merge Tree instead of a B-tree for indexing.

An LSM tree can provide better performance when we have a workload of random inserts that would otherwise overflow our page cache and start paging in data from disk to keep our index up to date.

LSM indexes can be selected from the command line like this:

```
> mongod --wiredTigerIndexConfigString "type=lsm,block_compressor=zlib"
```

The preceding command chooses `lsm` index type and `block_compressor` zlib for indexes in this `mongod` instance.

Encrypted

The encrypted storage engine was added to support a series of special use cases, mostly revolving around finance, retail, healthcare, education, and government.

We need to have encryption for the rest of our data if we have to comply to a set of regulations, including among others:

- PCI DSS for handling credit card information
- HIPAA for healthcare applications
- NIST for government
- FISMA for government
- STIG for government

This can be done in several ways and cloud services providers such as EC2 provide EBS storage volumes with built-in encryption.

Encrypted storage supports Intel's AES-NI equipped CPUs for acceleration of the encryption/decryption process.

The encryption algorithms supported are the following:

- AES-256, CBC (default)
- AES-256, GCM
- FIPS, FIPS-140-2

Encryption is supported at page level for better performance. When a change is made in a document, instead of re-encrypting/decrypting the entire underlying file, only the page that is affected gets modified.

Encryption key management is a huge aspect of encrypted storage security. Most specifications previously mentioned require key rotation at least once per year.

MongoDB's encrypted storage uses an internal database key per node. This key is wrapped by an external (master) key that must be used to start the node's `mongod` process. By using the underlying operating system's protection mechanisms such as mlock or VirtualLock, MongoDB can guarantee that the external key will never be leaked from memory to disk by page faults.

The external (master) key can be managed either by using the **Key Management Interoperability Protocol** (**KMIP**) or by using local key management via a keyfile.

MongoDB can achieve key rotation by performing rolling restarts of the replica set members. Using KMIP, MongoDB can rotate only the external key and not the underlying database files, delivering significant performance benefits.

Using KMIP is the recommended approach for encrypted data storage. Encrypted storage is based off of WiredTiger so all its advantages can be enjoyed using encryption as well. Encrypted storage is part of MongoDB Enterprise Edition, the paid offering by MongoDB.

Using MongoDB's encrypted storage provides the advantage of increased performance versus encrypted storage volumes. MongoDB's encrypted storage has an overhead of around 15% as compared to 25% or more for third-party encrypted storage solutions.

In most cases, if we need to use encrypted storage, we will know it way in advance from the application design phase and we can perform benchmarks against different solutions to choose the one that best fits our use case.

In-memory

MongoDB storage in-memory is a risky task with high rewards. Keeping data in-memory, can be up to 100,000 times faster than durable storage on disk.

Another advantage of using in-memory storage is that we can achieve predictable latency when we write or read data. Some use cases dictate for latency that does not deviate from normal no matter what the operation is.

On the other hand, by keeping data in-memory we are open to power loss and application failure where we can lose all of our data.

Using a replica set can safeguard against some classes of errors but we will always be more exposed to data loss if we store in data as opposed to storing on disk.

There are, however, some use cases in which we may not care that much about losing older data.

In the financial world, we may have the following:

- High-frequency trading/algorithmic trading where higher latency in the case of high traffic can lead to transactions not being fulfilled.
- Fraud detection systems. In this case, we are concerned about real-time detection being as fast as possible and we can safely store only the cases that require further investigation or the definitely positive ones to durable storage.
- Credit card authorizations, trade ordering reconciliation, and other high-traffic systems that demand a real-time answer.

In the web applications ecosystem, we have the following:

- Intrusion detection systems. Like fraud detection, we are concerned with detecting intrusion as fast as possible without so much concern for false positive cases.
- Product search cache. In this case, losing data is not mission-critical but rather a small inconvenience from the customer's perspective.
- Real-time personalized product recommendations. Again, a low-risk operation in terms of data loss, we can always rebuild the index even if we suffer data loss.

A major disadvantage of an in-memory storage engine is that our dataset has to fit in-memory. This means that we must know and keep track of our data usage so that we don't exceed the memory of our server.

Overall, using the MongoDB in-memory storage engine may be useful in some edge use cases but lacking durability in a database system can be a blocking factor in its adoption.

> In-memory storage is part of MongoDB Enterprise Edition, the paid offering by MongoDB.

MMAPv1

With the introduction of WiredTiger and the unquestionable benefits, such as document-level locking, many MongoDB users are questioning whether it's worth discussing MMAPv1 anymore.

In reality, the only cases that we should consider using MMAPv1 instead of WiredTiger would be the following:

- Legacy systems. If we have a system that fits our needs, we may upgrade to MongoDB 3.0+ and not transition to WiredTiger.
- Version downgrade. Once we upgrade to MongoDB 3.0+ and convert our storage to WiredTiger, we cannot downgrade to a version lower than 2.6.8. This should be kept in mind if we want the flexibility to downgrade at a later time.

As shown previously, WiredTiger is a better choice than MMAPv1 and we should use it whenever we get the chance to. This book is oriented around WiredTiger and assumes that we will be able to use the latest stable version of MongoDB (3.4 at the time of writing).

> MMAPv1, as of version 3.4, only supports collection-level locking, as opposed to the document-level locking supported by WiredTiger. This can lead to a performance penalty in high contention database loads and is one of the main reasons as to why we should use WiredTiger whenever possible.

MMAPv1 storage optimization

MongoDB by default uses the power of 2 allocation strategy. When a document is created, it will get allocated a power of 2 size, that is, `ceiling(document_size)`.

For example, if we create a document of 127 bytes, MongoDB will allocate 128 bytes (2^7). Whereas, if we create a document of 129 bytes, MongoDB will allocate 256 bytes (2^8). This is helpful when updating documents as we can update them and not move the underlying document on disk until it exceeds the space allocated.

If a document is moved on disk (that is, adding a new subdocument or an element in an array of the document that forces the size to exceed the allocated storage), a new power of 2 allocation size will be used.

If the operation doesn't affect its size (that is, changing an integer value from 1 to 2) the document will remain stored in the same physical location on disk. This concept is called **padding**. We can configure padding using the compact administration command as well.

When we move documents on disk, we have non-contiguous blocks of data stored, essentially *holes* in storage. We can prevent this from happening by setting `paddingFactor` at collection level.

`paddingFactor` has a default value of `1.0` (no padding) and a maximum of `4.0` (expand size by three times as much as the original document size). For example, a padding factor of `1.4` will allow the document to expand by 40% before getting moved on to a new location on disk.

For example, with our favorite `books` collection, to get 40% more space, we would do the following:

```
> db.runCommand ( { compact: 'books', paddingFactor: 1.4 } )
```

We can also set padding in terms of bytes per document. This way we get *x* bytes padding from the initial creation of each document in our collection:

```
> db.runCommand ( { compact: 'books', paddingBytes: 300 } )
```

This will allow a document created at 200 bytes to grow to 500 bytes. Whereas a document created at 4,000 bytes will be allowed to grow to 4,300 bytes.

We can eliminate holes altogether by running a compact command with no parameters but this means that every update that increases document size will have to move documents, essentially creating new holes in storage.

Mixed usage

When we have an application with MongoDB as the underlying database, we can set it up such that we use different replica sets for different operations at application level, matching their requirements.

For example, in our financial application, we can use a different connection pool for the fraud detection module utilizing in-memory nodes and a different one for the rest of our system shown as follows:

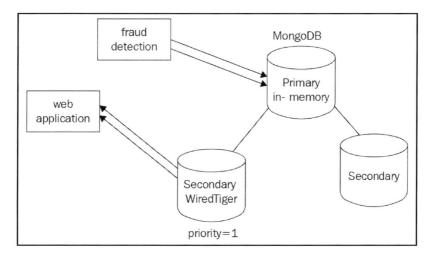

In addition, storage engine configuration in MongoDB is applied per node, which allows for some interesting setups.

As shown in the preceding architectural diagram, we can use a mix of different storage engines in different members of a replica set. In this case, we are using the in-memory engine for optimal performance in the primary node, whereas one of the secondaries uses WiredTiger to ensure data durability. We can use `priority=1` in the in-memory secondary node to make sure that if the primary fails, the secondary will get elected right away. If we don't do it, we risk having a failing primary server exactly when we have high load in the system and the secondary has not kept up with the primary's writes in-memory.

The mixed storage approach is widely used in microservice architecture. By decoupling service and database and using the appropriate database for each use case, we can easily horizontally scale our infrastructure.

All storage engines support a common baseline functionality, such as:

- Querying
- Indexing
- Replication
- Sharding
- Ops and Cloud Manager support
- Authentication and authorization semantics

Other storage engines

Modular MongoDB architecture allows for third parties to develop their own storage engines.

RocksDB

RocksDB is an embedded database for key-value data. It's a fork of LevelDB storing key-value pairs in arbitrary byte arrays. It was started at Facebook on 2012 and now serves as the backend for the interestingly named CockroachDB, the open source DB inspired by Google Spanner.

MongoRocks is a project backed by Percona and Facebook aiming to bring RocksDB backend to MongoDB. RocksDB can achieve higher performance than WiredTiger for some workloads and is worth investigating.

TokuMX

Another widely used storage engine is TokuMX by Percona. TokuMX was designed with both MySQL and MongoDB in mind but since 2016, Percona has focused its efforts on the MySQL version, instead switching over to RocksDB for MongoDB storage support.

Locking in MongoDB

Document- and collection-level locking is mentioned throughout this chapter and also in several other chapters in this book. It is important to understand how locking works and why it is important.

Database systems use the concept of locks to achieve **ACID (atomicity, consistency, isolation, durability)** properties. When there are multiple read or write requests coming in in parallel, we need to lock our data such that all readers and writers have consistent and predictable results.

MongoDB uses multi-granularity locking. The available granularity levels in descending order are as follows:

- Global
- Database
- Collection
- Document

The locks MongoDB and other databases use are the following in order of granularity:

- **IS**: Intent shared
- **IX**: Intent exclusive
- **S**: Shared
- **X**: Exclusive

If we use locking at a granularity level with shared (S) or exclusive (X), then all higher levels need to be locked with an intent lock of the same type.

Other rules for locks are as follows:

- A single database can simultaneously be locked in IS and IX mode
- An exclusive (X) lock cannot coexist with any other lock</li></li></li>
- A shared (S) lock can only coexist with intent shared (IS) locks

Reads and writes requesting locks are generally queued in **FIFO (first-in, first-out)** order. The only optimization that MongoDB will actually do is reordering requests according to the next request in queue to be serviced.

What this means is that if we have an *IS(1)* request coming up next and our current queue has the following:

IS(1)->IS(2)->X(3)->S(4)->IS(5)

1	2	3	4	5
IS	IS	X	S	IS

Then MongoDB will reorder requests like this:

IS(1)->IS(2)->S(4)->IS(5)->X(3)

1	2	4	5	3
IS	IS	S	IS	X

If during servicing the *IS(1)* request, new IS or S requests come in, let's say *IS(6)* and *S(7)* in that order, they will still be added at the end of the queue and won't be considered until the *X(3)* request is done with.

Our new queue will now look like this:

IS(2)->S(4)->IS(5)->X(3)->IS(6)->S(7)

2	4	5	3	6	7
IS	S	IS	X	IS	S

This is done to prevent starvation of the *X(3)* request which would end up getting pushed back in the queue all the time because new IS and S requests come in.

It is important to understand the difference between intent locks and locks themselves. WiredTiger storage engine will only use intent locks for global, database, and collection levels.

It uses intent locks at higher levels (that is, collection, database, global), when a new request comes in, and according to the compatibility matrix as follows:

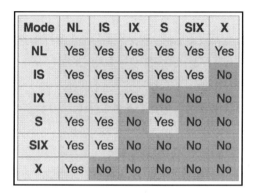

Mode	NL	IS	IX	S	SIX	X
NL	Yes	Yes	Yes	Yes	Yes	Yes
IS	Yes	Yes	Yes	Yes	Yes	No
IX	Yes	Yes	Yes	No	No	No
S	Yes	Yes	No	Yes	No	No
SIX	Yes	Yes	No	No	No	No
X	Yes	No	No	No	No	No

Source: https://en.wikipedia.org/wiki/Multiple_granularity_locking

MongoDB will first acquire intention locks in all ancestors before acquiring the lock on the document itself. This way, when a new request comes in, many times it can quickly identify if it cannot be serviced based on less granular locks.

WiredTiger will use S and X locks at the document level. The only exception to that is for typically infrequent and/or short-lived operations involving multiple databases. These will still require a global lock, similar to the behavior MongoDB had in pre 2.X versions.

 Administrative operations such as dropping a collection still require an exclusive database lock.

MMAPv1, as explained previously, uses collection-level locks. Operations that span a single collection but may or may not be spanning a single document will still lock up the entire collection. This is the main reason why WiredTiger is the preferred storage solution for all new deployments.

Lock reporting

We can inspect lock status using any of the following tools and commands:

- `db.serverStatus()` through the `locks` document

- `db.currentOp()` through the `locks` field

- `mongotop`

- `mongostat`

- MongoDB Cloud Manager

- MongoDB Ops Manager

Lock contention is a really important metric to keep track of as it can bring our database to its knees if it grows out of control.

 If we want to terminate an operation, we have to use the `db.killOp()` shell command.

Lock yield

A database with a database-level lock will not be really useful under stress and will end being locked up most of the time. A smart solution to that in the early versions of MongoDB was having operations yielding their locks based on some heuristics.

`update()` commands affecting multiple documents would yield their X lock to improve concurrency.

MMAPv1's predecessor in earlier versions of MongoDB would use these heuristics to predict whether data was already in-memory before performing the requested operation. If it wasn't, it would yield the lock until the underlying operating system pages data in-memory and then re-acquire the lock to continue with servicing the request.

The most notable exceptions to this are index scans, where the operation will not yield its lock and will just block on waiting for the data to get loaded from disk.

Since WiredTiger is only using intent locks at collection level and above, it doesn't really need these heuristics as intent locks don't block other readers and writers.

Commonly used commands and locks

The commonly used commands and locks are as follows:

Command	Lock
find()	S
it() (query cursor)	S
insert()	X
remove()	X
update()	X
mapreduce()	Both S and X, depending on the case. Some MapReduce chunks can run in parallel.
index()	**Foreground indexing**: Database lock. **Background indexing**: No lock, except for administrative commands which will return an error. Also, background indexing will take considerably more time.
aggregate()	S

Commands requiring a database lock

The following commands require a database lock. We should plan in advance before issuing them in a production environment:

- db.collection.createIndex() in the (default) foreground mode
- reIndex
- compact
- db.repairDatabase()
- db.createCollection() if creating a multiple GB capped collection

- db.collection.validate()
- db.copyDatabase() which may lock more than one database

We also have some commands that lock the entire database for a really short period of time:

- db.collection.dropIndex()
- db.getLastError()
- db.isMaster()
- Any rs.status() command
- db.serverStatus()
- db.auth()
- db.addUser()

These commands shouldn't take more than a few milliseconds to operate and so we shouldn't worry about it, except if we have automated scripts with these commands in place, in which case we must take note to throttle how often they would occur.

 In a sharded environment, each mongod applies its own locks, thus greatly improving concurrency.

In replica sets, our primary server must take all write operations. For these to be replicated correctly to the secondaries, we must lock the local database that holds the oplog of operations at the same time that we lock our primary document/collection/database. This is usually a short-lived lock that we shouldn't worry about.

Secondaries in replica sets will fetch write operations from the primary's local database's oplog, apply the appropriate X lock, and service reads once the X locks are done with.

From the long preceding explanation, it's evident that locking should be avoided at all costs in MongoDB. We should design our database so that we avoid as many X locks as possible and when we need to take X locks over one or multiple databases, do so in a maintenance window with a backup plan in case operations take longer than expected.

References

- https://docs.mongodb.com/manual/faq/concurrency/
- https://docs.mongodb.com/manual/core/storage-engines/
- https://www.mongodb.com/blog/post/building-applications-with-mongodbs-pluggable-storage-engines-part-1
- https://www.mongodb.com/blog/post/building-applications-with-mongodbs-pluggable-storage-engines-part-2
- https://docs.mongodb.com/manual/core/wiredtiger/
- https://docs.mongodb.com/manual/reference/method/db.collection.createIndex/#createindex-options
- https://docs.mongodb.com/manual/core/mmapv1/
- https://docs.mongodb.com/manual/reference/method/db.createCollection/#create-collection-storage-engine-options
- http://source.wiredtiger.com/mongodb-3.4/struct_w_t___s_e_s_s_i_o_n.html
- https://webassets.mongodb.com/microservices_white_paper.pdf?_ga=2.158920114.90404900.1503061618-355279797.1491859629
- https://webassets.mongodb.com/storage_engines_adress_wide_range_of_use_cases.pdf?_ga=2.125749506.90404900.1503061618-355279797.1491859629
- https://en.wikipedia.org/wiki/Multiversion_concurrency_control
- https://docs.mongodb.com/manual/reference/method/db.createCollection/#create-collection-storage-engine-options
- http://source.wiredtiger.com/mongodb-3.4/struct_w_t___s_e_s_s_i_o_n.html
- https://docs.mongodb.com/manual/reference/read-concern/
- https://www.percona.com/live/17/sessions/comparing-mongorocks-wiredtiger-and-mmapv1-performance-and-efficiency
- https://www.percona.com/blog/2016/06/01/embracing-mongorocks/
- https://www.percona.com/software/mongo-database/percona-tokumx
- https://www.slideshare.net/profyclub_ru/4-understanding-and-tuning-wired-tiger-the-new-high-performance-database-engine-in-mongodb-henrik-ingo-mongodb

Summary

In this chapter, we learned about different storage engines in MongoDB. We identified the pros and cons of each one and the use cases for choosing each storage engine.

We learned about using multiple storage engines, how we can use them, and the benefits.

A big part of this chapter was also dedicated to database locking, how it can happen, why it is bad, and how we can avoid it.

We split our operations by the lock they need. This way, when we design and implement our application, we can make sure that we have a design that locks our database as little as possible.

In the next chapter, we will learn about MongoDB and how we can use it to ingest and process big data.

9
Harnessing Big Data with MongoDB

In this chapter, we will learn more about how MongoDB fits into the wider big data landscape and ecosystem. We will contrast and compare MongoDB with message queuing systems such as Kafka and RabbitMQ. We will also discuss data warehousing technologies and how they can complement or replace our MongoDB cluster. Finally, we have a big data use case that will show all of the above in action and help us understand the big picture.

What is big data?

The internet has grown over the last few years and is not showing any signs of slowing down. Just in the last five years, internet users have grown from a little under 2 billion to around 3.7 billion, accounting for 50% of Earth's total population (up from 30% just 5 years ago).

With more internet users and networks evolving, every year adds increasingly more data to existing datasets. In 2016, global internet traffic was 1.2 zettabytes (which is 1.2 billion terabytes) and it is expected to grow to 3.3 zettabytes by 2021.

This enormous amount of data generates increased needs for processing and analysis. This has generated the need for databases and data stores in general that can scale and efficiently process our data.

The term big data was first coined in the 1980's by John Mashey and mostly came into play in the past decade with the explosive growth of the internet. Big data typically refers to datasets that are too large and complex to be processed by traditional data processing systems and need some kind of specialized system architecture to be processed.

Big data's defining characteristics are in general:

- Volume
- Variety
- Velocity
- Veracity
- Variability

Variety and variability refer to the fact that our data comes in different forms and our datasets have internal inconsistencies that need to be smoothed out by a data cleansing and normalization system before we can actually process our data.

Veracity refers to the uncertainty of the quality of data. Data quality may vary, having perfect data for some dates and missing datasets for others. This affects our data pipeline and how much we can invest in our data platforms, since even today one out of three business leaders don't completely trust the information they use to make business decisions.

Finally, velocity is probably the most important defining characteristic of big data (other than the obvious volume attribute) and it refers to the fact that big datasets not only that we have a large volume of data but also grow at an accelerated pace, making traditional storage using, for example, indexing a difficult task.

Big data landscape

Big data has evolved into a complex ecosystem affecting every sector of the economy. Going from hype to unrealistic expectations and back to reality, we now have big data systems implemented and deployed in most Fortune 1000 companies, delivering real value.

If we segment the companies that participate in the big data landscape by industry, we would probably come up with the following sections:

- Infrastructure
- Analytics
- Applications-enterprise
- Applications-industry
- Cross-infrastructure analytics

- Data sources and APIs
- Data resources
- Open source

From an engineering point of view, we are probably more concerned about the underlying technologies than their applications in different industry sectors.

Depending on our business domain, we may have data coming in from different sources: transactional databases, IoT sensors, application server logs, other websites via a web service API, or just plain web page content extraction:

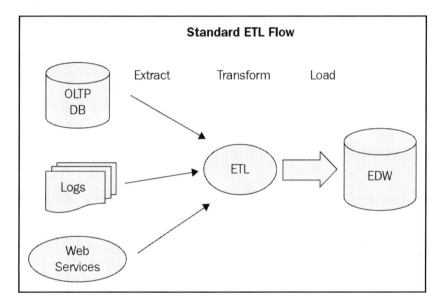

Message queuing systems

In most of the flows previously described, we have data being **extracted transformed and loaded** (ETL) into an **enterprise data warehouse** (EDW). To extract and transform this data we need a message queuing system to deal with spikes in traffic, endpoints being temporarily unavailable, and other issues that may affect the availability and scalability of this part of the system.

Message queues also provide decoupling between producers and consumers of messages. This allows for better scalability by partitioning our messages into different topics/queues.

Finally, using message queues we can have location-agnostic services, not caring about where the message producers sit, and provide interoperability between different systems.

In the message queuing world, the most popular systems in production at the time of writing this book are RabbitMQ, ActiveMQ, and Kafka. We will provide a small overview of them before we dive into our use case to bring all of them together.

Apache ActiveMQ

As explained best in Wikipedia, Apache ActiveMQ is an open source message broker written in Java together with a full **Java Message Service (JMS)** client.

It is the most mature implementation out of the three that we examine here and has a long history of successful production deployments. Commercial support is offered by many companies including Red Hat.

It is a fairly simple queuing system to set up and manage. It is based on the JMS client protocol and is the tool of choice for Java Enterprise Edition systems.

RabbitMQ

RabbitMQ on the other hand is written in Erlang and based on the AMQP protocol. AMQP is significantly more powerful and complicated than JMS as it allows for peer to peer messaging, request/reply, and publish/subscribe models for one-to-one or one-to-many message consuming.

RabbitMQ has gained popularity in the past five years and is nowadays the most searched for queuing system.

RabbitMQ's architecture is outlined below:

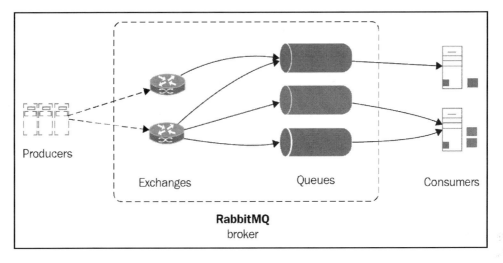

Scaling in RabbitMQ systems is performed by creating a cluster of RabbitMQ servers.

Clusters share data and state, which are replicated, but message queues are distinct per node. To achieve high availability we can also replicate queues in different nodes.

Apache Kafka

Kafka on the other hand is a queuing system that was first developed at LinkedIn for its own internal purposes. It is written in Scala and is designed from the ground up for horizontal scalability and the best performance possible.

Focusing on performance is a key differentiator for Apache Kafka but it means that in order to achieve performance we need to sacrifice something. Messages in Kafka don't hold unique IDs but are addressed by their offset in the log. Apache Kafka consumers are not tracked by the system; it is the responsibility of the application design to do so. Message ordering is implemented at the partition level and it is the responsibility of the consumer to identify if a message has been delivered already.

Exactly once semantics were introduced in version 0.11 and are part of the latest 1.0 release so that now messages can be both strictly ordered within a partition and always arrive exactly once at each consumer:

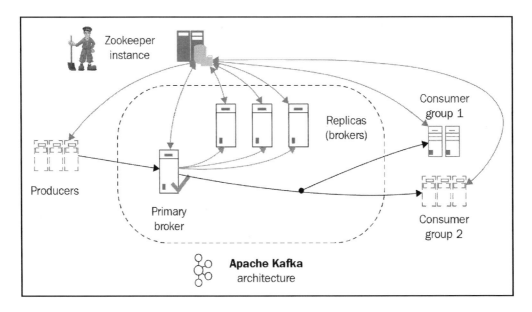

Data warehousing

Using a message queuing system is just the first step in our data pipeline design. At the other end of message queuing we would typically have a data warehouse to process the vast amount of data that arrives. There are numerous options there and it is not the main focus of this book to go over these or compare them but we will skim through two of the most widely used options, both from the Apache foundation: Apache Hadoop, and Apache Spark.

Apache Hadoop

The first, and probably still most widely used, framework for big data processing is Apache Hadoop. Its foundation is **Hadoop Distributed File System (HDFS)**. Developed at Yahoo! in the 2000's, it originally served as an open source alternative to **Google File System (GFS)**, a distributed file system that was serving Google's needs for distributed storage of its search index.

Hadoop also implemented a MapReduce alternative to Google's proprietary system, Hadoop MapReduce. Together with HDFS, they constitute a framework for distributed storage and computations. Written in Java, with bindings for most programming languages and many projects that provide abstracted and simple functionality, sometimes based on SQL querying, it is a system that can reliably be used to store and process TBs or even PBs of data.

In later versions, Hadoop became more modularized by introducing **Yet Another Resource Negotiator (YARN)** which provides the abstraction for applications to be developed on top of Hadoop. This has enabled several applications to be deployed on top of Hadoop such as Storm, Tez, Open MPI, Giraph, and of course Apache Spark as we will see in the next sections.

Hadoop MapReduce is a batch-oriented system, meaning that it relies on processing data in batches and is not designed for real-time use cases.

Apache Spark

Apache Spark is a cluster-computing framework from the University of California, Berkeley's AMPLab. Spark is not a substitute for the complete Hadoop ecosystem but mostly for the MapReduce aspect of a Hadoop cluster. Whereas Hadoop MapReduce uses on-disk batch operations to process data, Spark uses both in-memory and on-disk operations. As expected, it is faster with datasets that fit in memory and this is why it is more useful for real-time streaming applications but it can also be used with ease for datasets that don't fit in memory.

Apache Spark can run on top of HDFS using YARN or in a standalone mode as shown in the following diagram:

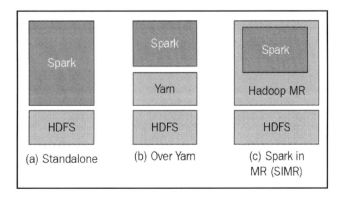

Reference: https://intellipaat.com/tutorial/spark-tutorial/

This means that in some cases (such as the one that we will use in our use case below) we can completely ditch Hadoop for Spark if our problem is really well defined and constrained within Spark's capabilities.

Spark can be up to 100 times faster than Hadoop MapReduce for in-memory operations. Spark offers user-friendly APIs for Scala (its native language), Java, Python, and Spark SQL (a variation of the SQL92 specification). Both Spark and MapReduce are resilient to failure. Spark uses **resilient distributed datasets (RDDs)** which are distributed across the whole cluster.

As we can see from the overall Spark architecture as follows, we can have several different modules of Spark working together for different needs, from SQL querying to streaming and machine learning libraries.

Spark comparison with Hadoop MapReduce

The Hadoop MapReduce framework is more commonly compared to Apache Spark, a newer technology that aims to solve problems in a similar problem space. Some of their most important attributes are summarized in the table that follows:

	Hadoop MapReduce	**Apache Spark**
Written in	Java	Scala
Programming model	MapReduce	Resilient distributed dataset
Client bindings	Most high-level languages	Java, Scala, Python
Ease of use	Moderate, with high-level abstractions (Pig, Hive, and so on)	Good
Performance	High throughput in batch	High throughput in Streaming and batch mode
Uses	Disk (I/O bound)	Memory, degrading performance if disk is needed
Typical node	Medium	Medium-large

As we can see from the preceding comparison, there are pros and cons for both technologies. Spark has arguably better performance, especially in problems that use fewer nodes. On the other hand, Hadoop is a mature framework with excellent tooling on top of it to cover almost every use case.

MongoDB as a data warehouse

Apache Hadoop is often described as the 800 lb gorilla in the room of big data frameworks. Apache Spark on the other hand, is more like a 200 lb cheetah for its speed and agility and performance characteristics, which allows it to work well in a subset of the problems Hadoop aims to solve.

MongoDB, on the other hand, can be described as the MySQL equivalent in the NoSQL world because of its adoption and ease of use. MongoDB also offers an aggregation framework, MapReduce capabilities, and horizontal scaling using sharding, which is essentially data partitioning at the database level.

So naturally, some people have been asking, Why not use MongoDB as our data warehouse, simplifying our architecture?

This is a pretty compelling argument and it may or may not be the case that it makes sense to use MongoDB as a data warehouse.

The advantages of such a decision are:

- Simpler architecture
- Less need for message queues, reducing latency in our system

The disadvantages:

- MongoDB's MapReduce framework is not a replacement for Hadoop's MapReduce. Even though they both follow the same philosophy, Hadoop can scale to accommodate larger workloads.
- Scaling MongoDB's document storage using sharding will hit a wall at some point. Whereas Yahoo! has reported using 42,000 servers at its largest Hadoop cluster, the largest MongoDB commercial deployments stand at 5 billion (Craigslist) compared to 600 nodes and PBs of data for Baidu, the internet giant dominating, among others, the Chinese internet search market.

There is more than an order of magnitude of difference in terms of scaling:

- MongoDB is mainly designed around being a real-time querying database based on stored data on disk, whereas MapReduce is designed around using batches and Spark is designed around using streams of data

Big data use case

Putting all of this into action, we will develop a fully working system using a data source, a Kafka message broker, an Apache Spark cluster on top of HDFS feeding a Hive table, and a MongoDB database.

Our Kafka message broker will ingest data from an API, streaming market data for an XMR/BTC currency pair. This data will be passed on to an Apache Spark algorithm on HDFS to calculate the price for the next ticker timestamp based on:

- The corpus of historical prices already stored on HDFS
- The streaming market data arriving from the API

This predicted price will then be stored in MongoDB using the MongoDB Connector for Hadoop.

MongoDB will also receive data straight from the Kafka message broker, storing it in a special collection with the document expiration date set to 1 minute. This collection will hold the latest orders with the goal of being used by our system to buy or sell, using the signal coming from the Spark ML system.

So for example, if the price is currently 10 and I have a bid for 9.5 but I expect the price to go down at the next market tick, then the system would wait. If we expect the price to go up in the next market tick then the system would increase the price to 10.01 to match the price in the next ticker.

Similarly, if the price is 10 and I bid for 10.5 but I expect the price to go down, I would adjust to 9.99 to make sure I don't overpay for it. But if the price is expected to go up, I would immediately buy to make a profit at the next market tick.

Schematically, our architecture looks like this:

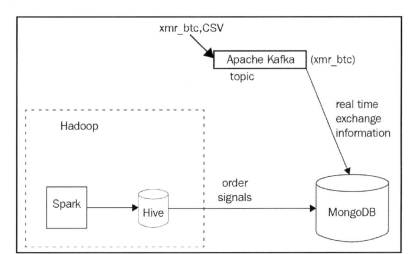

The API is simulated by posting JSON messages to a Kafka topic named xmr_btc. On the other end, we have a Kafka consumer importing real-time data to MongoDB.

We also have another Kafka consumer importing data to Hadoop, to be picked up by our algorithms, which sends recommendation data (signals) to a Hive table.

Finally, we export data from the Hive table into MongoDB.

Kafka setup

The first step in setting up the environment for our big data use case is to establish a Kafka node. Kafka is essentially a **first in, first-out** (**FIFO**) queue, so we will use the simplest single node (broker) setup. Kafka organizes data using topics, producers, consumers, and brokers.

Important Kafka terminology:

- A **broker** is essentially a node
- A **producer** is a process writing data to the message queue
- A **consumer** is a process reading data from the message queue
- A **topic** is the specific queue that we write to and read data from

A Kafka topic is further subdivided into a number of partitions. We can split data from a particular topic into multiple brokers (nodes) both when we write to the topic and also when we read our data at the other end of the queue.

After installing Kafka on our local machine or any cloud provider of our choice (there are excellent tutorials for EC2 to be found just a search away) we can create a topic using this single command:

```
$ kafka-topics --create --zookeeper localhost:2181 --replication-factor 1
--partitions 1 --topic xmr-btc
Created topic "xmr-btc".
```

This will create a new topic called `xmr-btc`.

> Deleting the topic is similar to creating by using:
> ```
> $ kafka-topics --delete --zookeeper localhost:2181 --
> topic xmr-btc
> ```

We can then get a list of all topics by issuing the following:

```
$ kafka-topics --list --zookeeper localhost:2181
xmr-btc
```

We can then create a command-line producer for our topic, just to test that we can send messages to the queue, like this:

```
$ kafka-console-producer --broker-list localhost:9092 --topic xmr-btc
```

Data on every line will be sent as a string encoded message to our topic and we can end the process by sending a SIGINT signal (typically *Ctrl + C*).

Afterwards, we can view the messages that are waiting in our queue by spinning up a consumer:

```
$ kafka-console-consumer --zookeeper localhost:2181 --topic xmr-btc --from-
beginning
```

This consumer will read all messages in our `xmr-btc` topic, starting from the beginning of history. This is useful for our test purposes, but we will change this configuration in real-world applications.

 You will keep seeing `zookeeper` in addition to `kafka` mentioned in the commands. Apache Zookeeper comes together with Apache Kafka and it's a centralized service that is used internally by Kafka for maintaining configuration information, naming, providing distributed synchronization, and providing group services.

Now have our broker set up, we can use the code at `https://github.com/agiamas/mastering-mongodb/tree/master/chapter_9` to start reading (consuming) and writing (producing) messages to the queue. For our purposes, we are using the `ruby-kafka` gem, developed by Zendesk.

For simplicity, we are using a single class to read from a file stored on disk and write to our Kafka queue.

Our `produce` method will be used to write messages to Kafka:

```
def produce
  options = { converters: :numeric, headers: true }
   CSV.foreach('xmr_btc.csv', options) do |row|
    json_line = JSON.generate(row.to_hash)
    @kafka.deliver_message(json_line, topic: 'xmr-btc')
  end
end
```

Our `consume` method will read messages from Kafka:

```
def consume
  consumer = @kafka.consumer(group_id: 'xmr-consumers')
  consumer.subscribe('xmr-btc', start_from_beginning: true)
  trap('TERM') { consumer.stop }
  consumer.each_message(automatically_mark_as_processed: false) do
|message|
    puts message.value
    if valid_json?(message.value)
      byebug
      MongoExchangeClient.new.insert(message.value)
      consumer.mark_message_as_processed(message)
    end
  end
  consumer.stop
end
```

Notice that we are using the consumer group API feature (added in Kafka 0.9) to get multiple consumers to access a single topic by assigning each partition to a single consumer. In the event of a consumer failure, its partitions will be reallocated to the remaining members of the group.

The next step is to write these messages to MongoDB.

First, we create our collection so that our documents expire after 1 minute. From the `mongo` shell:

```
> use exchange_data
> db.xmr_btc.createIndex( { "createdAt": 1 }, { expireAfterSeconds: 60 })
{
"createdCollectionAutomatically" : true,
"numIndexesBefore" : 1,
"numIndexesAfter" : 2,
"ok" : 1
}
```

This way we create a new database called `exchange_data` with a new collection called `xmr_btc` that has auto expiration after 60 seconds. For MongoDB to auto-expire documents, we need to provide a field with a `datetime` value to compare its value against the current server time. In our case this is the `createdAt` field.

For our use case, we will use the low-level mongo-ruby-driver. The code for `MongoExchangeClient` is as follows:

```
class MongoExchangeClient
  def initialize
    @collection = Mongo::Client.new([ '127.0.0.1:27017' ], database:
:exchange_data).database[:xmr_btc]
  end
  def insert(document)
    document = JSON.parse(document)
    document['createdAt'] = Time.now
    @collection.insert_one(document)
  end
end
```

This client connects to our local database, sets the `createdAt` field for the TTL document expiration, and saves the message to our collection.

With this setup, we can write messages to Kafka, read them at the other end of the queue, and write them into our MongoDB collection.

Hadoop setup

We can install Hadoop and use a single node for the use case in this chapter using the instructions from Apache Hadoop's website at: `https://hadoop.apache.org/docs/stable/hadoop-project-dist/hadoop-common/SingleCluster.html`.

After following these steps, we can browse the HDFS files in our local machine at: `http://localhost:50070/explorer.html#/`.

Assuming that our signals data is written in HDFS under the `/user/<username>/signals` directory, we will use the MongoDB Connector for Hadoop to export and import it into MongoDB.

MongoDB Connector for Hadoop is the officially supported library, allowing MongoDB data files or MongoDB backup files in BSON to be used as source or destination for Hadoop MapReduce tasks.

This means that we can also easily export to, and import data from, MongoDB when we are using higher-level Hadoop ecosystem tools such as Pig (a procedural high-level language), Hive (a SQL-like high-level language), and Spark (a cluster-computing framework).

Steps

The steps to set up Hadoop are:

1. Download JAR from the Maven repository at: `http://repo1.maven.org/maven2/org/mongodb/mongo-hadoop/mongo-hadoop-core/2.0.2/`.

2. Download `mongo-java-driver`: `https://oss.sonatype.org/content/repositories/releases/org/mongodb/mongodb-driver/3.5.0/`.

3. Create a directory (in our case named `mongo_lib`) and copy these two JARs in there with the following command:

   ```
   export
   HADOOP_CLASSPATH=$HADOOP_CLASSPATH:<path_to_directory>/mongo_lib/
   ```

Alternatively, we can copy these JARs under the `share/hadoop/common/` directory. As these JARs will need to be available in every node, for clustered deployment it's easier to use Hadoop's `DistributedCache` to distribute the JARs to all nodes.

4. The next step is to install Hive from: `https://hive.apache.org/downloads.html`.

    For this example, we used a MySQL server for Hive's metastore data. This can be a local MySQL server for development and is recommended to be a remote server for production environments.

5. Once we have Hive set up we just run the following:

    ```
    > hive
    ```

6. Then we add the three JARs (`mongo-hadoop-core`, `mongo-hadoop-driver`, and `mongo-hadoop-hive`) that we downloaded earlier:

    ```
    hive> add jar /Users/dituser/code/hadoop-2.8.1/mongo-hadoop-
    core-2.0.2.jar;
    Added [/Users/dituser/code/hadoop-2.8.1/mongo-hadoop-
    core-2.0.2.jar] to class path
    Added resources: [/Users/dituser/code/hadoop-2.8.1/mongo-hadoop-
    core-2.0.2.jar]
    hive> add jar /Users/dituser/code/hadoop-2.8.1/mongodb-
    driver-3.5.0.jar;
    Added [/Users/dituser/code/hadoop-2.8.1/mongodb-driver-3.5.0.jar]
    to class path
    Added resources: [/Users/dituser/code/hadoop-2.8.1/mongodb-
    driver-3.5.0.jar]
    hive> add jar /Users/dituser/code/hadoop-2.8.1/mongo-hadoop-
    hive-2.0.2.jar;
    Added [/Users/dituser/code/hadoop-2.8.1/mongo-hadoop-
    hive-2.0.2.jar] to class path
    Added resources: [/Users/dituser/code/hadoop-2.8.1/mongo-hadoop-
    hive-2.0.2.jar]
    hive>
    ```

And then assuming our data is in the table exchanges:

customerid	int
pair	string
time	timestamp
recommendation	int

We can also use Gradle or Maven to download the JARs in our local project. If we only need MapReduce, then we just download the mongo-hadoop-core JAR. For Pig/Hive/Streaming and so on, we must download the appropriate JARs from:
http://repo1.maven.org/maven2/org/mongodb/mongo-hadoop/.
Useful Hive commands:
show databases;
create table exchanges(customerId int, pair String, time TIMESTAMP, recommendation int);

7. Now that we are all set, we can create a MongoDB collection backed by our local Hive data:

```
hive> create external table exchanges_mongo (objectid STRING,
customerid INT,pair STRING,time STRING, recommendation INT) STORED
BY 'com.mongodb.hadoop.hive.MongoStorageHandler' WITH
SERDEPROPERTIES('mongo.columns.mapping'='{"objectid":"_id",
"customerid":"customerid","pair":"pair","time":"Timestamp",
"recommendation":"recommendation"}')
tblproperties('mongo.uri'='mongodb://localhost:27017/exchange_data.
xmr_btc');
```

8. Finally, we can copy all data from the exchanges' Hive table into MongoDB as follows:

```
hive> Insert into table exchanges_mongo select * from exchanges;
```

This way, we have established a pipeline between Hadoop and MongoDB using Hive, without any external server.

Hadoop to MongoDB pipeline

An alternative to using the MongoDB Connector for Hadoop is to use the programming language of our choice to export data from Hadoop and then write into MongoDB using the low-level driver or an ODM as described in previous chapters.

For example in Ruby there are a few options:

- WebHDFS on GitHub, which uses the WebHDFS or the HttpFS Hadoop API to fetch data from HDFS
- System calls, using the Hadoop command-line tool and Ruby's `system()` call

Whereas in Python we can use:

- HdfsCLI, which uses the WebHDFS or the HttpFS Hadoop API
- libhdfs, which uses a JNI-based native C wrapped around the HDFS Java client

All of these options require an intermediate server between our Hadoop infrastructure and our MongoDB server but on the other hand allow for more flexibility in the **extract transform load** (**ETL**) process of exporting/importing data.

Spark to MongoDB

MongoDB also offers a tool to directly query Spark clusters and export data to MongoDB. Spark is a cluster computing framework that typically runs as a YARN module in Hadoop, but can also run independently on top of other filesystems.

MongoDB Spark Connector can read and write to MongoDB collections from Spark using Java, Scala, Python, and R. It can also use aggregation and run SQL queries on MongoDB data after creating a temporary view for the dataset backed by Spark.

Using Scala, we can also use Spark Streaming, the Spark framework for data streaming applications built on top of Apache Spark.

References

- https://www.cisco.com/c/en/us/solutions/collateral/service-provider/visual-networking-index-vni/vni-hyperconnectivity-wp.html
- http://www.ibmbigdatahub.com/infographic/four-vs-big-data
- https://spreadstreet.io/database/
- http://mattturck.com/wp-content/uploads/2017/05/Matt-Turck-FirstMark-2017-Big-Data-Landscape.png
- http://mattturck.com/bigdata2017/
- https://dzone.com/articles/hadoop-t-etl
- https://www.cloudamqp.com/blog/2014-12-03-what-is-message-queuing.html
- https://www.linkedin.com/pulse/jms-vs-amqp-eran-shaham
- https://www.cloudamqp.com/blog/2017-01-09-apachekafka-vs-rabbitmq.html
- https://trends.google.com/trends/explore?date=all&q=ActiveMQ,RabbitMQ,ZeroMQ
- https://thenextweb.com/insider/2017/03/06/the-incredible-growth-of-the-internet-over-the-past-five-years-explained-in-detail/#.tnw_ALaObAUG
- https://static.googleusercontent.com/media/research.google.com/en//archive/mapreduce-osdi04.pdf
- https://en.wikipedia.org/wiki/Apache_Hadoop#Architecture
- https://wiki.apache.org/hadoop/PoweredByYarn
- https://www.slideshare.net/cloudera/introduction-to-yarn-and-mapreduce-2?next_slideshow=1
- https://www.mongodb.com/blog/post/mongodb-live-at-craigslist
- https://www.mongodb.com/blog/post/mongodb-at-baidu-powering-100-apps-across-600-nodes-at-pb-scale
- http://www.datamation.com/data-center/hadoop-vs.-spark-the-new-age-of-big-data.html
- https://www.mongodb.com/mongodb-data-warehouse-time-series-and-device-history-data-medtronic-transcript
- https://www.mongodb.com/blog/post/mongodb-debuts-in-gartner-s-magic-quadrant-for-data-warehouse-and-data-management-solutions-for-analytics
- https://www.infoworld.com/article/3014440/big-data/five-things-you-need-to-know-about-hadoop-v-apache-spark.html
- https://www.quora.com/What-is-the-difference-between-Hadoop-and-Spark

- https://iamsoftwareengineer.wordpress.com/2015/12/15/hadoop-vs-spark/?iframe=truetheme_preview=true
- https://www.infoq.com/articles/apache-kafka
- https://stackoverflow.com/questions/42151544/is-there-any-reason-to-use-rabbitmq-over-kafka
- https://medium.com/@jaykreps/exactly-once-support-in-apache-kafka-55e1fdd0a35f
- https://www.slideshare.net/sbaltagi/apache-kafka-vs-rabbitmq-fit-for-purpose-decision-tree
- https://techbeacon.com/what-apache-kafka-why-it-so-popular-should-you-use-it
- https://github.com/zendesk/ruby-kafka
- http://zhongyaonan.com/hadoop-tutorial/setting-up-hadoop-2-6-on-mac-osx-yosemite.html
- https://github.com/mtth/hdfs
- http://wesmckinney.com/blog/outlook-for-2017/
- http://wesmckinney.com/blog/python-hdfs-interfaces/
- https://acadgild.com/blog/how-to-export-data-from-hive-to-mongodb/
- https://sookocheff.com/post/kafka/kafka-in-a-nutshell/
- https://www.codementor.io/jadianes/spark-mllib-logistic-regression-du107neto
- http://ondra-m.github.io/ruby-spark/
- https://amodernstory.com/2015/03/29/installing-hive-on-mac/
- https://www.infoq.com/articles/apache-spark-introduction
- https://cs.stanford.edu/~matei/papers/2010/hotcloud_spark.pdf

Summary

In this chapter, we learned about the big data landscape and how MongoDB compares with and fares against message queuing systems and data warehousing technologies. Using a big data use case, we learned how to integrate MongoDB with Kafka and Hadoop from a practical perspective.

In the next chapter, we will turn to replication and cluster operations, and discuss replica sets, the internals of elections, and the setting up and administration of our MongoDB cluster.

10
Replication

Replication has been one of the most useful features of MongoDB since the very early days. In general, replication refers to the process of synchronizing data across different servers.

The upsides for replication:

- Protect from data loss
- High availability of data
- Disaster recovery
- Avoiding downtime for maintenance
- Scaling reads since we can read from multiple servers
- Scaling writes (only if we can write to multiple servers)

In this chapter, we will also discuss cluster operations on a replica set. Administration tasks such as maintenance, resyncing a member, changing the oplog size, reconfiguring a member, and chained replication will be covered later in this chapter.

Replication

There are different approaches to replication. The approach MongoDB takes is logical replication with a master-slave, which we will explain in more detail further on in this chapter.

Logical or physical replication

In logical replication, we have our master/primary server performing operations and then the slave/secondary server tails a queue of operations from the master and applies the same operations in the same order. In the example of MongoDB, the oplog (operations log) keeps a track of operations that have happened on the primary server and applies them in the exact same order on the secondary server.

Logical replication is useful for a wide array of applications such as information sharing, data analysis, and **Online Analytical Processing (OLAP)** reporting.

In physical replication, data gets copied on the physical level, at a lower level than database operations. This means that we are not applying the operations, but copying the bytes that were affected by these operations. It also means that we can gain better efficiency since we are using low level structures to transfer data. We can also be sure that the state of the database is exactly the same, since they are identical, byte for byte.

What is typically missing from physical replication is knowledge about the database structure, which means that it is harder (if not impossible) to copy some collections from a database and ignore others.

Physical replication is typically suited to more rare circumstances like disaster recovery where a full and exact copy of everything including data, indexes, the internal state of the database in a journal, and redoing/undoing logs is of crucial importance to bringing the application back to the exact state it was.

Replication is the process of synchronizing data across multiple servers. Replication provides redundancy and increases data availability with multiple copies of data on different database servers. Replication protects a database from the loss of a single server. Replication also allows you to recover from hardware failure and service interruptions. With additional copies of the data, you can dedicate one to disaster recovery, reporting, or backup.

Different high availability types

In high availability, we have several configurations that we can use. Our primary server is called the **hot server** as it can process each and every request coming in.

Our secondary server can be any of these states:

- Cold
- Warm
- Hot

A secondary cold server is a server that is there just in case the primary server goes offline, without any expectation of it holding the data and state that the primary server had.

A secondary warm server receives periodic updates of data from the primary server but is typically not entirely up to date with the primary server. It can be used for some non real-time analytics reporting, to offload the main server, but will typically not be able to pick up the transactional load of the primary server if it goes down.

A secondary hot server always keeps an up to date copy of the data and state from the primary server. It usually waits in a *hot standby* state ready to take over when the primary server goes down.

MongoDB has both the hot and warm server type of functionality as we will explore in the following sections.

 Most database systems employ a similar notion of primary /secondary servers so, conceptually, everything from MongoDB gets applied there too.

Architectural overview

MongoDB's replication can be seen in the following diagram:

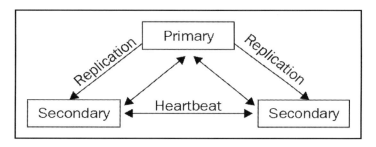

https://docs.mongodb.com/master/replication/

The primary server is the only one that can take writes at any time. The secondary servers are in a hot standby state, ready to take over if the primary server fails. Once the primary server fails, an election takes place regarding which secondary server will become primary.

We can also have arbiter nodes. Arbiter nodes do not hold any data and their sole purpose is only to participate in the election process.

We must always have an odd number of nodes (including arbiters). Three, five, and seven are all fine so that in the event of the primary (or more servers) failing we have a majority of votes in the election process.

When other members of a replica set don't hear from the primary for more than 10 seconds (configurable), an eligible secondary will start the election process to vote for a new primary. The first secondary to hold the election and win the majority will become the new primary. All remaining servers will now replicate from the new primary server, keeping their roles as secondaries but syncing up from the new primary.

 A replica set can have up to 50 members, but only up to seven of them can vote in the election process.

The setup for our replica set after the new election will be as follows:

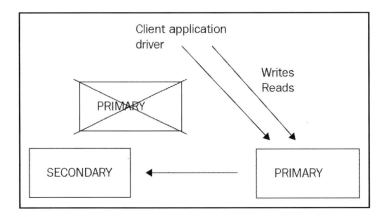

How do elections work?

All servers in a replica set maintain regular communication with every other member via a heartbeat. The heartbeat is a small packet sent regularly to verify that all members are operating normally.

Secondary members also communicate with the primary to get the latest updates from the oplog and apply them to their own data.

 The information here refers to the latest replication election protocol, version 1, which was introduced in MongoDB v3.2.

Schematically, we can see how this works:

When the primary member goes down, all secondaries will miss a heartbeat or more. They will be waiting up until `settings.electionTimeoutMillis` time passes (default 10 seconds) and then the secondaries start one or more rounds of elections to find the new primary.

For a server to be elected as primary from the secondaries it must have two properties:

- Belong in a group of voters that have 50%+1 of the votes
- Be the most up-to-date secondary in this group

In the simple example of three servers with one vote each, once we lose the primary, the other two servers will each have one vote, so in total two-thirds, and as such the one with the most up-to-date oplog will be elected primary.

Now consider a more complex setup:

- Seven servers (one primary, six secondaries)
- One vote each

We lose the primary and the six remaining servers have network connectivity issues resulting in a network partition:

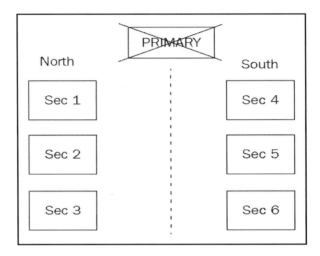

Partition North:

- Three servers (one vote each)

Partition South:

- Three servers (one vote each)

Each partition doesn't have any knowledge of what happened to the rest of the servers. Now when they hold elections no partition can establish majority as they have three out of seven votes. No primary will get elected from either partition.

This problem can be overcome by having, for example, one server having three votes.

Now our overall cluster setup looks as follows:

- Server #1 - one vote
- Server #2 - one vote
- Server #3 - one vote
- Server #4 - one vote
- Server #5 - one vote
- Server #6 - one vote
- Server #7 - three votes

After losing Server #1, now our partitions look as follows:

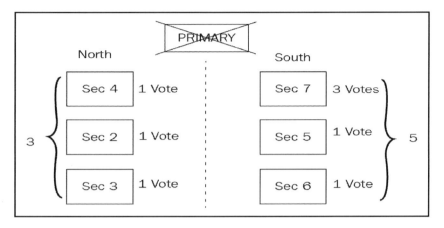

Partition North:

- Server #2 - one vote
- Server #3 - one vote
- Server #4 - one vote

Partition South:

- Server #5 - one vote
- Server #6 - one vote
- Server #7 - three votes

Partition South has three servers with a total of five out of nine votes. The secondary among servers #5 ,#6, and #7 that is most up to date according to its oplog entries will be elected as primary.

What is the use case for a replica set?

MongoDB offers most of the advantages for using a replica set and then some more:

- Protecting from data loss
- High availability of data
- Disaster recovery

- Avoiding downtime for maintenance
- Scaling reads since we can read from multiple servers
- Helping design for geographically dispersed services
- Data privacy

The most notable item missing from the list in the introduction to our chapter is scaling writes. This is because in MongoDB, we can only have one primary and only this primary can take writes from our application server.

When we want to scale write performance, we typically design and implement sharding, which is the topic of the next chapter.

Two interesting properties of the way MongoDB replication is implemented are geographically dispersed services and data privacy.

It is not uncommon for our application servers to be located in multiple data centers across the globe. Using replication, we can have a secondary server as close to the application server as possible. What this means is that our reads will be fast, as if it was local, and we will get a latency performance penalty just for our writes. This, of course, requires some planning at the application level so that we maintain two different pools of connections to our database which can be easily done either using the official MongoDB drivers or when using higher level ODMs.

The second interesting property of MongoDB's replication design is implementing data privacy. When we have servers geographically dispersed across different data centers, we can enable replication per database. By keeping a database out of the replication process we can make sure that our data stays confined in the data center that we need. We can also set up different replication schemas per database in the same MongoDB server so that we have multiple replication strategies according to our data privacy needs, excluding some servers from our replica sets if it is not allowed by our data privacy regulations.

Setting up a replica set

In this section, we will go through the most common deployment procedures to set up a replica set.

Converting a standalone server to a replica set

To convert a standalone server to a replica set, we first need to cleanly shut down the mongo server:

```
> use admin
> db.shutdownServer()
```

Then we start the server with the `--replSet` configuration option via the command line or using a configuration file, as explained in the next section.

First, we connect via the mongo shell to the new replica set enabled instance as follows:

```
> rs.initiate()
```

Now, we have the first server of our replica set. We can add the other servers (which must have also been started with `--replSet`) by using the mongo shell as follows:

```
> rs.add("<hostname><:port>")
```

> Double check the replica set configuration, using `rs.conf()`. Verify the replica set status, using `rs.status()`.

Creating a replica set

Starting a MongoDB server as part of a replica set is as easy as setting it in the configuration via the command line:

```
> mongod --replSet "xmr_cluster"
```

This is fine for development purposes. For production environments it's recommended that we use a configuration file instead:

```
> mongod --config <path-to-config>
```

Here, `<path-to-config>` can be as follows:

```
/etc/mongod.conf
```

This configuration file has to be in YAML format.

YAML does not support tabs. Convert tabs to spaces using your editor of choice.

A sample, simple as possible configuration file looks as follows:

```
systemLog:
  destination: file
  path: "/var/log/mongodb/mongod.log"
  logAppend: true
storage:
  journal:
      enabled: true
processManagement:
  fork: true
net:
  bindIp: 127.0.0.1
  port: 27017
replication:
  oplogSizeMB: <int>
  replSetName: <string>
```

Root level options define the section which leaf level options apply to, by nesting.

Regarding replication, the mandatory options are `oplogSizeMB` (the oplog size for the member in MB) and `replSetName` (the replica set name, such as `xmr_cluster`).

We can also set the following on the same level as `replSetName`:

```
secondaryIndexPrefetch: <string>
```

This is only available for the MMAPv1 storage engine and refers to the indexes on secondaries that will get loaded into memory before applying operations from the oplog.

It defaults to `all` and available options are `none` and `_id_only` to load no indexes into memory and only load the default index created on `_id` fields.

```
enableMajorityReadConcern: <boolean>
```

This is the configuration setting to enable read preference of `majority` for this member.

After we have started all replica set processes on different nodes, we log in to one of the nodes using `mongo` from the command line with the appropriate `host:port`.

Then we need to initiate the cluster from one member.

If we use configuration files it is as follows:

```
> rs.initiate()
```

Or we can pass in configuration as a document parameter:

```
> rs.initiate( {
    _id : "xmr_cluster",
    members: [ { _id : 0, host : "host:port" } ]
})
```

We can verify that the cluster got initiated by using `rs.conf()` in the shell.

Following that, we add each other member to our replica set using the `host:port` that we have defined in our networking setup:

```
> rs.add("host2:port2")
> rs.add("host3:port3")
```

The minimum number of servers we must use for a HA replica set is 3. We could replace one of the servers with an arbiter but this is not recommended. Once we add all servers and wait a bit, we can check the status of our cluster by using `rs.status()`.

Oplog by default will be 5% of free disk space. If we want to define it when we create our replica set we can do so by passing the command-line parameter `--oplogSizeMB` or `replication.oplogSizeMB` in our configuration file. An oplog size can not be more than 50 GB.

Read preference

By default, all writes and reads go/come from the primary server. Secondary servers are replicating data but not used for querying.

In some cases, it may be beneficial to change this and start taking reads from secondaries.

MongoDB official drivers support five levels of read preference:

Read preference mode	Description
primary	Default mode. All operations read from the current replica set primary.
primaryPreferred	In most situations, operations read from the primary but if it is unavailable, operations read from secondary members.
secondary	All operations read from the secondary members of the replica set.
secondaryPreferred	In most situations, operations read from secondary members but if no secondary members are available, operations read from the primary.
nearest	Operations read from member of the replica set with the least network latency, irrespective of the member's type.

Using any read preference other than primary can be beneficial for asynchronous operations that are not extremely time sensitive. Reporting servers, for example, can take reads from secondaries instead of the primary as we may be fine with a small delay in our aggregations data at the benefit of incurring more read load on our primary server.

Geographically distributed applications will also benefit by reading from secondaries as these will have significantly lower latency.

Although probably counter intuitive, just changing the read preference from primary to secondary will not significantly increase the total read capacity of our cluster. This is because all members of our cluster are taking roughly the same write load from clients' writes and replication for primary and secondaries respectively.

More importantly though, reading from a secondary may return stale data which has to be dealt with at the application level. Reading from different secondaries that may have variable replication lag as compared to our primary writes may result in reading documents out of their insertion order (non-monotonic reads).

With all the preceding caveats, it is still a good idea to test reading from secondaries if our application design supports it. An additional configuration option that can help us avoid reading stale data is as follows:

```
maxStalenessSeconds
```

Based on a coarse estimation from each secondary as to how far behind the primary it is, we can set this to a value of 90 (seconds) or more to avoid reading stale data.

Given that secondaries know how far behind they are from the primary but don't accurately or aggressively estimate it, this should be treated as an approximation rather than basing our design on this setting.

Write concern

Write operations in MongoDB replica sets will, by default, get acknowledged once the write has been acknowledged by the primary server. If we want to change this behavior we can do it in two different ways.

We can request a different write concern per operation in cases where we want to make sure that a write has propagated to multiple members of our replica set before marking it as completed as follows:

```
> db.mongo_books.insert(
  { name: "Mastering MongoDB", isbn: "1001" },
  { writeConcern: { w: 2, wtimeout: 5000 } }
)
```

In the preceding example, we are waiting for the write to be confirmed by two servers (primary plus any one of the secondaries). We are also setting a timeout of 5000 milliseconds to avoid our write from blocking in cases where the network is slow or we just don't have enough servers to acknowledge the request.

We can also change the default write concern across the entire replica set, as follows:

```
> cfg = rs.conf()
> cfg.settings.getLastErrorDefaults = { w: "majority", wtimeout: 5000 }
> rs.reconfig(cfg)
```

Here, we set the write concern to majority with a timeout, again, of 5 seconds. The write concern majority makes sure that our writes will propagate to at least *n/2+1* servers, where *n* is the number of our replica set members.

> The write concern majority is useful if we have a read preference of majority as well, as it ensures that every write with w: 'majority' will also be visible with the same read preference.
>
> If we set w>1 it's useful to also set wtimeout:<milliseconds> together with it. wtimeout will return from our write operation once the timeout has been reached, thus not blocking our client for an indefinite period of time.
>
> It's recommended to set j: true as well. j: true will wait for our write operation to be written to the journal before acknowledging it. w>1 together with j: true will wait for the number of servers that we have specified to write to the journal before acknowledging.

Custom write concern

We can also identify our replica set members by different tags (that is, reporting, east-coast servers, HQ servers) and specify a custom write concern per operation.

Using the usual procedure of connecting to the primary via mongo shell as follows:

```
> conf = rs.conf()
> conf.members[0].tags = { "location": "UK", "use": "production",
"location_uk":"true"  }
> conf.members[1].tags = { "location": "UK", "use": "reporting",
"location_uk":"true"  }
> conf.members[2].tags = { "location": "Ireland", "use": "production"  }
```

We can now set a custom write concern as follows:

```
> conf.settings = { getLastErrorModes: { UKWrites : { "location_uk": 2} } }
```

And after applying it as follows:

```
> rs.reconfig(conf)
```

We can now start using it by setting `writeConcern` in our writes as follows:

```
> db.mongo_books.insert({<our insert object>}, { writeConcern: { w:
"UKWrites" } })
```

This means that our write will only be acknowledged if the `UKWrites` write concern is satisfied, which in turn will be satisfied by at least two servers with tag `location_uk` verifying it. Since we only have two servers located in the UK, we can make sure that with this custom write concern we have written our data to all of our UK-based servers.

Priority settings for replica set members

MongoDB allows us to set different priority levels for each member. This allows for some interesting applications and topologies to be implemented.

To change the priority after we have set up our cluster, we have to connect using the mongo shell to our primary and get the configuration object (hereby named as `cfg`):

```
> cfg = rs.conf()
```

Then we can change the members subdocument `priority` attribute to the value of our choice:

```
> cfg.members[0].priority = 0.778
> cfg.members[1].priority = 999.9999
```

Default `priority` is 1 for every member. Priority can be set from 0 (never become a primary) to 1000 in floating point precision.

Higher priority members will be the first to call an election when the primary steps down and the most likely to win the election.

Custom priorities should be configured with great consideration of all different network partitions. Setting priorities the wrong way may lead to elections not being able to elect a primary, thus stopping all writes to our MongoDB replica set.

If we want to prevent a secondary from becoming a primary, we can set its priority to 0 as explained in the following section.

Priority zero replica set members

In some cases, for example if we have multiple data centers, we will want some of the members to never be able to become a primary server.

In a scenario with multiple data center replication, we may have our primary data center with one primary and one secondary based in the UK and a secondary server located in Russia. In this case, we don't want our Russia-based server to become primary as it would incur latency on our application servers based in the UK. In this case, we will set up our Russia-based server with `priority 0`.

Replica set members with `priority 0` also can't trigger elections. In all other aspects they are identical to every other member in the replica set. To change the priority of a replica set member, we must first get the current replica set configuration by connecting via mongo shell to the primary server:

```
> cfg = rs.conf()
```

This will output the config document which contains configuration for every member in our replica set. In the `members` subdocument we can find the `priority` attribute which we have to set to `0`:

```
> cfg.members[2].priority = 0
```

Finally, we need to reconfigure the replica set with the updated configuration:

```
rs.reconfig(cfg)
```

Make sure we have the same version of MongoDB running in every node or else there may be unexpected behavior. Avoid reconfiguring the replica set cluster during high volume periods. Reconfiguring a replica set may force an election for a new primary, which will close all active connections and may lead to a downtime of 10-30 seconds. Try to identify the lowest traffic time window to run maintenance operations like reconfigure and always have a recovery plan in case something goes wrong.

Hidden replica set members

Hidden replica set members are used for special tasks. They are invisible to clients, will not show up in `db.isMaster()` mongo shell command and similar administration commands and for all purposes will not be taken into account by clients (that is, read preference options).

They can vote for elections but will never become a primary server.

A hidden replica set member will only sync up to the primary server and doesn't take reads from the clients. As such, it has the same write load as the primary server (for replication purposes) but no read load on its own.

Because of the previously mentioned characteristics, reporting is the most common application of a hidden member. We can connect directly to this member and use it as the data source of truth for OLAP.

To set up a hidden replica set member, we follow a similar procedure to the `priority 0`. After we connect via mongo shell to our primary, we get the configuration object, identify the member in the members subdocument that corresponds to the member we want to set as hidden, and subsequently set its `priority` to 0 and its `hidden` attribute to `true`. Finally, we have to apply the new configuration by calling `rs.reconfig(config_object)` with the `config_object` that we used as a parameter:

```
> cfg = rs.conf()
> cfg.members[0].priority = 0
> cfg.members[0].hidden = true
> rs.reconfig(cfg)
```

A hidden replica set member can also be used for backup purposes. However, as we can see in the next section, we may want to use other options either at the physical level or if we want to replicate data at the logical level. Consider using a delayed replica set instead.

Delayed replica set members

In many cases, we want to have a node that holds a copy of our data at an earlier point in time. This helps recover from a big subset of human errors like accidentally dropping a collection or an upgrade going horrendously wrong.

A delayed replica set member has to be `priority 0` and `hidden = true`.

A delayed replica set member can vote for elections but will never be visible to clients (`hidden = true`) and will never become a primary (`priority 0`).

Following on from the preceding examples:

```
> cfg = rs.conf()
> cfg.members[0].priority = 0
> cfg.members[0].hidden = true
> cfg.members[0].slaveDelay = 7200
> rs.reconfig(cfg)
```

This will set the `member[0]` to a delay of 2 hours. Two important factors for deciding the delta time period between the primary and delayed secondary server are:

- Enough oplog size on the primary
- Enough time for maintenance to finish before the delayed member starts picking up data

Maintenance window in hours	Delay	Oplog size on primary in hours
0.5	[0.5,5)	5

Production considerations

Deploy each `mongod` instance on a separate physical host. If using VMs make sure they map to different underlying physical hosts.

Use the `bind_ip` option to make sure our server maps to a specific network interface and port address.

Use firewalls to block access to any other port and/or only allow access between application servers and MongoDB servers. Even better, set up a VPN so that our servers communicate with each other in a secure, encrypted fashion.

Connecting to a replica set

Connecting to a replica set is not fundamentally different to connecting to a single server. In this section, we will show some examples using the official mongo-ruby-driver.

First we need to set our host and options objects:

```
client_host = ['hostname:port']
client_options = {
 database: 'signals',
 replica_set: 'xmr_btc'
}
```

In the preceding example, we are getting ready to connect to `host:port` hostname, in database signals in the `replica_set xmr_btc`.

Calling the initializer on `Mongo::Client` will now return a client object that contains a connection to our replica set and database:

```
client = Mongo::Client.new(client_host, client_options)
```

The client object then has the same options as it has when connecting to a single server.

MongoDB uses auto-discovery after connecting to our `client_host` to identify the other members of our replica set, be they the primary or secondaries.
The client object should be used as a singleton, created once and reused across our code base.

Having a singleton client object is a rule that can be overridden in some cases. We should create different client objects if we have different classes of connections to our replica set.

An example would be having a client object for most operations and then another client object for operations that are okay with reading just from secondaries:

```
client_reporting = client.with(:read => { :mode => :secondary })
```

This Ruby MongoDB client command will return a copy of the `MongoDB:Client` object with a read preference secondary that can be used, for example, for reporting purposes.

Some of the most useful options that we can use in our `client_options` initialization object are as follows:

Option	Description	Type	Default
replica_set	As used in our example, the replica set name.	String	none
write	The write concern options as a hash object. Available options are w, wtimeout, j, fsync. That is, to specify writes to two servers, with journaling, flushing to disk (fsync) true and a timeout of 1 second: { write: { w: 2, j: true, wtimeout: 1000, fsync: true } }	Hash	{ w: 1 }

read	The read preference mode as a hash. Available options are `mode` and `tag_sets`. That is, to limit reads from secondary servers that have tag `UKWrites`: `{ read:` `{ mode: :secondary,` `tag_sets: [ "UKWrites" ]` `}` `}`	Hash	`{ mode: primary }`
user	The name of the user to authenticate with.	String	none
password	The password of the user to authenticate with.	String	none
connect	Using `:direct`, we can force treat a replica set member as a standalone server, bypassing auto discovery. Other options: `:direct`, `:replica_set`, `:sharded`.	Symbol	none
heartbeat_frequency	How often replica set members will communicate to check if they are all alive.	Float	`10`
database	Database to connect.	String	`admin`

Similar to connecting to a standalone server, there are also options around SSL and authentication used in the same way.

We can also configure the connection pool by setting the following:

```
min_pool_size(defaults to 1 connection),
max_pool_size(defaults to 5),
wait_queue_timeout(defaults to 1 in seconds).
```

The MongoDB driver will try to reuse existing connections if available, or else open a new connection. Once the pool limit has been reached the driver will block waiting for a connection to be released to use it.

Replica set administration

Administration for a replica set can be significantly more complex than what is needed for single server deployments. In this section, instead of trying to exhaustively cover all different cases we will focus on some of the most common administration tasks that we will have to perform and how to do them.

How to perform maintenance on replica sets

If we have some maintenance tasks that we have to perform in every member in a replica set, we always start with the secondaries first. First we connect via mongo shell to one of the secondaries. Then we stop this secondary:

```
> use admin
> db.shutdownServer()
```

Then, using the same user that was connected to the mongo shell in the previous step, we restart the mongo server as a standalone server in a different port:

```
> mongod --port 95658 --dbpath <wherever our mongoDB data resides in this host>
```

The next step is to connect to this `mongod` server (which is using `dbpath`):

```
> mongo --port 37017
```

At this point, we can safely perform all administrative tasks on our standalone server without affecting our replica set operations. When we are done, we shut down the standalone server in the same way that we did in the first step.

Then, we can restart our server in the replica set using the command line or the configuration script that we normally use. The final step is to verify that everything works fine by connecting to the replica set server and getting its replica set status:

```
> rs.status()
```

The server should initially be in `state: RECOVERING` and once it has caught up with the secondary back in `state: SECONDARY` as it was before starting the maintenance.

We will repeat the same process for every secondary server. In the end, we have to perform maintenance on the primary. The only difference in the process for our primary is that we will start by stepping down our primary into secondary before every other step that we did for secondaries:

```
> rs.stepDown(600)
```

By using the argument, we prevent our secondary from being elected as a master for 10 minutes. This should be enough time to shutdown the server and continue with our maintenance as we did with the secondaries.

Resyncing a member of a replica set

Secondaries sync up with the primary by replaying the contents of the oplog. If our oplog is not large enough or we encounter network issues (partitioning, underperforming network, or just an outage of the secondary server) for a period of time larger than the oplog then MongoDB cannot use the oplog to catch up to the primary anymore.

At this point we have two options:

- The more straightforward option is to delete our dbpath directory and restart the mongod process. In this case, MongoDB will start an initial sync from scratch. This option has the downside of putting a strain on our replica set and our network as well.
- The more complicated (from an operational standpoint) option is to copy data files from another well-behaving member of the replica set. This goes back to the contents of Chapter 8, *Monitoring, Backup, and Security*. The important thing to keep in mind is that a simple file copy will most probably not suffice as data files will have changed from the time that we start copying to the time that the copying has ended.

Thus, we need to be able to take a snapshot copy of the filesystem under our data directory.

Another point of consideration is that by the time we start our secondary server with the newly copied files, our MongoDB secondary server will, again, try to sync up to the primary using the oplog. So, if our oplog has again fallen so far behind the primary that it can't find the entry on our primary server, this method will fail too.

Keep a sufficiently sized oplog. Don't let data grow out of hand in any replica set member. Design, test, and deploy sharding early on.

Changing the oplog size

Hand in hand with the previous operational tip, we may need to rethink and resize our oplog as our data grows. Operations become more complicated and time consuming as our data grows and we need to adjust our oplog size to accommodate for it.

The first step is to restart our MongoDB secondary server as a standalone server, an operation that has been described in the *How to perform maintenance on replica sets* section.

Then, we take a backup of our existing oplog:

```
> mongodump --db local --collection 'oplog.rs' --port 37017
```

And keep a copy of this data just in case.

Then we connect to our standalone database:

```
> use local
> db = db.getSiblingDB('local')
> db.temp.drop()
```

Up until now we connected to the local database and deleted the `temp` collection just in case it had any leftover documents.

The next step is to get the last entry of our current oplog and save it in the `temp` collection:

```
> db.temp.save( db.oplog.rs.find( { }, { ts: 1, h: 1 } ).sort( {$natural :
-1} ).limit(1).next() )
```

This entry will be used when we restart our secondary to keep track of where it has reached in oplog replication.

```
> db = db.getSiblingDB('local')
> db.oplog.rs.drop()
```

Now, we delete our existing oplog and in the next step we will create a new oplog of 4 GB in size:

```
> db.runCommand( { create: "oplog.rs", capped: true, size: (4 * 1024 * 1024
* 1024) } )
```

The next step is to copy the one entry from our `temp` collection back to our oplog:

```
> db.oplog.rs.save( db.temp.findOne() )
```

Finally, we clean shutdown our server from the `admin` database using the `db.shutdownServer()` command and restart our secondary as a member of the replica set.

We repeat this process for all secondary servers and as a last step, we repeat the procedure for our primary member after we step the primary down first using the following:

```
> rs.stepDown(600)
```

As with every other step.

Reconfiguring a replica set when we have lost the majority of our servers

This is only intended as an interim solution and a last resort when we are faced with downtime and disrupted cluster operations. When we lose the majority of our servers and we still have enough servers to start a replica set (maybe including some quickly spawned arbiters) we can force a reconfiguration with the surviving members only.

First we get the replica set configuration document:

```
> cfg = rs.conf()
```

And using `printjson(cfg)` we identify the members that are still operational. Let's say that these are 1, 2, and 3:

```
> cfg.members = [cfg.members[1] , cfg.members[2] , cfg.members[3]]
> rs.reconfig(cfg, {force : true})
```

By using `force: true` we are forcing this reconfiguration to happen. Of course, we need to have at least three surviving members in our replica set for this to work.

It's important to remove the failing servers as soon as possible by killing the processes and/or taking them out of the network to avoid unintended consequences as these servers may believe that they are still part of a cluster that doesn't acknowledge them anymore.

Chained replication

Replication in MongoDB usually happens from the primary to the secondaries. In some cases, we may want to replicate from another secondary instead of the primary. Chained replication helps alleviate the primary from read load but at the same time increases average replication lag for the secondary that chooses to replicate from a secondary. This makes sense as replication first has to go from the primary to the secondary (1) and then from this server to another secondary (2).

Chained replication can be enabled (and disabled respectively) with the following `cfg` command:

```
> cfg.settings.chainingAllowed = true
```

In cases where `printjson(cfg)` doesn't reveal a settings subdocument, then we need to create an empty one first:

```
> cfg.settings = { }
```

If there is a settings document already, the preceding command will result in deleting its settings, leading to potential data loss.

Cloud options for a replica set

We can set up and operate a replica set from our own servers but we can reduce our operational overhead by using a **database as a service (DBaaS)** provider to do it. The two most widely used MongoDB cloud providers are mLab (former MongoLab) and MongoDB Atlas, the native offering from MongoDB Inc.

In this section, we will go over these options and how they fare against using our own hardware and data centers.

mLab

mLab is one of the most popular cloud DBaaS providers for MongoDB. It has been offered since 2011 and is considered a stable and mature provider.

After signing up, we can easily deploy a replica set cluster in a set of cloud servers without any operational overhead. Configuration options include AWS, Microsoft Azure, or Google Cloud as the underlying server provider.

There are multiple sizing options for the latest MongoDB version. There is no support at the time of writing for the MMAPv1 storage engine.

There are multiple regions for each provider (US, Europe, Asia). Most notably, the regions missing are AWS China, AWS US Gov, and AWS Germany regions.

MongoDB Atlas

MongoDB Atlas is a newer offering from MongoDB Inc., launched in Summer 2016. Similar to MLab, it offers deployment of single server, replica set, or sharded clusters through a web interface.

It offers the latest MongoDB version. The only storage option is WiredTiger. There are multiple regions for each provider (US, Europe, Asia).

Most notably, the regions missing are AWS China and AWS US Gov regions.

In both (and most others) providers we can't have a cross region replica set. This is prohibitive if we want to deploy a truly global service, serving users from multiple data centers around the globe with our MongoDB servers being as close to the application servers as possible.

Running costs for cloud hosted services can be significantly higher than setting these up in our own servers. What we gain in convenience and time to market, we may have to pay in operational cost.

Replica set limitations

A replica set is great when we understand why we need it and what it cannot do.

A replica set:

- Will not scale horizontally; we need sharding for it
- Will introduce replication issues if our network is flaky
- Will make debugging issues more complex if we use secondaries for reads and these have fallen behind our primary server

On the flip side, as explained in previous sections of this chapter, a replica set can be a great choice for replication, data redundancy, conforming with data privacy, backups, and even recovery from errors caused by humans or otherwise.

Summary

In this chapter, we discussed replica sets and how to administer them. Starting from an architectural overview of replica sets and replica set internals around elections, we took a deep dive into setting up and configuring a replica set.

We learned how to perform various administration tasks with replica sets and the main options when we want to outsource operations to a cloud DBaaS provider.

Finally, we identified some of the limitations that replica sets in MongoDB currently have. In the next chapter, we will move on to one of the most interesting concepts in MongoDB, the one that makes it achieve horizontal scaling, sharding.

11
Sharding

Sharding was one of the features that MongoDB offered from an early stage, since version 1.6 was released in August 2010. Sharding is the ability to horizontally scale out our database by partitioning our datasets across different servers—the shards. Foursquare and Bitly are two of the most famous early customers for MongoDB that were also using sharding from its inception all the way to the general availability release.

In this chapter, we will learn how to design a sharding cluster and how to make the single most important decision around it—choosing the shard key. We will also learn about different sharding techniques and how to monitor and administrate sharded clusters. We will discuss the `mongos` router and how it is being used to route our queries across different shards. Finally, we will learn how we can recover from errors in our shard.

Advantages of sharding

In database systems and computing systems in general, we have two ways to improve performance. The first one is to simply replace our servers with more powerful ones, keeping the same network topology and systems architecture. This is called **vertical scaling**.

An advantage of vertical scaling is that it is simple from an operational standpoint, especially with cloud providers such as Amazon making it as easy as a few clicks to replace an m2.medium with an m2.extralarge server instance.

Another advantage is that we don't need to make any code changes and there is little to no risk of something going catastrophically wrong.

The main disadvantage of vertical scaling is that there is a limit to it; we can only get as powerful servers as our cloud provider can provide to us.

A related disadvantage is that getting more powerful servers is generally not a linear but an exponential cost increase. Similar to precious gemstones, five cheap servers are almost always cheaper than one server with all the aggregate computing power of the five cheap ones. So, even if our cloud provider offers more powerful instances, we will hit the cost effectiveness barrier before we hit the limit of our department's credit card.

The second way to improve performance is by using the same servers in capacity and increase the number of them. This is called horizontal scaling.

Horizontal scaling offers the advantage of being able to scale theoretically to infinity and practically enough for real-world applications. The main disadvantage is that it can be operationally more complex and requires code change and careful designing of the system upfront.

Horizontal scaling is more complex from a system aspect as well because it requires communication between the different servers over network links that are not as reliable as interprocess communication on a single server.

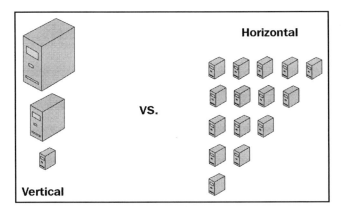

Reference: http://www.pc-freak.net/images/horizontal-vs-vertical-scaling-vertical-and-horizontal-scaling-explained-diagram.png

To understand scaling, it's important to understand the limitations of single server systems. A server is typically bound by one or more of the following characteristics:

- **CPU**: A CPU-bound system is one that is limited by our CPU's speed. A task such as multiplication of matrices that can fit in RAM will be CPU bound because there is a specific number of steps that have to be performed in CPU without any disk or memory access needed for the task to complete. CPU usage is the metric that we need to keep track of in this case.

- **I/O**: I/O or input-output-bound systems are similarly limited by the speed of our storage system (HDD or SSD). A task such as reading large files from a disk to load into memory will be I/O bound as there is little to do in terms of CPU processing; the bulk majority of time is spent reading the files from the disk. The important metrics to keep track of are all the metrics related to disk access, reads per second, and writes per second as compared to the practical limit of our storage system.

- **Memory and cache**: Memory- and cache-bound systems are restricted by the amount of available RAM memory and/or the cache size that we have assigned to them. A task that multiplies matrices larger than our RAM size will be memory bound as it will need to page in/out data from disk to perform the multiplication. The important metric to keep track of is the memory used. This may be misleading in MongoDB MMAPv1 as the storage engine will allocate as much memory as possible through the filesystem cache.

In the WiredTiger storage engine on the other hand, if we don't allocate enough memory for the core MongoDB process, we may get *Out of memory* errors killing it, and this is something that we want to avoid at all costs.

Monitoring memory usage has to be done both directly through the operating system and indirectly by keeping a track of page in/out data. An increasing number of memory paging is often an indication that we are running short of memory and the operating system is using virtual address space to keep up.

 MongoDB, being a database system, is generally memory and I/O bound. Investing in SSD and more memory for our nodes is almost always a good investment. Most systems are a combination of one or more of the preceding limitations. Once we add more memory, our system may become CPU bound as complex operations are almost always a combination of CPU, I/O, and memory usage.

MongoDB's sharding is simple enough to set up and operate, and this has contributed to its huge success over the years as it provides the advantages of horizontal scaling without requiring a large commitment of engineering and operations resources.

That being said, it's really important to get sharding right from the beginning as it is extremely difficult from an operational standpoint to change the configuration once it has been set up. Sharding should not be an afterthought but rather a key architecture design decision from an early point in time.

Architectural overview

A sharded cluster is comprised of the following elements:

- Two or more shards. Each shard must be a replica set.
- One or more query routers (mongos). mongos provides an interface between our application and the database.
- A replica set of config servers. Config servers store metadata and configuration settings for the entire cluster.

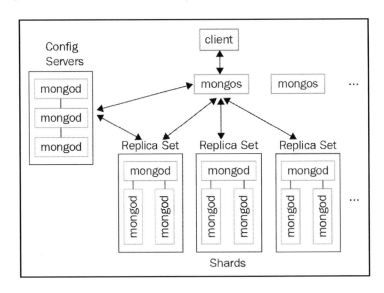

Reference: https://www.infoq.com/news/2010/08/MongoDB-1.6

We can't have a shard composed of a single server.

Development, continuous deployment, and staging environments

In preproduction environments it may be an overkill to use the full set of servers, and for efficiency reasons, we may opt to use a more simplified architecture.

The simplest possible configuration that we can deploy for sharding is the following:

- One `mongos` router
- One sharded replica set with one MongoDB server and two arbiters
- One replica set of config servers with one MongoDB server and two arbiters

This should be strictly used for development and testing as this architecture defies most of the advantages that a replica set provides such as high availability, scalability, and replication of data.

 Staging is strongly recommended to mirror our production environment in servers, configuration, and (if possible) dataset requirements too to avoid surprises at deployment time.

Planning ahead on sharding

As we will see in the next sections, sharding is complicated and expensive operation-wise. It is important to plan ahead and make sure that we start the sharding process long before we hit our system's limits.

Some rough guidelines on when to start sharding:

- CPU utilization of <70% on an average
- I/O and especially write capacity is <80%
- Memory utilization <70% on an average

As sharding helps with write performance, it's important to keep an eye on our I/O write capacity and requirements from our application.

 Don't wait until the last minute to start sharding in an already busy-to-the-neck MongoDB system; it can have unintended consequences.

Sharding setup

Sharding is performed at the collection level. We can have collections that we don't want or need to shard for several reasons. We can leave these collections unsharded.

These collections will be stored in the primary shard. The primary shard is different for each database in MongoDB.

The primary shard is automatically selected by MongoDB when we create a new database in a sharded environment. MongoDB will pick the shard that has the least data stored at the moment of creation.

If we want to change the primary shard at any other point, we can issue the following command:

```
> db.runCommand( { movePrimary : "mongo_books", to : "UK_based" } )
```

We thus move the database named `mongo_books` to the shard named `UK_based`.

Choosing the shard key

Choosing our shard key is the most important decision we need to make. The reason is that once we shard our data and deploy our cluster, it becomes very difficult to change the shard key.

First, we will go through the process of changing the shard key.

Changing the shard key

There is no command or simple procedure to change the shard key in MongoDB. The only way to change the shard key involves backing up and restoring all of our data, something that may range from being extremely difficult to impossible in high-load production environments.

The steps if we want to change our shard key are as follows:

1. Export all data from MongoDB.
2. Drop the original sharded collection.
3. Configure sharding with the new key.
4. Presplit the new shard key range.
5. Restore our data back into MongoDB.

From these steps, step 4 is the one that needs some more explanation.

MongoDB uses chunks to split data in a sharded collection. If we bootstrap a MongoDB sharded cluster from scratch, chunks will be calculated automatically by MongoDB. MongoDB will then distribute the chunks across different shards to ensure that there are an equal number of chunks in each shard.

The only case in which we cannot really do this is when we want to load data into a newly sharded collection.

The reasons are threefold:

1. MongoDB creates splits only after an `insert` operation.
2. Chunk migration will copy all of the data in that chunk from one shard to another.
3. The `floor(n/2)` chunk migrations can happen at any given time, where *n* is the number of shards we have. Even with three shards, this is only a `floor(1.5)=1` chunk migration at a time.

These three limitations combined mean that letting MongoDB to figure it out on its own will definitely take much longer and may result in an eventual failure. This is why we want to presplit our data and give MongoDB some guidance on where our chunks should go.

Considering our example of the `mongo_books` database and the `books` collection, this would be:

```
> db.runCommand( { split : "mongo_books.books", middle : { id : 50 } } )
```

The `middle` command parameter will split our key space in documents that have `id<=50` and documents that have `id>50`. There is no need for a document to exist in our collection with `id=50` as this will only serve as the guidance value for our partitions.

In this example, we chose `50` assuming that our keys follow a uniform distribution (that is, the same count of keys for each value) in the range of values from `0` to `100`.

We should aim to create at least 20-30 chunks to grant MongoDB flexibility in potential migrations. We can also use `bounds` and `find` instead of `middle` if we want to manually define the partition key, but both parameters need data to exist in our collection before applying them.

Choosing the correct shard key

After the previous section, it's now self-evident that we need to take into great consideration the choice of our shard key as it is something that we have to stick with.

A great shard key has three characteristics:

- High cardinality
- Low frequency
- Non-monotonically changing in value

We will go over the definitions of these three properties first to understand what they mean.

High cardinality means that the shard key must have as many distinct values as possible. A Boolean can take only values of `true`/`false`, and so it is a bad shard key choice.

A 64-bit long value field that can take any value from $-(2^{63})$ to $2^{63} - 1$ and is a good example in terms of cardinality.

Low frequency directly relates to the argument about high cardinality. A low-frequency shard key will have a distribution of values as close to a perfectly random / uniform distribution.

Using the example of our 64-bit long value, it is of little use to us if we have a field that can take values ranging from $-(2^{63})$ to $2^{63} - 1$ only to end up observing the values of 0 and 1 all the time. In fact, it is as bad as using a Boolean field, which can also take only two values after all.

If we have a shard key with high frequency values, we will end up with chunks that are indivisible. These chunks cannot be further divided and will grow in size, negatively affecting the performance of the shard that contains them.

Non-monotonically changing values mean that our shard key should not be, for example, an integer that always increases with every new insert. If we choose a monotonically increasing value as our shard key, this will result in all writes ending up in the last of all of our shards, limiting our write performance.

> If we want to use a monotonically changing value as the shard key, we should consider using hash-based sharding.

In the next section, we will describe different sharding strategies and their advantages and disadvantages.

Range-based sharding

The default and the most widely used sharding strategy is range-based sharding. This strategy will split our collection's data into chunks, grouping documents with nearby values in the same shard.

For our example database and collection, `mongo_books` and `books` respectively, we have:

```
> sh.shardCollection("mongo_books.books", { id: 1 } )
```

This creates a range-based shard key on `id` with ascending direction. The direction of our shard key will determine which documents will end up in the first shard and which ones in the subsequent ones.

This is a good strategy if we plan to have range-based queries as these will be directed to the shard that holds the result set instead of having to query all shards.

Hash-based sharding

If we don't have a shard key (or can't create one) that achieves the three goals mentioned previously, we can use the alternative strategy of using hash-based sharding.

In this case, we are trading data distribution with query isolation.

Hash-based sharding will take the values of our shard key and hash them in a way that guarantees close to uniform distribution. This way we can be sure that our data will evenly distribute across shards.

The downside is that only exact match queries will get routed to the exact shard that holds the value. Any range query will have to go out and fetch data from all shards.

For our example database and collection (`mongo_books` and `books` respectively), we have:

```
> sh.shardCollection("mongo_books.books", { id: "hashed" } )
```

Similar to the preceding example, we are now using the `id` field as our hashed shard key.

> Suppose we use fields with float values for hash-based sharding. Then we will end up with collisions if the precision of our floats is more that 2^53. These fields should be avoided where possible.

Coming up with our own key

Range-based sharding does not need to be confined to a single key. In fact, in most cases, we would like to combine multiple keys to achieve high cardinality and low frequency.

A common pattern is to combine a low-cardinality first part (but still having as distinct values more than two times the number of shards that we have) with a high-cardinality key as its second field. This achieves both read and write distribution from the first part of the sharding key and then cardinality and read locality from the second part.

On the other hand, if we don't have range queries, we can get away by using hash-based sharding on a primary key as this will exactly target the shard and document that we are going after.

To make things more complicated, these considerations may change depending on our workload. A workload that consists almost exclusively (say 99.5%) of reads won't care about write distribution. We can use the built-in `_id` field as our shard key and this will only add 0.5% load in the last shard. Our reads will still be distributed across shards.

Unfortunately, in most cases, this is not simple.

Location-based data

Due to government regulations and the desire to have our data as close to our users as possible, there is often a constraint and need to limit data in a specific data center. By placing different shards at different data centers, we can satisfy this requirement.

> Every shard is essentially a replica set. We can connect to it like we would connect to a replica set for administrative and maintenance operations. We can query one shard's data directly but the results will only be a subset of the full sharded result set.

Sharding administration and monitoring

Sharded MongoDB environments have some unique challenges and limitations compared to single-server or replica set deployments. In this section, we will explore how MongoDB balances our data across shards using chunks and how we can tweak it if we need. Together, we will explore some of the shard's design limitations.

Balancing data – how to track and keep our data balanced

One of the advantages of sharding in MongoDB is that it is mostly transparent to the application and requires minimal administration and operational effort.

One of the core tasks that MongoDB needs to perform continuously is balancing data between shards. No matter whether we implement range- or hash-based sharding, MongoDB will need to calculate bounds for the hashed field to be able to figure out on which shard to direct every new document insert or update. As our data grows, these bounds may need to get readjusted to avoid having a hot shard that ends up with a majority of our data.

For the sake of this example, let's assume that there is a data type named `extra_tiny_int` with integer values from [-12, 12). If we enable sharding on this `extra_tiny_int` field, the initial bounds of our data will be the whole range of values denoted by `$minKey: -12` and `$maxKey: 11`.

After we insert some initial data, MongoDB will generate chunks and recalculate the bounds for each chunk to try and balance our data.

 By default, the initial number of chunks created by MongoDB is 2*number of shards.

In our case of two shards and four initial chunks, the initial bounds will be calculated as:

Chunk1: [-12..-6)

Chunk2: [-6..0)

Chunk3: [0..6)

Chunk4: [6,12) where [is inclusive and) is not inclusive.

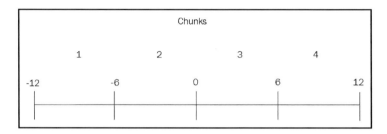

After we insert some data, our chunks will look like:

ShardA

Chunk1 Chunk2

-12,-8,-7 -6

ShardB

Chunk3   Chunk4

0, 2   7,8,9,10,11,11,11,11

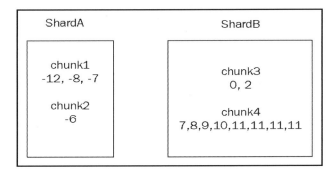

In this case, we observe that *Chunk4* has more items than any other chunk.

MongoDB will first split *Chunk4* into two new chunks, attempting to keep the size of each chunk under a certain threshold (64 MB by default).

Now, instead of *Chunk4*, we have:

Chunk4A

7,8,9,10

Chunk4B

11,11,11,11

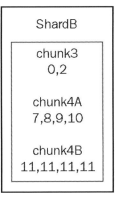

With the new bounds being:

Chunk4A: [6,11)

Chunk4B: [11,12)

Notice that *Chunk4B* can only hold one value. This is now an indivisible chunk—a chunk that can not be broken down into smaller ones anymore—and will grow in size unbounded, causing potential performance issues down the line.

This clarifies why we need to use a high-cardinality field as our shard key and why something like Boolean that only has `true`/`false` values is a bad selection for a shard key.

In our case, we now have two chunks in *ShardA* and three chunks in *ShardB*. According to the following table:

Number of chunks	Migration threshold
<20	2
20-79	4
>=80	8

We have not reached our migration threshold yet, since *3-2 = 1*.

The migration threshold is calculated as the number of chunks in the shard with the highest count of chunks and the number of chunks in the shard with the lowest count of chunks:

Shard1 -> 85 chunks

Shard2 -> 86 chunks

Shard3 -> 92 chunks

In the preceding example, balancing will not occur until *Shard3* (or *Shard2*) reaches 93 chunks because the migration threshold is 8 for >=80 chunks and the difference between *Shard1* and *Shard3* is still 7 chunks (92-85).

If we continue adding data in *Chunk4A*, it will eventually be split into *Chunk4A1* and *Chunk4A2*.

Now we have four chunks in *ShardB* (*Chunk3*, *Chunk4A1*, *Chunk4A2*, and *Chunk4B*) and two chunks in *ShardA* (*Chunk1* and *Chunk2*).

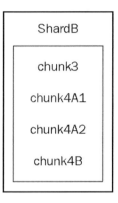

The MongoDB balancer will now migrate one chunk from *ShardB* to *ShardA* as 4-2 = 2, reaching the migration threshold for <20 chunks. The balancer will adjust the boundaries between the two shards to be able to query more effectively (targeted queries).

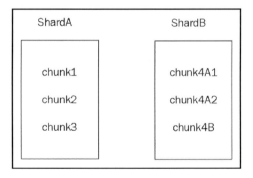

As seen in the preceding diagram, MongoDB will try to split >64 MB chunks into half in terms of size. Bounds between the two resulting chunks may be completely uneven if our data distribution is uneven to begin with. MongoDB can split chunks into smaller ones but cannot merge them automatically. We need to manually merge chunks, a delicate and operationally expensive procedure.

Chunk administration

Most of the times, we should leave chunk administration to MongoDB. The case for manually managing chunks comes mostly in the initial load of data when we change our configuration from replica set to sharding.

Moving chunks

To move a chunk manually, we need to issue the following command after connecting to mongos and the admin database:

```
> db.runCommand( { moveChunk : 'mongo_books.books' ,
                   find : {id: 50},
                   to : 'shard1.packtdb.com' } )
```

Using the preceding command, we move the chunk containing the document with id: 50 (this has to be the shard key) from the collection books of database mongo_books to the new shard named shard1.packtdb.com.

We can also define more explicitly the bounds of the chunk that we want to move. Now the syntax is:

```
> db.runCommand( { moveChunk : 'mongo_books.books' ,
                bounds :[ { id : <minValue> } ,
   { id : <maxValue> } ],
                to : 'shard1.packtdb.com' } )
```

Here, minValue and maxValue are the values that we get from db.printShardingStatus().

In the example used previously, for *Chunk2*, `minValue` would be −6 and `maxValue` would be 0.

 Do not use find in hash-based sharding. Use bounds instead.

Changing the default chunk size

To change the default chunk size, we need to connect to a `mongos` router and consequently to the `config` database.

Then we issue the following command to change our global `chunksize` to 16 MB:

```
> db.settings.save( { _id:"chunksize", value: 16 } )
```

The main reasoning behind changing `chunksize` comes from cases where the default `chunksize` of 64 MB can cause more I/O than our hardware can handle. In this case, defining a smaller `chunksize` will result in more frequent but less data-intensive migrations.

Changing the default chunk size has several drawbacks:

- Creating more splits by defining a smaller chunk size cannot be undone automatically.
- Increasing the chunk size will not force any chunk migration; instead chunks will grow through inserts and updates until they reach the new size.
- Lowering the chunk size may take quite some time to complete.
- Automatic splitting to comply with the new chunk size if it is lower will only happen on insert or update. We may have chunks that don't get any write operations and thus will not be changed in size.

The chunk size can be [1…, 1024] MB.

Jumbo chunks

In some edge cases, we may end up with jumbo chunks, chunks that are larger than the chunk size and can not be split by MongoDB. We may also run into the same situation if the number of documents in our chunk exceeds the maximum document limit.

These chunks will have the `jumbo` flag enabled. Ideally MongoDB will keep track of whether it can split the chunk, and as soon as it can, it will. However, we may decide that we want to manually trigger the split before MongoDB does.

The way to do so is as follows.

Connect via shell to your `mongos` router and run the following:

```
> sh.status(true)
```

Identify the chunk that has `jumbo` in its description:

```
databases:
...
mongo_books.books
...
chunks:
...
            shardB    2
            shardA    2
      { "id" : 7 } -->> { "id" : 9 } on : shardA Timestamp(2, 2) jumbo
```

Invoke `splitAt()` or `splitFind()` manually to split the chunk on the `books` collection of database `mongo_books` at id=8:

```
> sh.splitAt( "mongo_books.books", { id: 8 })
```

 `splitAt()` will split based on the split point we define. The two new splits may or may not be balanced.

Alternatively, if we want to leave it to MongoDB to find where to split in our chunk, we can use `splitFind`:

```
> sh.splitFind("mongo_books.books", {id: 7})
```

`splitFind` now will try to find the chunk that the `id:7` query belongs to and automatically define the new bounds for the split chunks so that they are roughly balanced.

In both cases, MongoDB will try to split the chunk, and if successful, it will remove the jumbo flag from it.

If the preceding operation is unsuccessful, then and only then should we try stopping the balancer first, while also verifying the output and waiting for any pending migrations to finish first:

```
> sh.stopBalancer()
> sh.getBalancerState()
```

This should return `false`:

```
> use config
while( sh.isBalancerRunning() ) {
        print("waiting...");
        sleep(1000);
}
```

Wait for any *waiting...* messages to stop printing. Then find the jumbo flagged chunk in the same way as before.

Finally update the `chunks` collection in your `config` database of the `mongos` router, like this:

```
> db.getSiblingDB("config").chunks.update(
  { ns: "mongo_books.books", min: { id: 7 }, jumbo: true },
  { $unset: { jumbo: "" } }
)
```

The preceding command is a regular `update()` command, with the first argument being the `find()` part to find which document to update and the second argument being the operation to apply to it (`$unset: jumbo flag`).

After all this is done, we re-enable the balancer:

```
> sh.setBalancerState(true)
```

And connect to the `admin` database to flush the new configuration to all nodes:

```
> db.adminCommand({ flushRouterConfig: 1 } )
```

Always back up the `config` database before modifying any state manually.

Merging chunks

As we have seen previously, usually MongoDB will adjust the bounds for each chunk in our shard to make sure that our data is equally distributed. This may not work in some cases, especially when we define the chunks manually, if our data distribution is surprisingly unbalanced, or if we have many delete operations in our shard.

Having empty chunks will invoke unnecessary chunk migrations and give MongoDB a false impression of which chunk needs to be migrated where. As we have explained before, the threshold for chunk migration is dependent on the number of chunks that each shard holds. Having empty chunks may or may not trigger the balancer when it's needed.

Chunk merging can only happen when at least one of the chunks is empty and only between neighboring chunks.

To find empty chunks, we need to connect to the database that we want to inspect (in our case, mongo_books) and do runCommand with dataSize set as follows:

```
> use mongo_books
> db.runCommand({
  "dataSize": "mongo_books.books",
  "keyPattern": { id: 1 },
  "min": { "id": -6 },
  "max": { "id": 0 }
})
```

dataSize follows the database_name.collection_name pattern, whereas keyPattern is the shard key that we have defined for this collection.

min and max values should be calculated by the chunks that we have in this collection. In our case, we entered *ChunkB's* details from the example earlier in this chapter.

If the bounds of our query (which, in our case, are the bounds of *ChunkB*) return no documents, the result will resemble the following:

```
{ "size" : 0, "numObjects" : 0, "millis" : 0, "ok" : 1 }
```

Now that we know that *ChunkB* has no data, we can merge it with another chunk (only *ChunkA* in the use case described before) like this:

```
> db.runCommand( { mergeChunks: "mongo_books.books",
             bounds: [ { "id": -12 },
                       { id: 0 } ]
        } )
```

On success, this will return MongoDB's default ok status message:

```
{ "ok" : 1 }
```

We can then verify that we only have one chunk on *ShardA* by invoking
`sh.status()` again.

Adding and removing shards

Adding a new shard to our cluster is as easy as connecting to `mongos`, connecting to the
`admin` database, and invoking `runCommand` with:

```
> db.runCommand( {
addShard: "mongo_books_replica_set/rs01.packtdb.com:27017", maxSize: 18000,
name: "packt_mongo_shard_UK"
} )
```

This adds a new shard from the replica set named `mongo_books_replica_set` from host
`rs01.packtdb.com` running on port `27017`. We also define the `maxSize` of data for this
shard as 18,000 MB (or we can set it to `0` for no limit) and the name of the new shard as
`packt_mongo_shard_UK`.

> This operation will take quite some time to complete as chunks will have
> to be rebalanced and migrated to the new shard.

Removing a shard, on the other hand, requires more involvement since we have to make
sure that we won't lose any data on the way.

First we need to make sure that the balancer is enabled using `sh.getBalancerState()`.

Then, after identifying the shard we want to remove using any one of the `sh.status()`,
`db.printShardingStatus()`, or `listShards` admin commands, we connect to the
`admin` database and invoke `removeShard`:

```
> use admin
> db.runCommand( { removeShard: "packt_mongo_shard_UK" } )
```

The output should contain this part:

```
...
   "msg" : "draining started successfully",
   "state" : "started",
...
```

Then if we invoke the same command again, we get:

```
> db.runCommand( { removeShard: "packt_mongo_shard_UK" } )
...
"msg" : "draining ongoing",
   "state" : "ongoing",
   "remaining" : {
      "chunks" : NumberLong(2),
      "dbs" : NumberLong(3)
   },
...
```

The remaining document in the result contains the number of chunks and DBs that are still being transferred. In our case it's two and three respectively.

 All the commands need to be executed in the admin database.

An extra complication in removing a shard can arise if the shard we want to remove serves as the primary shard for one or more of the databases that it contains.

The primary shard is allocated by MongoDB when we initiate sharding, so when we remove the shard, we need to manually move these databases to a new shard.

We will know whether we need to perform this operation by a section of the result from removeShard() like this:

```
...
   "note" : "you need to drop or movePrimary these databases",
      "dbsToMove" : [
         "mongo_books"
      ],
...
```

So we need `movePrimary` for our `mongo_books` database. The way to do it is again from the `admin` database:

 Wait for all chunks to finish migrating before running this command.

The result should contain the following before proceeding:

```
..."remaining" : {
    "chunks" : NumberLong(0) }...
> db.runCommand( { movePrimary: "mongo_books", to: "packt_mongo_shard_EU"
})
```

This command will invoke a blocking operation, and when it returns, it should have a result like this:

```
{ "primary" : "packt_mongo_shard_EU", "ok" : 1 }
```

Invoking the same `removeShard()` command after we are all done should return a result like:

```
> db.runCommand( { removeShard: "packt_mongo_shard_UK" } )

... "msg" : "removeshard completed successfully",
    "state" : "completed",
    "shard" : "packt_mongo_shard_UK"
    "ok" : 1
...
```

After we get to `state: completed` and `ok: 1`, it is safe to remove our `packt_mongo_shard_UK` shard.

Removing a shard is naturally more involving than adding one. We need to allow some time, hope for the best, and plan for the worst when performing potentially destructive operations on our live cluster.

Sharding limitations

Sharding comes with great flexibility, but unfortunately there are a few limitations in the way we can perform some operations.

We will highlight the most important ones here:

- The `group()` database command does not work. `group()` should not be used anyway; use `aggregate()` and the aggregation framework instead, or `mapreduce()`.
- `db.eval()` does not work. `db.eval()` should not be used regardless and should be disabled in most cases for security reasons.
- The `$isolated` option in updates does not work.

This is a functionality that is missing in sharded environments. The `$isolated` option for `update()` provides the guarantee that if we update multiple documents at once, other readers and writers will not see some of the documents updated with the new value and the others still having the old value.

The way this is implemented in unsharded environments is by holding a global write lock and/or serializing operations to a single thread to make sure that every request for the documents affected by `update()` will not be accessed by other threads/operations.

This affects concurrency and performance seriously and makes it prohibitive to implement in a sharded environment.

- The `$snapshot` operator in queries is not supported. `$snapshot` in the `find()` cursor prevents documents from appearing more than once in the results as a result of being moved to a different location on disk after an update. `$snapshot` is operationally expensive and often not a hard requirement. The way to substitute it is by using an index for our queries on a field whose keys will not change for the duration of the query.

- The indexes cannot cover our queries if our queries do not contain the shard key. Results in sharded environments will come from the disk and not exclusively from the index. The only exception is if we query only on the built-in `_id` field and return only the `_id` field, in which case MongoDB can still cover the query using built-in indexes.

- The `update()` and `remove()` operations work differently. All `update()` and `remove()` operations in a sharded environment must include either the `_id` of the documents to be affected or the shard key. Otherwise, the `mongos` router will have to do a full table scan across all collections, databases, and shards, which would be operationally very expensive.

- Unique indexes across shards need to contain the shard key as a prefix of the index. In other words, to achieve uniqueness of documents across shards, we need to follow the data distribution that MongoDB follows for the shards.

- **Shard key limitations**: The shard key has to be up to 512 bytes. The shard key index has to be in ascending order on the key field that gets sharded and optionally other fields as well, or a hashed index on it.

The shard key value in a document is also immutable. If our shard key for our `User` collection is `email`, then we cannot update the `email` value for any user after we set it.

Querying sharded data

Querying our data using a MongoDB shard is different than a single server deployment or a replica set. Instead of connecting to the single server or the primary of the replica set, we connect to the `mongos` router which decides which shard to ask for our data. In this section we will explore how the query router operates and showcase how similar to a replica set this is for the developer, using Ruby.

The query router

The query router, also known as `mongos` process, acts as the interface and entry point to our MongoDB cluster. Applications connect to it instead of connecting to the underlying shards and replica sets; `mongos` executes queries, gathers results, and passes them to our application.

`mongos` doesn't hold any persistent state and is typically low on system resources.

 `mongos` is typically hosted in the same instance as the application server.

It is acting as a proxy for requests. When a query comes in, `mongos` will examine and decide which shards need to execute the query and establish a cursor in each one of them.

Find

If our query includes the shard key or a prefix of the shard key, `mongos` will perform a targeted operation, only querying the shards that hold the keys that we are looking for.

For example, with a composite shard key of `{_id, email, address}` on our collection `User`, we can have a targeted operation with any of the following queries:

```
> db.User.find({_id: 1})
> db.User.find({_id: 1, email: 'alex@packt.com'})
> db.User.find({_id: 1, email: 'janluc@packt.com', address: 'Linwood
Dunn'})
```

All three of them are either a prefix (the first two) or the complete shard key.

On the other hand, a query on `{email, address}` or `{address}` will not be able to target the right shards, resulting in a broadcast operation.

A broadcast operation is any operation that doesn't include the shard key or a prefix of the shard key and results in `mongos` querying every shard and gathering results from them. It's also known as a **scatter-and-gather operation** or a **fanout query**.

 This behavior is a direct result of the way indexes are organized and is similar to the behavior that we identified in the relevant chapter about indexing.

Sort/limit/skip

If we want to sort our results, there are two options:

- If we are using the shard key in our sort criteria, then `mongos` can determine the order in which it has to query the shard or shards. This results in an efficient and, again, targeted operation.
- If we are not using the shard key in our sort criteria, then as with a query without sort, it's going to be a fanout query. To sort the results when we are not using the shard key, the primary shard executes a distributed merge sort locally before passing on the sorted result set to `mongos`.

Limit on queries is enforced on each individual shard and then again at the `mongos` level as there may be results from multiple shards.

Skip, on the other hand, cannot be passed on to individual shards and will be applied by `mongos` after retrieving all the results locally.

> If we combine the skip and limit operators, `mongos` will optimize the query by passing both values to individual shards. This is particularly useful in cases such as pagination. If we query without sort and the results are coming from more than one shard, `mongos` will round-robin across shards for the results.

Update/remove

In document modifier operations like update and remove, we have a similar situation to find. If we have the shard key in the find section of the modifier, then `mongos` can direct the query to the relevant shard.

If we don't have the shard key in the find section, then it will again be a fanout operation.

> `UpdateOne`, `replaceOne`, and `removeOne` operations must have the shard key or the `_id` value.

In essence, we have the following cases for operations with sharding:

Type of operation	Query topology
`insert`	Must have the shard key
`update`	Can have the shard key
Query with shard key	Targeted operation
Query without shard key	Scatter gather/fanout query
Indexed/sorted query with shard key	Targeted operation
Indexed/sorted query without shard key	Distributed sort merge

Reference: http://learnmongodbthehardway.com/schema/sharding/

Querying using Ruby

Connecting to a sharded cluster using Ruby is no different than connecting to a replica set.

Using the Ruby official driver we have to configure the client object to define the set of `mongos` **servers:**

```
client = Mongo::Client.new('mongodb://key:password@mongos-server1-
host:mongos-server1-port,mongos-server2-host:mongos-server2-
port/admin?ssl=true&authSource=admin')
```

The mongo-ruby-driver will then return a client object that is no different than connecting to a replica set from the Mongo Ruby client.

We can then use the client object like we did in previous chapters, with all the caveats around how sharding behaves differently than a standalone server or a replica set with regards to querying and performance.

Performance comparison with replica sets

Developers and architects are always looking out for ways to compare performance between replica sets and sharded configurations.

The way MongoDB implements sharding, it is based on top of replica sets. Every shard in production should be a replica set.

The main difference in performance comes from fan out queries. When we are querying without the shard key, MongoDB's execution time is limited by the worst-performing replica set.

In addition, when using sorting without the shard key, the primary server has to implement the distributed merge sort on the entire dataset. This means that it has to collect all data from different shards, merge-sort them, and pass them as sorted to `mongos`.

In both cases, network latency and limitations in bandwidth can slow down operations as opposed to a replica set.

On the flip side, by having three shards, we can distribute our working set requirements across different nodes, thus serving results from RAM instead of reaching out to the underlying storage, HDD or SSD.

On the other hand, writes can be sped up significantly since we are no longer bound by a single node's I/O capacity but we can have writes in as many nodes as there are shards.

Summing up, in most cases and especially for the cases that we are using the shard key, both queries and modification operations will be significantly sped up by sharding.

 The shard key is the single most important decision in sharding and should reflect and apply to our most common application use cases.

Sharding recovery

In this section, we will explore different failure types and how we can recover in a sharded environment.

Mongos

mongos is a relatively lightweight process that holds no state. In the case that the process fails we can just restart it or spin up a new process in a different server. It's recommended that mongos processes co-locate in the same server as our application and so it makes sense to connect from our application using the set of mongos servers that we have co-located in our application servers to ensure high availability of mongos processes.

Mongod process

A mongod process failing in a sharded environment is no different than it failing in a replica set. If it is a secondary, the primary and the other secondary (assuming three-node replica sets) will continue as usual.

If it is a mongod process acting as a primary, then an election round will start to elect a new primary in this shard (which is really; a replica set).

In both cases, we should actively monitor and try to repair the node as soon as possible as our availability can be impacted.

Config server

Starting from MongoDB 3.4, config servers are also configured as a replica set. A config server failing is no different than a regular `mongod` process failing. We should monitor, log and repair the process.

A shard goes down

Losing an entire shard is pretty rare and in many cases can be attributed to network partitioning rather than failing processes. When a shard goes down, all operations that would go to this shard will fail. We can (and should) implement fault tolerance in our application level, allowing our application to resume for the operations that can be completed.

Choosing a shard key that can easily map on our operational side can also help; for example, if our shard key is based on location, we may lose the EU shard but will still be able to write and read data regarding US-based customers through our US shard.

The entire cluster goes down

If we lose the entire cluster, we can't do anything other than get it back up and running as soon as possible.

It's important to have monitoring and a proper process in place to understand what needs to be done, when and by who should this ever happen.

Recovering when the entire cluster goes down is essentially restoring from backups and setting up new shards, which is complicated and will take time.

Dry testing this on staging environment is also advisable, and so is investing in regular backups via MongoDB Ops Manager or any other backup solution.

 A member from each shard's replica set could be in a different location for disaster recovery purposes.

References

- *Scaling MongoDB* by Kristina Chodorow
- *MongoDB: The Definitive Guide* by Kristina Chodorow and Michael Dirolf
- `https://docs.mongodb.com/manual/sharding/`
- `https://www.mongodb.com/blog/post/mongodb-16-released`
- `https://github.com/mongodb/mongo/blob/r3.4.2-rc0/src/mongo/s/commands/cluster_shard_collection_cmd.cpp#L469`
- `https://www.mongodb.com/blog/post/sharding-pitfalls-part-iii-chunk-balancing-and`
- `http://plusnconsulting.com/post/mongodb-sharding-and-chunks/`
- `https://github.com/mongodb/mongo/wiki/Sharding-Internals`
- `http://learnmongodbthehardway.com/schema/sharding`

Summary

In this chapter, we explored sharding, one of the most interesting features of MongoDB. We started from an architectural overview of sharding and moved on to how we can design a shard and especially choose the right shard key.

We learned more about monitoring, administration, and the limitations that come with sharding. We also learned about `mongos`, the mongo sharding router that directs our queries to the correct shard. Finally, we discussed recovery from common failure types in a MongoDB sharded environment.

The next chapter on fault tolerance and high availability will offer some useful tips and tricks that I didn't manage to get to in the first 11 chapters.

12
Fault Tolerance and High Availability

In this chapter, we will try to fit in the information that we didn't manage to discuss in the previous chapters, and place emphasis on some others. Throughout the previous 11 chapters we have gone all the way through the basic concepts, to effective querying, to administration and data management, ending in scaling and high-availability concepts.

In the following sections, we will dive deeper into how our application design should be accommodating and proactive with regard to our database needs.

Day-to-day operations are another large area that we will discuss, including tips and best practices that can help us avoid nasty surprises down-the-line.

In light of recent attempts by ransomware to infect and hold hostage MongoDB servers, we will offer more tips around security.

Finally, we will try to sum up the advice given in a series of checklists that should be followed to ensure that best practices are being properly set up and followed.

Application design

In this section, we will describe the most useful tips for application design that we have not covered or emphasized enough in the previous chapters.

Schema-less doesn't mean schema design-less

A big part of MongoDB's success can be attributed to the increased popularity of ORM/ODMs. Especially with languages such as JavaScript and the MEAN stack, the developer can use JavaScript from the frontend (Angular/Express) to the backend (Node.js) to the database (MongoDB). This is many times coupled with an **Object Document Mapper (ODM)** that abstracts away the internals of the database, mapping collections to Node.js models.

The major advantage is that developers don't need to fiddle with database schema design as this is automatically provided by the ODM. The downside is that database collections and schema design are left up to the ODM, which does not have the business domain knowledge of different fields and access patterns.

In the case of MongoDB and other NoSQL-based databases, this boils down to making architectural decisions based not only on immediate needs but also on what needs to be done down-the-line. On an architectural level this may mean that, instead of a monolithic approach, we can combine different database technologies for our diverse and evolving needs using a graph database for graph-related querying, a relational database for hierarchical unbounded data, and MongoDB for JSON retrieval, processing, and storage.

In fact, many of MongoDB's successful use cases come from the exact fact that it's not being used as a one-size-fits-all solution, but only for the use cases that make sense.

Read performance optimization

In this section, we will discuss some tips for optimizing read performance.

Consolidating read querying

We should aim to have as few queries as possible. This can be achieved by embedding information into subdocuments instead of having separate entities. This may lead to an increased write load, as we have to keep the same data point in multiple documents and maintain their values everywhere when they change in one place.

The design consideration here is:

- Read performance benefits from data duplication/denormalization
- Data integrity benefits from data references (DBRef or in-application code using an attribute as a foreign key)

We should denormalize especially if our read/write ratio is too high (our data rarely changes value but gets accessed several times in between), if our data can afford to be inconsistent for brief periods of time, and most importantly if we absolutely need our reads to be as fast as possible and are willing to pay the price in consistency/write performance.

The most obvious candidates for fields that we should denormalize (embed) are dependent fields. If we have an attribute or a document structure that we don't plan to query on its own but only as part of a contained attribute/document, then it makes sense to embed it rather than have it in a separate document/collection.

Using our Mongo books example, a book can have a related data structure named review that refers to a review from a reader of the book. If our most common use case is showing a book along with its associated reviews, then we can embed reviews into the book document.

The downside to this design is that, when we want to find all book reviews by a user, this will be costly as we will have to iterate all books for associated reviews. Denormalizing users and embedding their reviews in there too can be a solution to this problem.

A counter example is data that can grow unbounded. In our example here, embedding reviews along with heavy metadata can lead to an issue if we hit the 16 MB document size limit. A solution here is to distinguish between data structures that we expect to grow rapidly and those that won't, and keep an eye on their size through monitoring processes that query our live dataset at off-peak times and report on attributes that may pose a risk down the line.

 Don't embed data that can grow unbounded.

When we embed attributes, we have to decide as to whether we will use a subdocument or an enclosing array.

When we have a unique identifier to access the subdocument, then we should embed it as a subdocument. If we don't know exactly how to access it or we need the flexibility to be able to query for an attribute's values, then we should embed it in an array.

For example, with our `books` collection, if we decide to embed reviews into each book document we have the following two designs:

With array:

A book document:

```
{
Isbn: '1001',
Title: 'Mastering MongoDB',
Reviews: [
{ 'user_id': 1, text: 'great book', rating: 5 },
{ 'user_id': 2, text: 'not so bad book', rating: 3 },
]
}
```

With embedded document:

A book document::

```
{
Isbn: '1001',
Title: 'Mastering MongoDB',
Reviews:
{ 'user_id': 1, text: 'great book', rating: 5 },
{ 'user_id': 2, text: 'not so bad book', rating: 3 },
}
```

The array structure has the advantage that we can directly query MongoDB for all reviews with `rating` > 4 through the embedded array reviews.

Using the embedded document structure on the other hand, we can retrieve all reviews the same way as we would do using the array, but if we want to filter on them it has to be done on the application side rather than on the database side.

Defensive coding

More of a generic principle, defensive coding refers to a set of practices and software design that ensure the continuing function of a piece of software under unforeseen circumstances.

It prioritizes code quality, readability, and predictability.

Readability is best explained by John F. Woods in his *comp.lang.c++* post on September 24, 1991:

> *"Always code as if the guy who ends up maintaining your code will be a violent psychopath who knows where you live. Code for readability."*

Our code should be readable and understandable by humans as well as machines. With code quality metrics as derived by static analysis tools, code reviews, and bugs reported/resolved, we can estimate the quality of our code base and aim for a certain threshold at each sprint or when we are ready to release.

Code predictability, on the other hand, means that we should always have expected results in unexpected inputs and program state.

These principles apply to every software system. In the context of system programming using MongoDB, there are some extra steps that we must take to ensure code predictability and subsequently quality is measured by the number of resulting bugs.

MongoDB limitations that will result in the loss of database functionality should be monitored and evaluated on a periodic basis:

- **Document size limit**: We should keep an eye on collections that we expect to have documents growing the most, running a background script to examine document sizes and alert us if we have documents approaching the limit (16 MB), or the average size has grown significantly since the last check.
- **Data integrity checks**: If we are using denormalization for read optimization then it's a good practice to check for data integrity. Through a software bug or a database error, we may end up with inconsistent duplicate data among collections.
- **Schema checks**: If we don't want to use the document validation feature of MongoDB but rather have a lax document schema, it's still a good idea to periodically run scripts to identify fields that are present in our documents and their frequency. Then along with relative access patterns, we can identify if these fields can be identified and consolidated. This is mostly useful if we are ingesting data from another system where data input changes over time, which may result in a wildly varying document structure on our end.

- **Data storage checks**: This mostly applies if using MMAPv1, where document padding optimization can help performance. By keeping an eye on document size relative to its padding we can make sure that our size-modifying updates won't incur a move of the document in physical storage.

These are the basic checks that we should implement when defensively coding for our MongoDB application. On top of this, we need to defensively code our application-level code to make sure that when failures occur in MongoDB our application will continue operating, maybe with degraded performance but still operational.

An example of this is replica set failover and failback. When our replica set master fails, there is a brief period before the other members of the replica set detect this failure and the new master is elected, promoted, and operational. During this brief period of time, we should make sure that our application continues operating in read-only mode instead of throwing 500 errors. In most cases, electing a new primary is done in seconds, but in some cases we may end up in the minority end of a network partition, not being able to contact a master for a long period of time. Similarly, some secondaries may end up in a recovering state (for example, if they fall way behind the master in replication); our application should be able to pick a different secondary in this case.

Designing for secondary access is one of the most useful examples of defensive coding. Our application should weigh between fields that can only be accessed by the primary to ensure data consistency and fields that are okay to be updated in near-real-time instead of in real time, in which case we can read these from secondary servers. By keeping track of replication lag for our secondaries using automated scripts, we can have a view of our cluster's load and how safe it is to enable this functionality.

Another defensive coding practice is to always perform writes with journaling on. Journaling helps to recover from server crashes and power failures.

Finally, we should aim to use replica sets as early as possible. Other than the performance and workload improvements, they help us to recover from server failures.

Monitoring integrations

All of this adds up to greater adoption of monitoring tools and services. As much as we can script some of them, integrating with cloud and on-premise monitoring tools can help us achieve more in less time.

The metrics that we keep a track of should be the ones that either:

- Detect failures
- Prevent failures

Failure detection is a reactive process, where we should have clear protocols in place for what happens when each of the failure detection flags go off. For example, what should the recovery steps be if we lose a server, a replica set, or a shard?

Failure prevention on the other hand is a proactive process, designed to help us catch early problems before they become a potential source of failure in the future. For example, CPU/storage/memory usage should be actively monitored with yellow and red thresholds and clear processes put in place as to what we should do in the event we reach either threshold.

Operations

When connecting to our production MongoDB servers, we want to make sure that our operations are as lightweight as possible (and certainly non-destructive) and do not alter the database state in any sense.

Two useful utilities we can chain to our queries are as follows:

```
> db.collection.find(query).maxTimeMS(999)
```

Our query will only take up to 999 ms and then return an exceeded time limit error.

```
> db.collection.find(query).maxScan(1000)
```

Our query will examine at most 1,000 documents to find results and then return (no error raised).

Whenever we can, we should bind our queries by time or document result size to avoid running unexpectedly long queries that may affect our production database.

A common reason for accessing our production database is troubleshooting degraded cluster performance. This can be investigated via cloud monitoring tools as described in previous chapters.

`db.currentOp()` through the MongoDB shell will give us a list of all current operations. We can then isolate the ones that have large `.secs_running` values and identify them through the `.query` field.

If we want to kill an in-progress operation that takes a long time, we need to note the value of the `.opid` field and pass it on `db.killOp(<opid>)`.

Finally, it's important to recognize from an operational standpoint that everything may go wrong. We must have a backup strategy in place that is implemented consistently. Most importantly, we should practice restoring from backups to make sure that they work as intended.

Security

After the recent waves of ransomware locking MongoDB administrators out of their servers and asking for cryptocurrency payments to unlock them, many developers have become more security-conscious. Security is one of the items on a checklist that we as developers may not prioritize highly enough due to the optimistic belief that it won't happen to us. The truth is that, in the modern internet landscape, everyone may become a target of automated or directed attacks, so security should always be taken into account from the early stages of design until after production deployment.

Enabling security by default

Every database, other than maybe local development servers, should be set up with the following in the `mongod.conf` file:

```
auth = true
```

 SSL should be always enabled, as described in the relevant Chapter 7, *Monitoring, Backup and Security*.

REST and HTTP status interfaces should be disabled by adding the following lines in `mongod.conf`:

```
nohttpinterface = true
rest = false
```

Access should be restricted only between application servers and MongoDB servers and only in the interfaces that are needed. Using `bind_ip` we can force MongoDB to listen to specific interfaces instead of the default bind to every interface-available behavior:

```
bind_ip = 10.10.0.10,10.10.0.20
```

Isolating our servers

We should secure our infrastructure perimeter with AWS VPC or the equivalent from the cloud provider of our choice. As an extra layer of security, we should isolate our servers in a cloud of their own, only allowing external connections to reach our application servers and never directly connect to our MongoDB servers.

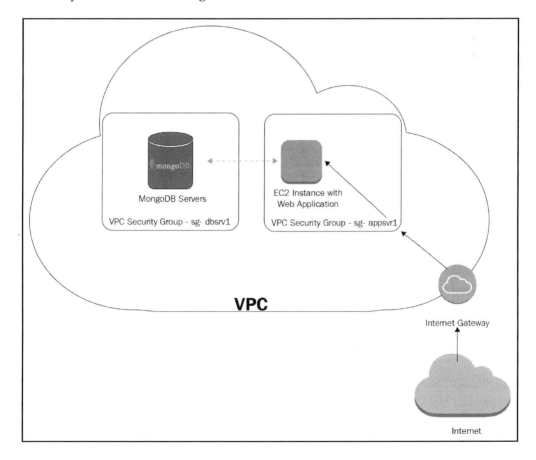

We should invest in role-based authorization. Security lies not in only protecting against data leaks caused by external actors, but also in making sure that internal actors have the appropriate level of access to our data. Using role-based authorization in the MongoDB level, we can make sure that our users have the appropriate level of access.

Consider Enterprise Edition for large deployments. Enterprise Edition offers some convenient features around security, more integrations with well-known tools, and should be evaluated for large deployments with an eye on changing needs as we transition from a single replica set to an enterprise-complex architecture.

Checklists

Operations require the completion of many tasks of varying time and complexity to be marked as done. A good practice is to keep a set of checklists with all the tasks that need to be performed and their order of significance. This will ensure that we don't let something slip through.

A deployment and security checklist, for example, could be:

- **Hardware**:
    - **Storage**: How much disk space is needed per node? What is the growth rate?
    - **Storage technology**: Do we need SSD versus HDD? What is the throughput of our storage?
    - **RAM**: What is the expected working set? Can we fit it in the RAM? If not, are we going to be okay with SSD instead of HDD? What is the growth rate?
    - **CPU**: Usually not a concern for MongoDB, but could be if we plan to run CPU-intensive jobs in our cluster (for example, aggregation, MapReduce).
    - **Network**: What are the network links between servers? This is usually trivial if we are using a single data center but can get complicated if we have multiple data centers and/or offsite servers for disaster recovery.

- **Security**:
    - Enable auth.
    - Enable SSL.
    - Disable REST/HTTP interface.
    - Isolate our servers (for example, VPC).
    - Authorization is enabled. With power comes great responsibility. Make sure power users are the ones that you trust. Don't give potentially destructive powers to inexperienced users.

A monitoring and operations checklist:

- **Monitoring**:
    - Usage of hardware mentioned above (CPU, memory, storage, network).
    - Health checks using Pingdom or an equivalent service to make sure that we get a notification when one of our servers fails.
    - Client performance monitoring: Integrate periodic mystery shopper tests, using the service in a manual or automated way as a customer from an end-to-end perspective in order to find out if it behaves as expected. We don't want to learn about application performance issues from our customers.
    - Use MongoDB Cloud Manager monitoring—it has a free tier, can provide useful metrics, and is the tool that MongoDB engineers can take a look at if we run into issues and need their help, especially as part of support contracts.

- **Disaster recovery**:
    - **Evaluate risk**: What is the risk from the business perspective of losing MongoDB data? Can we recreate this dataset and, if yes, how costly is it in terms of time and effort needed?
    - **Devise a plan**: Have a plan for each failure scenario, with the exact steps that we need to take in case it happens.
    - **Test the plan**: Having a dry run of every recovery strategy is as important as having one. Many things can go wrong in disaster recovery and having an incomplete plan, or one that fails in each purpose, is something that we shouldn't allow to happen under any circumstance.

- **Have an alternative to the plan**: No matter how well we devise a plan and test it, anything can go wrong during planning, testing, or execution. We need to have a backup plan for our plan in case we can't recover our data using plan A. This is also called plan B, or the last resort plan. It doesn't have to be efficient, but it should alleviate any business reputation risk.
- **Load test**: We should make sure we load test our application end to end before deployment with a realistic workload. This is the only way to ensure that our application will behave as expected.

References

- `http://mo.github.io/2017/01/22/mongo-db-tips-and-tricks.html`
- `https://studio3t.com/whats-new/tips-for-sql-users-new-to-mongodb/`
- `https://www.hostreview.com/blog/170327-top-7-mongodb-performance-tips-must-know`
- `https://groups.google.com/forum/#!msg/comp.lang.c++/rYCO5yn4lXw/oITtSkZOtoUJ`

Summary

In this chapter, we covered some areas that were not detailed in previous chapters. It is important to apply best practices according to our workload requirements. Read performance is usually what we want to optimize for, and this is why we discussed consolidating queries and denormalization of our data.

Operations are also important when we go from deployment to ensuring the continuous performance and availability of our cluster.

Security is something that we don't think about until it affects us. This is why we should invest the time beforehand in planning, to make sure that we have the measures we need in place to be sufficiently secure.

Finally, we introduced the concept of checklists to keep track of our tasks and make sure we complete all of them before major operational events (deployment, cluster upgrades, moving to sharding from replica sets, and so on).

Index

Y

Made in the USA
Middletown, DE
15 August 2018